TALES FROM HERODOTUS

TALES FROM HERODOTUS

Edited and selected for easy Greek reading by

G. S. Farnell & Marie Goff
with Introduction by
E. P. C. Cotter

Published by Bristol Classical Press
General Editor: John H. Betts

(by arrangement with Macmillan Education Ltd)

Cover illustration: Herodotus, from a portrait bust, Dresden [drawing by Emma Faull].
Additional drawings for this edition have been prepared by Emma Faull, Patrick
Harrison and Jean Bees. The photograph on p.viii is produced by permission of
the Trustees of the British Museum.

First published in 1963 by Macmillan Education Ltd.

Reprinted by permission of Macmillan Education Ltd.
Reprinted by Bristol Classical Press 1983, 1992

Bristol Classical Press
is an imprint of
Gerald Duckworth & Co. Ltd.
The Old Piano Factory
48 Hoxton Square, London N1 6PB

ISBN 0-86292-091-4

Printed in Great Britain by
Booksprint, Bristol

CONTENTS

LIST OF ILLUSTRATIONS

LIST OF MAPS AND PLANS

PLAYING AT KNUCKLEBONES
Terra-cotta group in the British Museum

viii

INTRODUCTION

DEVELOPMENT OF GREEK HISTORY

It is interesting to reflect that though poetry had reached the excellence that we find in the Epic as early as the ninth century before Christ, and continued to develop through the hexameter, the elegiac, the iambic, and the lyric metres, it is not until the sixth century that we find prose used as a literary medium.

Many names, mostly Ionian, have survived, but our information about nearly all of them is very limited. The two outstanding prose writers or λογογράφοι before Herodotus were Hecataeus and Hellanicus.

Hecataeus, a native of Miletus, was celebrated not only as a historian but also as an influence in Ionian politics. He did his best to prevent his fellow countrymen from starting the Ionian revolt. His shrewd analysis of the tremendous power of Persia made it clear to him that such an undertaking could only result in disaster. He wrote Genealogies and a Περίοδος γῆς and had a reputation as a geographer. He is credited with having made a map with which to illustrate his Περίοδος γῆς.

With Hecataeus the prose chronicle emerges from the state of vague anonymity and bears the stamp of the individual, as may be seen from the opening remarks in his Genealogies:

Ἑκαταῖος Μιλήσιος ὧδε μυθεῖται· τάδε γράφω ὥς μοι ἀληθέα δοκέει εἶναι· οἱ γὰρ Ἑλλήνων λόγοι πολλοί τε καὶ γελοῖοι, ὡς ἐμοὶ φαίνονται, εἰσίν.

Hellanicus, a contemporary of Herodotus, wrote works that fall into three classes, topographical, genealogical, and chronological. In the first class there was an *Atthis*, which is referred to in the first book of Thucydides. In the second class we hear of a *Deucali-oneia* and *Argolica*. In the third class we find a list of the priestesses of Hera at Argos, to which there would seem to be some connection in the second chapter of Thucydides ii. He was industrious and conscientious, but Thucydides finds fault with his dates and he is also dubbed ἐν τοῖς πρώτοις ψευδόμενον.

HERODOTUS

Accorded the title 'Father of History' by Cicero, Herodotus is the link between the earlier λογογράφοι and the later historians represented by Thucydides, for with him we see the start of genuine critical treatment of historical facts. There is a correlation of cause and effect instead of a mere compilation of detached incidents.

Herodotus was well educated. His knowledge of Greek literature, especially the Homeric poems, colours his whole work. In fact his history is Homeric in its conception and in its design. Longinus calls him ὁμηρικώτατος. So extensive a knowledge of literature implies an inquisitive mind and, beyond that, the industry to satisfy it.

HIS LIFE

The traditional date of his birth is 484 B.C. Though this date cannot be determined with certainty, it is likely to be right, because Herodotus does not claim to have been alive when the recorded events took place, but he does claim to have been on intimate terms with those that were.

From Suidas we learn that his birthplace was Halicarnassus, and that his parents, of good position, were Lyxes and Dryo. These names are of no significance, but we are also told that he was related to Panyasis, the epic poet, who wrote works on Heracles and the colonisation of Ionia. Panyasis was an ardent patriot, actively engaged in an attempt to overthrow Lygdamis who had become tyrant of Halicarnassus about 460 B.C. The attempt failed, Panyasis was put to death, and Herodotus was forced to take refuge in Samos.

A few years later, after the overthrow of Lygdamis in which he may or may not have been involved, Herodotus returned to Halicarnassus. He seems to have found the city no longer congenial for he started on his career of wandering. He made his home in Athens and eventually in 443 B.C. settled in Thurii, an Athenian colony of Magna Graecia, and presumably died there, if we are to believe the epitaph of Stephanus:

'Ηρόδοτον Λύξεω κρύπτει κόνις ἥδε θανόντα
'Ιάδος ἀρχαίης ἱστορίης πρύτανιν,
Δωριέων βλαστόντα πάτρης ἄπο, τῶν γὰρ ἄτλητον
μῶμον ὑπεκπροφυγὼν Θούριον ἔσχε πάτρην.

The date of his death is a matter of conjecture. Internal evidence would show that it was soon after the outbreak of the Peloponnesian war, and 424 B.C. may be taken as approximately correct.

HIS TRAVELS

Our information about his later life and extensive

travels is scanty. In Egypt he seems to have gone as far south as Elephantine. Eastwards he reached Susa and Ecbatana, northwards the Black Sea and the Dnieper. He was familiar with the islands of the Aegean and travelled widely in Greece itself, visiting Athens, Thebes, Sparta, Olympia, Delphi, and Dodona.

Interesting questions arise in connection with this travelling. What was the object of it? How did Herodotus find sufficient funds to make it possible? It has been suggested that he travelled as an ἔμπορος. This may have been true, but the natural conclusion drawn from his history is that learning not commerce was his object. He was much like a modern on a lecture tour — in quest of knowledge and post-graduate study, but giving lectures to defray the cost of the tour. Herodotus was a professional reciter, a prose rhapsodist.

Diyllus tells us that he received ten talents from the Athenian treasury. Now, as Gilbert Murray pointed out, a sum of this size was surely no fee for a series of lectures, but must have been the grateful recognition of some important service to the state. It is undeniably true that Herodotus must have acquired much more information than that actually published in his history. Could Herodotus have been a high class intelligence agent?

His History

It has been the vogue, from the earliest times to the present day, to censure Herodotus as a historian and to compare him unfavourably with Thucydides. This negative attitude of thought greets every pioneer. Progress is the law of nature, and it is as senseless to

criticise Herodotus for his history as it is to laugh at the
Pilgrim Fathers' crossing of the Atlantic in two months
because we can now do it in a few hours. Is it not more
rational to praise Herodotus for his pioneering in the
field of historical criticism and at the same time to
admire the advancement in Thucydides?

A more intelligent appreciation of the aims of each of
these two historians would prevent this unjustified
criticism. Herodotus says unequivocally that his object
in writing is: ' that past events may not pass from the
memory of men through lapse of time, and that the
great and marvellous achievements of Greek and bar-
barian alike may not be lost in oblivion, and especially
the reasons for their going to war with each other '.
Thucydides, on the other hand, states that he is not
interested in the past events for themselves but only in
their relation to the present and future, that mankind
may learn a lesson from them.

One of the charges levelled at Herodotus is that the
whole tenor of his history is too theological. It is imbued
with the sentiment that we find in the *Oedipus Tyrannus*
of Sophocles:

$$\mu\eta\delta\acute{\epsilon}\nu' \ \acute{o}\lambda\beta\acute{\iota}\zeta\epsilon\iota\nu \ \pi\rho\grave{\iota}\nu \ \ddot{a}\nu$$
$$\tau\acute{\epsilon}\rho\mu\alpha \ \tauo\hat{\upsilon} \ \beta\acute{\iota}o\upsilon \ \pi\epsilon\rho\acute{a}\sigma\eta \ \mu\eta\delta\grave{\epsilon}\nu \ \grave{a}\lambda\gamma\epsilon\iota\nu\grave{o}\nu \ \pi\alpha\theta\acute{\omega}\nu.$$

This is clearly seen in the story of Polycrates. The
doctrine of Nemesis is the *deus ex machina* which provides a religious solution for all problems, moral, social,
and political. This, it is alleged, prevents logical
analysis and blinds Herodotus to the true causes that
underlie events.

It is also claimed that Herodotus is far too given to

the miraculous. Juvenal, a first-century A.D. satirist, says in this connection

quid Graecia mendax
audet in historia.

In company with other ancient critics, Juvenal, for instance, doubted that a canal had been dug through mount Athos, at the time of the Persian invasion, but modern travellers have found undeniable evidence of it. Here, indeed, is proof that Herodotus was not basing his history on fable.

There are undoubtedly inconsistencies in the history. The description of the Persians as water-drinkers does not accord with their wine-drinking at the time when Cyrus is planning revolt from the Medes. But to one painting on so wide a canvas, with impressions culled from so many sources, this may be forgiven.

Perhaps the critics are most justified when they accuse Herodotus of inability to detect the predisposing causes of events. He is content to ascribe cause to person, oblivious of the fact that it is the progress of human thought that results in great events such as the overthrow of tyranny, the abolition of slavery, and the reform of child labour, and that individuals are merely the instruments through which progressive thinking is manifested.

Modern research is constantly showing that statements of Herodotus, once ridiculed, rest on a basis of fact. This introduction makes no real attempt to whitewash Herodotus because Herodotus does not need whitewashing. No critic, however severe, can deny his gift for telling a story. In this respect Hero-

dotus is a consummate artist. His narrative flows
with the life and charm of the *Odyssey*. As Dionysius
says:

παρεσκεύασε τῇ κρατίστῃ ποιήσει τὴν πεζὴν φράσιν
ὁμοίαν γενέσθαι.

Though the εἰρομένη λέξις of Herodotus is quite
unlike the epigrammatic terseness of Tacitus, both
have the incomparable gift of making a story live.
And to the great story-teller much is forgiven because
he has given much.

THE SELECTED TALES

The twenty selections give ample scope for studying
the versatility of Herodotus, as he moves from one
mood to another. In the stories of Mycerinus and
the Lydian games we get a sense of the Gilbertian
paradox of the *Pirates of Penzance*. In the ' Oldest
Race upon Earth ' we see a practical experiment in
human behaviourism, an idea that has occurred to
all of us and has been used by modern novelists. The
sketch of Amasis is a psychological study of inverted
logic, while the ' Blinding of Euenius ' depicts a
cynicism foreign to Herodotus' wide charity. We see
the mystery and horror of Edgar Allan Poe in the
story of Cyrus, in the ' Capture of Babylon ' we have
Zopyrus as the Double Agent. The ' Babylonian Wife-
market ' is an amusing study in economics, and
Alcmaeon emerging from the treasury of Croesus is a
comic strip character. The reply of Hippocleides οὐ
φροντὶς Ἱπποκλείδῃ is sheer theatre — what would
not an actor give for such a line? Finally, in the

' Power of Custom ' there is a pointed rebuke to bigoted insularity.

No one can be bored by Herodotus. He compels the reader's attention by his stories, for their application is to all ages, past, present and future.

The selections in this text were adapted from the passages in Herodotus indicated below.

Herodotus, from a portrait bust, Dresden

TALES FROM HERODOTUS

I. How Games were invented by the Lydians to relieve their Distress in Time of Famine

Φασὶν οἱ Λυδοὶ τὰς παιγνίας τὰς νῦν σφίσι τε καὶ
Ἕλλησι καθεστώσας ἑαυτῶν ἐξεύρημα γενέσθαι, ὧδε περὶ
αὐτῶν λέγοντες. ἐπὶ Ἄτυος τοῦ Μάνου βασιλέως σιτο-
δεία ἰσχυρὰ ἀνὰ τὴν Λυδίαν πᾶσαν ἐγένετο, καὶ οἱ Λυδοὶ

5 τέως μὲν διῆγον λιπαροῦντες, μετὰ δέ, ὡς οὐκ ἐπαύετο, ἄκη
ἐζήτουν, ἄλλος δὲ ἄλλο ἐπεμηχανᾶτο. ἐξηυρέθη δὴ οὖν
τότε καὶ τῶν κύβων καὶ τῶν ἀστραγάλων καὶ τῆς σφαίρας
καὶ τῶν ἄλλων πασῶν παιγνιῶν τὰ εἴδη, πλὴν πεττῶν·
τούτων γὰρ τὴν ἐξεύρεσιν οὐκ οἰκειοῦνται οἱ Λυδοί.
10 ἐποίουν δὲ ὧδε, πρὸς τὸν λιμὸν ἐξευρόντες τὰς παιγνίας·
τὴν μὲν ἑτέραν τῶν ἡμερῶν ἔπαιζον πᾶσαν, ἵνα δὴ μὴ
ζητοῖεν σιτία, τὴν δὲ ἑτέραν ἐσιτοῦντο παυόμενοι τῶν
παιγνιῶν. τοιούτῳ τρόπῳ διῆγον ἐπ' ἔτη δυοῖν δέοντα
εἴκοσιν.

PLAYING AT DRAUGHTS
Terra-cotta group from Athens

II. How the Egyptian King Psammetichus
discovered the Oldest Race on Earth

Οἱ Αἰγύπτιοι, πρὶν μὲν ἢ Ψαμμήτιχον σφῶν βασιλεῦσαι, ἐνόμιζον ἑαυτοὺς πρώτους γενέσθαι πάντων ἀνθρώ-
πων· ἐπειδὴ δὲ Ψαμμήτιχος βασιλεύσας ἠθέλησεν εἰδέναι

οἵτινες γένοιντο πρῶτοι, ἀπὸ τούτου (χρόνου) νομίζουσι
Φρύγας προτέρους γενέσθαι ἑαυτῶν, τῶν δὲ ἄλλων ἑαυτούς. 5
Ψαμμήτιχος δὲ ὡς οὐκ ἐδύνατο πυνθανόμενος πόρον
οὐδένα τούτου ἀνευρεῖν, οἳ γένοιντο πρῶτοι ἀνθρώπων,
ἐπιτεχνᾶται τοιόνδε. παιδία δύο νεογνὰ ἀνθρώπων τῶν
ἐπιτυχόντων δίδωσι ποιμένι τρέφειν, ἐντειλάμενος μηδένα
ἀντίον αὐτῶν μηδεμίαν φωνὴν ἱέναι, ἐν στέγῃ δὲ ἐρήμῃ 10
ἐφ᾽ ἑαυτῶν κεῖσθαι αὐτά, καὶ ἐν ὥρᾳ τὸν ποιμένα ἐπάγειν
αὐτοῖς αἶγας, πλήσαντα δὲ τοῦ γάλακτος τἆλλα διαπ-
ράττεσθαι. ταῦτα δ᾽ ἐποίει τε καὶ ἐνετέλλετο ὁ Ψαμμήτιχος,
ἐθέλων ἀκοῦσαι ἥντινα φωνὴν ῥήξουσι πρώτην οἱ παῖδες,
ἀπαλλαχθέντων τῶν ἀσήμων κνυζημάτων. ἅπερ οὖν καὶ 15
ἐγένετο· ὡς γὰρ διετὴς χρόνος ἐγεγόνει, τῷ ποιμένι
ἀνοίγοντι τὴν θύραν καὶ εἰσιόντι τὰ παιδία ἀμφότερα
προσπίπτοντα " βέκος " ἐφώνουν, ὀρέγοντα τὰς χεῖρας.

Τὰ μὲν δὴ πρῶτα ἀκούσας ἥσυχος ἦν ὁ ποιμήν· ὡς
δὲ πολλάκις φοιτῶντι αὐτῷ καὶ ἐπιμελομένῳ πολὺ ἦν 20
τοῦτο τὸ ἔπος, οὕτω δὴ σημήνας τῷ δεσπότῃ ἤγαγε τὰ
παιδία εἰς ὄψιν τὴν ἐκείνου. ἀκούσας δὲ καὶ αὐτὸς ὁ
Ψαμμήτιχος, ἐπυνθάνετο οἵτινες ἀνθρώπων " βέκος " τι
καλοῦσι· πυνθανόμενος δὲ ηὕρισκε Φρύγας καλοῦντας τὸν
ἄρτον. οὕτω συνεχώρησαν Αἰγύπτιοι, τοιούτῳ σταθμησάμ- 25
ενοι πράγματι, τοὺς Φρύγας πρεσβυτέρους εἶναι ἑαυτῶν.

III. How Crocodiles are worshipped by some
Egyptians, captured and eaten by Others

Τοῖς μὲν δὴ τῶν Αἰγυπτίων ἱεροί εἰσιν οἱ κροκόδειλοι,
τοῖς δ᾽ οὔ, ἀλλ᾽ ἅτε πολεμίους περιέπουσι. οἱ δὲ περί τε
Θήβας καὶ τὴν Μοίρεως λίμνην οἰκοῦντες καὶ κάρτα
ἡγοῦνται αὐτοὺς εἶναι ἱερούς. ἕνα δὲ ἑκάτεροι τρέφουσι
κροκόδειλον, δεδιδαγμένον εἶναι χειροήθη· ἀρτήματα δὲ 5

εἰς τὰ ὦτα ἐνθέντες καὶ ἀμφιδέας περὶ τοὺς προσθίους
πόδας, καὶ σιτία ἀποτακτὰ διδόντες καὶ ἱερεῖα, περιέπουσιν ὡς
κάλλιστα ζῶντας· ἀποθανόντας δὲ ταριχεύοντες θάπτουσιν
ἐν ἱεραῖς θήκαις.

10 Οἱ δὲ περὶ Ἐλεφαντίνην πόλιν οἰκοῦντες καὶ ἐσθίουσιν
αὐτούς, οὐχ ἡγούμενοι ἱεροὺς εἶναι. ἄγραι δὲ αὐτῶν
πολλαὶ καθεστήκασι καὶ παντοῖαι· ἣ δ᾽ ἔμοιγε δοκεῖ
ἀξιωτάτη ἀφηγήσεως εἶναι ταύτην γράφω. ἐπειδὰν
νῶτον ὑὸς δελεάσῃ τις περὶ ἄγκιστρον, μεθίησι εἰς μέσον
15 τὸν ποταμόν· αὐτὸς δὲ ἐπὶ τοῦ χείλους τοῦ ποταμοῦ ἔχων
δέλφακα ζωήν, ταύτην τύπτει. ἐπακούσας δὲ τῆς φωνῆς
ὁ κροκόδειλος ἵεται κατὰ τὴν φωνήν· ἐντυχὼν δὲ τῷ
νώτῳ καταπίνει, οἱ δὲ ἕλκουσι. ἐπειδὰν δὲ ἐξελκυσθῇ
εἰς γῆν, πρῶτον ἁπάντων ὁ θηρευτὴς πηλῷ κατέπλασεν
20 αὐτοῦ τοὺς ὀφθαλμούς· τοῦτο δὲ ποιήσας κάρτα εὐπετῶς
τὰ λοιπὰ χειροῦται· μὴ ποιήσας δὲ σὺν πόνῳ.

MUMMY OF A CROCODILE IN THE BRITISH MUSEUM

IV. STORY OF MYCERINUS

*How Mycerinus, who governed the Egyptians justly after they had
been grievously oppressed by his predecessors, was fated to
die in six years' time, and how, by turning night into day, he
contrived to live twelve years in six.*

Μυκερίνῳ τὰ μὲν τοῦ πατρὸς ἔργα ἀφήνδανε· ὁ δὲ τά
τε ἱερὰ ἀνέῳξε, καὶ τὸν λεών, τετρυμένον εἰς τὸ ἔσχατον
κακοῦ, ἀνῆκε πρὸς ἔργα τε καὶ θυσίας· δίκας δὲ αὐτοῖς
πάντων βασιλέων δικαιοτάτας ἔκρινεν. ὄντι δὲ ἠπίῳ τῷ

STATUETTE OF MYCERINUS

A plaster cast in the British Museum of the original statue
which is in the Gizeh Museum, Cairo

5 Μυκερίνῳ κατὰ τοὺς πολίτας καὶ ταῦτα ἐπιτηδεύοντι
πρῶτον κακῶν ἦρξεν ἡ θυγάτηρ ἀποθανοῦσα, ἣ μόνον
αὐτῷ ἦν ἐν τοῖς οἰκίοις τέκνον. μετὰ δὲ τὸ τῆς θυγατρὸς
πάθος, δεύτερα τούτῳ τῷ βασιλεῖ τάδε ἐγένετο. ἦλθεν
αὐτῷ μαντεῖον ἐκ Βουτοῦς πόλεως, ὡς μέλλοι ἓξ ἔτη
10 μόνον βιοὺς τῷ ἑβδόμῳ τελευτήσειν. ὁ δὲ δεινὸν ποιησάμενος ἔπεμψεν εἰς τὸ μαντεῖον τῷ θεῷ ὀνείδισμα, ἀντι-
μεμφόμενος τάδε, " Ὁ μὲν πατὴρ ἐμοῦ καὶ πάτρως,
ἀποκλείσαντες τὰ ἱερά, καὶ θεῶν οὐ μεμνημένοι ἀλλὰ καὶ
τοὺς ἀνθρώπους φθείροντες, ἐβίωσαν ἐπὶ πολὺν χρόνον·
15 ἐγὼ δ᾽ εὐσεβὴς ὢν μέλλω ταχέως οὕτω τελευτήσειν."

Ἐκ δὲ τοῦ χρηστηρίου τούτου αὐτῷ δεύτερον ἦλθε
λέγον, " Τούτων ἕνεκα καὶ συνταχύνει σοι ὁ βίος· οὐ γὰρ
πεποίηκας ὃ χρεὼν ἦν ποιεῖν. δεῖ γὰρ Αἴγυπτον κακοῦσθαι
ἐπ᾽ ἔτη πεντήκοντά τε καὶ ἑκατόν· καὶ οἱ μὲν δύο βασιλεῖς
20 οἱ πρὸ σοῦ γενόμενοι ἔμαθον τοῦτο, σὺ δὲ οὔ."

Ταῦτα ἀκούσας ὁ Μυκερῖνος, ὡς κατακεκριμένων ἤδη
οἱ τούτων, λύχνα ποιησάμενος πολλά, ἀνάψας αὐτὰ ὅπως
γίγνοιτο νύξ, ἔπινέ τε καὶ ηὐπάθει οὔθ᾽ ἡμέρας οὔτε
νυκτὸς ἀνιείς, εἴς τε τὰ ἕλη καὶ τὰ ἄλση πλανώμενος καὶ
25 ἵνα γῆς πυνθάνοιτο εἶναι ἐνηβητήρια ἐπιτηδειότατα.
ταῦτα δὲ ἐμηχανᾶτο ἐθέλων τὸ μαντεῖον ψευδόμενον
ἀποδεῖξαι, ἵνα οἱ δώδεκα ἔτη ἀντὶ ἓξ ἐτῶν γένοιτο, τῶν
νυκτῶν ἡμερῶν ποιουμένων.

V. STORIES OF AMASIS, WHO USURPED THE THRONE OF EGYPT

(a) How, in spite of his low birth, he induced his subjects to respect him.

Ἀπρίου δὲ καθῃρημένου ἐβασίλευσεν Ἄμασις. τὰ μὲν
δὴ πρῶτα κατώνοντο τὸν Ἄμασιν Αἰγύπτιοι καὶ ἐν

οὐδεμιᾷ μοίρᾳ μεγάλῃ ἦγον, ἅτε δὴ δημότην τὸ πρὶν
ὄντα καὶ οἰκίας οὐκ ἐπιφανοῦς· μετὰ δὲ σοφίᾳ αὐτοὺς ὁ
Ἄμασις οὐκ ἀγνωμοσύνῃ προσηγάγετο. ἦν αὐτῷ ἄλλα 5
τε ἀγαθὰ μυρία καὶ ποδανιπτὴρ χρυσοῦς ἐν ᾧ αὐτός τε ὁ
Ἄμασις καὶ οἱ δαιτυμόνες πάντες τοὺς πόδας ἑκάστοτε
ἐναπενίζοντο. τοῦτον οὖν κατακόψας ἄγαλμα δαίμονος
ἐξ αὐτοῦ ἐποιήσατο, καὶ ἵδρυσεν ὅπου ἦν ἐπιτηδειότατον·
οἱ δὲ Αἰγύπτιοι φοιτῶντες πρὸς τὸ ἄγαλμα ἐσέβοντο 10
μεγάλως.

Μαθὼν δὲ ὁ Ἄμασις συγκαλέσας Αἰγυπτίους ἐξέφηνε
φὰς ἐκ τοῦ ποδανιπτῆρος τὸ ἄγαλμα γεγονέναι, εἰς ὃν
πρότερον μὲν οἱ Αἰγύπτιοι ἐνεμοῖέν τε καὶ πόδας ἐναπονίζοιντο, τότε δὲ μεγάλως σέβοιντο. ἤδη οὖν, ἔφη λέγων, 15
ὁμοίως αὐτὸς τῷ ποδανιπτῆρι πεπραγέναι· εἰ γὰρ πρότερον
εἴη δημότης, ὅμως ἐν τῷ παρόντι εἶναι αὐτῶν βασιλεύς·
καὶ τιμᾶν τε καὶ προμηθεῖσθαι ἑαυτοῦ ἐκέλευε.

(b) How he justified his relaxation.

Τοιούτῳ μὲν τρόπῳ προσηγάγετο τοὺς Αἰγυπτίους
ὥστε δικαιοῦν δουλεύειν. ἐχρῆτο δὲ καταστάσει πραγμάτων τοιᾷδε· τὸ μὲν ὄρθριον, μέχρι πληθούσης ἀγορᾶς,
προθύμως ἔπραττε τὰ προσφερόμενα πράγματα· τὸ δὲ
ἀπὸ τοῦδε ἔπινέ τε καὶ κατέσκωπτε τοὺς συμπότας καὶ 5
ἦν μάταιός τε καὶ παιγνιήμων.

Ἀχθεσθέντες δὲ τούτοις οἱ φίλοι αὐτοῦ ἐνουθέτουν
αὐτόν, τοιάδε λέγοντες, " Ὦ βασιλεῦ, οὐκ ὀρθῶς σεαυτοῦ
προύστηκας, εἰς τὸ ἄγαν φλαῦρον προάγων σεαυτόν. σὲ
γὰρ χρῆν ἐν θρόνῳ σεμνῷ σεμνὸν θακοῦντα δι᾽ ἡμέρας 10
πράττειν τὰ πράγματα· καὶ οὕτως Αἰγύπτιοί τ᾽ ἂν ἠπίσ-
ταντο ὡς ὑπ᾽ ἀνδρὸς μεγάλου ἄρχονται, καὶ ἄμεινον σὺ
ἂν ἤκουες· νῦν δὲ ποιεῖς οὐδαμῶς βασιλικά."

Ὁ δὲ ἠμείβετο τοῖσδε αὐτούς, " Οἱ τὰ τόξα κεκτημένοι,

15 ἐπὴν μὲν δέωνται χρῆσθαι, ἐντείνουσιν· ἐπὴν δὲ χρή-
σωνται, ἐκλύουσιν· εἰ γὰρ δὴ τὸν πάντα χρόνον ἐντετα-
μένα εἴη, ἐκραγείη ἄν, ὥστε εἰς τὸ δέον οὐκ ἂν ἔχοιεν
αὐτοῖς χρῆσθαι. οὕτω δὴ καὶ ἀνθρώπου κατάστασις· εἰ
ἐθέλοι κατεσπουδάσθαι ἀεὶ μηδὲ εἰς παιγνίαν τὸ μέρος
20 ἑαυτὸν ἀνιέναι, λάθοι ἂν ἤτοι μανεὶς ἢ ἀπόπληκτος γενόμενος·
ἃ ἐγὼ ἐπιστάμενος μέρος ἑκατέρῳ νέμω."

(c) Former spendthrift and dishonest habits of Amasis; his unexpected treatment, after his accession to the throne, of the
oracular shrines which had encouraged his practices.

Λέγεται δὲ ὁ Ἄμασις, καὶ ὅτε ἦν ἰδιώτης, φιλοπότης
εἶναι καὶ φιλοσκώμμων καὶ οὐδαμῶς κατεσπουδασμένος
ἀνήρ· ὅπως δὲ αὐτὸν πίνοντά τε καὶ εὐπαθοῦντα ἐπιλείποι
τὰ ἐπιτήδεια, ἔκλεπτεν ἂν περιών. οἱ δὲ φάμενοι αὐτὸν
5 ἔχειν τὰ ἑαυτῶν χρήματα ἀρνούμενον ἦγον ἂν ἐπὶ μαντεῖον
ὅπου ἑκάστοις εἴη. πολλάκις μὲν δὴ καὶ ἡλίσκετο ὑπὸ
τῶν μαντείων, πολλάκις δὲ καὶ ἀπέφευγεν.

Ἐπεὶ δὲ καὶ ἐβασίλευσεν, ἐποίησε τοιάδε· ὅσοι μὲν
αὐτὸν τῶν θεῶν ἀπέλυσαν μὴ φώρα εἶναι, τούτων μὲν
10 τῶν ἱερῶν οὔτε ἐπεμέλετο οὔτε εἰς ἐπισκευὴν ἐδίδου
οὐδέν· οὐδὲ φοιτῶν ἔθυεν αὐτοῖς ὡς οὐδενὸς οὖσιν ἀξίοις,
ψευδῆ δὲ μαντεῖα κεκτημένοις· ὅσοι δὲ αὐτὸν κατέδησαν
φῶρα εἶναι, τούτων, ὡς ἀληθῶς θεῶν ὄντων καὶ ἀψευδῆ
μαντεῖα παρεχομένων, τὰ μάλιστα ἐπεμέλετο.

VI. How Arion was saved by a Dolphin

Ἀρίων ὁ κιθαρῳδός, τὸν πολὺν τοῦ χρόνου διατρίβων
παρὰ Περιάνδρῳ τῷ Κορίνθου τυράννῳ, ἐπεθύμησε πλεῦ-
σαι εἰς Ἰταλίαν τε καὶ Σικελίαν. ἐργασάμενος δὲ χρήματα
μεγάλα, ἠθέλησεν ὀπίσω εἰς Κόρινθον ἀφικέσθαι. ὡρμᾶτο

μέν νυν ἐκ Τάραντος, πιστεύων δὲ οὐδαμοῖς μᾶλλον ἢ 5
Κορινθίοις, ἐμισθώσατο πλοῖον ἀνδρῶν Κορινθίων. οἱ δὲ
ἐν τῷ πελάγει ἐπεβούλευον, τὸν Ἀρίονα ἐκβαλόντες,
ἔχειν τὰ χρήματα. ὁ δέ, συνεὶς τοῦτο, ἐλίσσετο, χρήματα
μὲν αὐτοῖς προϊείς, ψυχὴν δὲ παραιτούμενος. οὔκουν δὴ
ἔπειθεν, ἀλλ᾽ ἐκέλευον αὐτὸν οἱ πορθμεῖς ἢ διαχρῆσθαι 10
ἑαυτόν, ὡς ταφῆς ἐν γῇ τύχοι, ἢ ἐκπηδᾶν εἰς τὴν θάλατταν
τὴν ταχίστην. ἀπειληθεὶς δὲ ὁ Ἀρίων εἰς ἀπορίαν,
παρῃτήσατο αὐτοὺς περιδεῖν αὐτὸν ἐν τῇ σκευῇ πάσῃ
στάντα ἐν τοῖς ἑδωλίοις ᾆσαι· ᾄσας δὲ ὑπεδέχετο ἑαυτὸν
κατεργάσεσθαι. 15

ARION ON A DOLPHIN
Coin of Methymna in Lesbos

Οἱ δέ, εἰσῆλθε γὰρ αὐτοῖς ἡδονὴ εἰ μέλλοιεν ἀκού-
σεσθαι τοῦ ἀρίστου ἀνθρώπων ἀοιδοῦ, ἀνεχώρησαν ἐκ τῆς
πρύμνης εἰς μέσην ναῦν. ὁ δέ, ἐνδύς τε πᾶσαν τὴν σκευὴν
καὶ λαβὼν τὴν κιθάραν, στὰς ἐν τοῖς ἑδωλίοις διεξῆλθε
νόμον τὸν ὄρθιον· τελευτῶντος δὲ τοῦ νόμου ἔρριψεν εἰς 20
τὴν θάλατταν ἑαυτὸν ὡς εἶχε σὺν τῇ σκευῇ πάσῃ.
Καὶ οἱ μὲν ἀπέπλεον εἰς Κόρινθον· τὸν δὲ Ἀρίονα
δελφίς, ὡς λέγουσι, ὑπολαβὼν ἐξήνεγκεν ἐπὶ Ταίναρον.
ἀποβὰς δὲ ἐχώρει εἰς Κόρινθον σὺν τῇ σκευῇ, καὶ ἀφικόμενος ἀφηγεῖτο πᾶν τὸ γεγονός. Περίανδρος δὲ ὑπὸ 25
ἀπιστίας Ἀρίονα μὲν ἐν φυλακῇ εἶχεν οὐδαμῇ μεθιείς,
ἀνακῶς δὲ εἶχε τῶν πορθμέων. ὡς δὲ ἄρα παρῆσαν,

κληθέντας αὐτοὺς ἤρετο εἴ τι λέγοιεν περὶ Ἀρίονος. φαμένων δὲ ἐκείνων ὡς εἴη τε σῶς περὶ Ἰταλίαν καὶ
30 λίποιεν εὖ πράττοντα ἐν Τάραντι, ἐπεφάνη αὐτοῖς ὁ Ἀρίων, ὥσπερ ἔχων ἐξεπήδησε. καὶ οἱ δὲ ἐκπλαγέντες οὐκ εἶχον ἔτι ἐλεγχόμενοι ἀρνεῖσθαι.

VII. Story of Euenius

(a) *He neglects the sacred sheep of Apollonia, and is punished with blindness by his fellow-citizens.*

Ἔστιν ἐν τῇ Ἀπολλωνίᾳ ἱερὰ ἡλίου πρόβατα, ἃ τὰς μὲν ἡμέρας βόσκεται παρὰ ποταμόν τινα, τὰς δὲ νύκτας ᾑρημένοι ἄνδρες, οἱ πλούτῳ τε καὶ γένει δοκιμώτατοι τῶν ἀστῶν, φυλάττουσιν ἐνιαυτὸν ἕκαστος· περὶ πολλοῦ
5 γὰρ δὴ ποιοῦνται οἱ Ἀπολλωνιᾶται τὰ πρόβατα ταῦτα ἐκ θεοπροπίου τινός· ἐν δὲ ἄντρῳ αὐλίζονται ἀπὸ τῆς πόλεως ἑκάς. ἔνθα δὴ τότε ὁ Εὐήνιος οὗτος ᾑρημένος ἐφύλαττε.

Καί ποτε αὐτοῦ κατακοιμηθέντος, λύκοι εἰς τὸ ἄντρον
10 εἰσελθόντες διέφθειραν τῶν προβάτων ὡς ἑξήκοντα. ὁ δέ, ὡς ᾔσθετο, εἶχε σιγῇ καὶ ἔφραζεν οὐδενί, ἐν νῷ ἔχων ἀντικαταστήσειν ἄλλα πριάμενος. οἱ δὲ Ἀπολλωνιᾶται ὡς ἐπύθοντο, οὐ γὰρ ἔλαθεν αὐτοὺς ταῦτα γενόμενα, ὑπαγαγόντες αὐτὸν ὑπὸ δικαστήριον κατέκριναν τῆς
15 ὄψεως στερηθῆναι.

(b) *The gods declare that the punishment is excessive, and that Euenius must be given whatever compensation he chooses to claim.*

Ἐπεὶ δὲ τὸν Εὐήνιον ἐξετύφλωσαν, αὐτίκα μετὰ ταῦτα οὔτε πρόβατα αὐτοῖς ἔτικτεν οὔτε γῆ ἔφερεν ὁμοίως καρπόν. ἐπερωτωμένοις δὲ αὐτοῖς ἔν τε Δωδώνῃ καὶ

ἐν Δελφοῖς τὸ αἴτιον τοῦ παρόντος κακοῦ, τοιάδε ἔφραζον
οἱ θεοί, "'Αδίκως τὸν φύλακα τῶν ἱερῶν προβάτων 5
Εὐήνιον τῆς ὄψεως ἐστερήσατε· ἡμεῖς γὰρ ἐφωρμήσαμεν
τοὺς λύκους, οὐ πρότερόν τε παυσόμεθα τιμωροῦντες
ἐκείνῳ πρὶν ἂν δίκας δῶτε ἃς ἂν αὐτὸς ἕληται καὶ δικαιοῖ·
τούτων δὲ τελουμένων αὐτοὶ δώσομεν Εὐηνίῳ δόσιν
τοιαύτην ἣν ἔχοντα πολλοὶ ἀνθρώπων μακαριοῦσιν αὐτόν." 10

(c) *The Apolloniates trick Euenius into making only a moderate
demand. The gods bestow in addition the gift of prophecy.*

Οἱ δὲ 'Απολλωνιᾶται ἀπόρρητα ποιησάμενοι τὰ χρηστήρια ταῦτα, προύθεσαν ἀστοῖς τισι διαπρᾶξαι· οἱ δὲ
αὐτοῖς διέπραξαν ὧδε· καθημένου Εὐηνίου ἐν θάκῳ,
ἐλθόντες παρίζοντο αὐτῷ, καὶ λόγους ἄλλους ἐποιοῦντο
εἰς ὃ κατέβαινον συλλυπούμενοι τῷ πάθει. ταύτῃ δὲ 5
ὑπάγοντες ἠρώτων τίνα δίκην ἂν ἕλοιτο, εἰ ἐθέλοιεν
'Απολλωνιᾶται δίκας ὑποστῆναι δώσειν τῶν ποιηθέντων.
ὁ δὲ οὐκ ἀκηκοὼς τὸ θεοπρόπιον εἵλετο, εἰπὼν ὅτι εἰ
δοθεῖεν αὐτῷ ἀγροί τινες κάλλιστοι ὄντες τῶν ἐν τῇ
'Απολλωνίᾳ, καὶ οἴκησις πρὸς τούτοις, ἣν ᾔδει καλλίστην 10
οὖσαν τῶν ἐν πόλει, τὸ λοιπὸν ἀμήνιτος ἂν εἴη, καὶ αὕτη
ἡ δίκη ἂν ἀποχρώη. καὶ ὁ μὲν ταῦτα ἔλεγεν, οἱ δὲ
πάρεδροι εἶπον ὑπολαβόντες, "Εὐήνιε, ταύτην τὴν δίκην
'Απολλωνιᾶται τῆς ἐκτυφλώσεως ἐκτίνουσι κατὰ θεο-
πρόπια τὰ γενόμενα." 15
'Ο μὲν δὴ πρὸς ταῦτα δεινὰ ἐποιεῖτο, ἐντεῦθεν πυθόμενος
τὸν πάντα λόγον, ὡς ἐξαπατηθείς· οἱ δὲ διδόασιν αὐτῷ
ἃ εἵλετο. καὶ μετὰ ταῦτα αὐτίκα ἔμφυτον μαντικὴν
εἶχεν ὥστε καὶ ὀνομαστὸς γενέσθαι.

VIII. Story of Cyrus the Great, King of Persia

[The career of Cyrus is outlined in the Index of Names under
Κῦρος. *The subsequent history of the Persian Empire up to
its culmination in the wars with Greece may be followed by
reading the accounts of Cyrus's successors, Cambyses,
Darius, and Xerxes.*

*The story of Cyrus's parentage as related in the following
excerpt from Herodotus has no basis in fact.]*

A. INFANCY OF CYRUS

§ 1. *As a result of a dream, Astyages, king of the Medes, determines to destroy the new-born child Cyrus. He orders
Harpagus to put the boy to death.*

Οἱ τῶν Μάγων ὀνειροπόλοι ἐσήμαινον τῷ Ἀστυάγει
ἐξ ὄψεώς τινος ὅτι μέλλοι ὁ τῆς θυγατρὸς αὐτοῦ γόνος
βασιλεύσειν ἀντὶ ἐκείνου. ταῦτα δὴ οὖν φυλαττόμενος
ὁ Ἀστυάγης, ὡς ἐγένετο ὁ Κῦρος, καλέσας τὸν Ἅρπαγον,
5 ἄνδρα οἰκεῖον καὶ πιστότατον τῶν Μήδων καὶ πάντων
τῶν ἑαυτοῦ ἐπίτροπον, ἔλεγεν αὐτῷ τοιάδε, " Ἅρπαγε,
πρᾶγμα ὃ ἄν προσθῶ, μηδαμῶς παραχρήσῃ. λάβε τὸν
Μανδάνης παῖδα, φέρων δὲ εἰς σεαυτοῦ ἀπόκτεινον· μετὰ
δὲ θάψον ᾧτινι ἂν τρόπῳ αὐτὸς βούλῃ." ὁ δὲ ἀμείβεται,
10 " Ὦ βασιλεῦ, εἴ τοι φίλον τοῦτο οὕτω γίγνεσθαι, χρὴ δὴ
τό γ᾽ ἐμὸν ὑπηρετεῖσθαι ἐπιτηδείως."

Τούτοις ἀμειψάμενος ὁ Ἅρπαγος, ὡς αὐτῷ παρεδόθη τὸ
παιδίον, ᾔει κλάων εἰς τὰ οἰκία. παρελθὼν δὲ ἔφραζε τῇ
ἑαυτοῦ γυναικὶ τὸν πάντα ὑπ᾽ Ἀστυάγους ῥηθέντα λόγον.
15 ἡ δὲ πρὸς αὐτὸν λέγει, " Νῦν οὖν τί σοι ἐν νῷ ἐστι
ποιεῖν;" ὁ δὲ ἀμείβεται, " Οὐχ ᾗ ἐνετέλλετο Ἀστυάγης·
οὐδ᾽ εἰ παραφρονήσει τε καὶ μανεῖται κάκιον ἢ νῦν μαίνεται,

οὐκ ἔγωγε προσθήσομαι τῇ γνώμῃ αὐτοῦ, οὐδ' εἰς φόνον
τοιοῦτον ὑπηρετήσω. πολλῶν δὲ ἔνεκα οὐ φονεύσω τὸ
παιδίον· καὶ ὅτι αὐτῷ μοι συγγενές ἐστι, καὶ ὅτι Ἀστυάγης 20
μέν ἐστι γέρων καὶ ἄπαις ἄρσενος γόνου. εἰ δὲ μελλήσει
ἡ τυραννίς, τούτου τελευτήσαντος, εἰς τὴν θυγατέρα ταύτην
ἀναβήσεσθαι, ἧς νῦν τὸν υἱὸν κτείνει Ἀστυάγης δι' ἐμοῦ,
λείπεται τὸ ἐντεῦθεν ἐμοὶ κινδύνων ὁ μέγιστος· ἀλλὰ τῆς
μὲν ἀσφαλείας ἔνεκα ἐμοὶ δεῖ τοῦτον τὸν παῖδα τελευτᾶν· 25
δεῖ μέντοι τινὰ τῶν Ἀστυάγους φονέα αὐτοῦ γενέσθαι,
καὶ μὴ τῶν ἐμῶν."

§ 2. *Harpagus transfers the task of slaying the child to one of
Astyages' own herdsmen.*

Ταῦτα εἶπε καὶ αὐτίκα ἄγγελον ἔπεμπεν ἐπὶ βουκόλον
τινὰ τῶν Ἀστυάγους, ὃν ἠπίστατο νομάς τε ἐπιτηδειο-
τάτας νέμοντα καὶ ὄρη θηριωδέστατα, ᾧ ὄνομα ἦν Μιτρα-
δάτης. ἐπεὶ οὖν ὁ βουκόλος σπουδῇ πολλῇ ἀφίκετο
καλούμενος, ἔλεγεν ὁ Ἅρπαγος τάδε, " Κελεύει σε 5
Ἀστυάγης τὸ παιδίον τοῦτο λαβόντα θεῖναι εἰς τὸ ἐρημότατον τῶν ὀρῶν, ὅπως ἂν τάχιστα διαφθαρείη. καὶ
τάδε τοι ἐκέλευσεν εἰπεῖν, ὅτι, ἐὰν μὴ ἀποκτείνῃς αὐτό,
ἀλλά τινι τρόπῳ περιποιήσῃς, ὀλέθρῳ τῷ κακίστῳ σε
διαχρήσεται· ἐφορᾶν δὲ ἐκκείμενον τέταγμαι ἐγώ." 10

§ 3. *The herdsman returns home with the child and relates the
story to his wife.*

Ταῦτα ἀκούσας ὁ βουκόλος καὶ ἀναλαβὼν τὸ παιδίον
ᾔει τὴν αὐτὴν ὁδὸν ὀπίσω, καὶ ἀφικνεῖται εἰς τὴν ἔπαυλιν.
τούτῳ δ' ἄρα καὶ αὐτῷ ἡ γυνὴ ἐν ἐκείνῃ τῇ ἡμέρᾳ παῖδα
ἔτεκεν. ἐπεὶ δὲ ἀπενόστησεν ὁ βουκόλος, ἡ γυνὴ ἤρετο
εὐθὺς ὅ τι οὕτω προθύμως Ἅρπαγος αὐτὸν μεταπέμψαιτο. 5
ὁ δὲ εἶπεν, " Ὦ γύναι, εἶδόν τε εἰς πόλιν ἐλθὼν καὶ
ἤκουσα ὃ μὴ ἰδεῖν ὤφελον. οἶκος μὲν πᾶς Ἁρπάγου

κλαυθμῷ κατείχετο· ἐγὼ δὲ ἐκπλαγεὶς ᾖα εἴσω. ὡς δὲ
τάχιστα εἰσῆλθον, ὁρῶ παιδίον προκείμενον, ἀσπαῖρόν τε
10 καὶ κραυγανώμενον, κεκοσμημένον χρυσῷ τε καὶ ἐσθῆτι
ποικίλῃ. Ἅρπαγος δέ, ὡς εἶδέ με, ἐκέλευε τὴν ταχίστην
ἀναλαβόντα τὸ παιδίον οἴχεσθαι φέροντα καὶ θεῖναι ἔνθα
θηριωδέστατον εἴη τῶν ὀρῶν, πόλλ' ἀπειλήσας εἰ μὴ
ταῦτα ποιήσαιμι. ἐγὼ δὲ ἀναλαβὼν ἔφερον, καὶ καθ'
15 ὁδὸν πυνθάνομαι τὸν πάντα λόγον ἐκ θεράποντος, ὃς ἐμὲ
προπέμπων ἔξω πόλεως ἐνεχείρισε τὸ βρέφος, ὡς ἄρα
Μανδάνης τε εἴη παῖς καὶ Καμβύσου, καὶ Ἀστυάγης
ἐντέλλεται ἀποκτεῖναι αὐτόν. νῦν τε ὅδε ἐστίν."

§ 4. *The wife implores the herdsman to spare the child. At her
suggestion he exposes their own dead infant on the mountains
instead of Cyrus, and they bring up Cyrus as their son.*

Ἅμα δὲ ταῦτα ἔλεγεν ὁ βουκόλος καὶ ἐκκαλύψας ἀπε-
δείκνυε. ἡ δέ, ὡς εἶδε τὸ παιδίον μέγα τε καὶ εὐειδὲς
ὄν, δακρύσασα καὶ λαβομένη τῶν γονάτων τοῦ ἀνδρός,
ἐχρῇζε μηδαμῶς ἐκθεῖναι αὐτό. ὁ δὲ οὐκ ἔφη οἷός τε
5 εἶναι ἄλλως αὐτὰ ποιεῖν· ἐπιφοιτήσειν γὰρ κατασκόπους
ἐξ Ἁρπάγου ἐποψομένους· ἀπολεῖσθαί τε αὐτὸς κάκιστα
ἐὰν μὴ ταῦτα ποιήσῃ. ὡς δὲ οὐκ ἔπειθεν ἄρα τὸν ἄνδρα,
δεύτερα λέγει ἡ γυνὴ τάδε, "Ἐπεὶ τοίνυν οὐ δύναμαί σε
πείθειν μὴ ἐκθεῖναι, ὅμως ὧδε σὺ ποίησον, εἰ δὴ πᾶσα
10 ἀνάγκη ὀφθῆναι παιδίον ἐκκείμενον· τέτοκα γὰρ καὶ
ἐγώ, τέθνηκε δὲ τὸ βρέφος· τοῦτο μὲν φέρων πρόθες,
τὸν δὲ τῆς Ἀστυάγους θυγατρὸς παῖδα ὡς ἐξ ἡμῶν
ὄντα τρέφωμεν. καὶ οὕτως οὔτε σὺ ἁλώσει ἀδικῶν τοὺς
δεσπότας, οὔτε ἡμῖν κακῶς βεβουλευμένον ἔσται· ὅ τε
15 γὰρ τεθνηκὼς βασιλείας ταφῆς κυρήσει, καὶ ὁ περιὼν
οὐκ ἀπολεῖ τὴν ψυχήν."

Κάρτα τε ἔδοξε τῷ βουκόλῳ εὖ λέγειν ἡ γυνή, καὶ

αὐτίκα ἐποίει ταῦτα· ὃν μὲν ἔφερε θανατώσων παῖδα,
τοῦτον μὲν παραδίδωσι τῇ ἑαυτοῦ γυναικί· τὸν δὲ ἑαυτοῦ,
νεκρὸν ὄντα, λαβὼν ἔθηκεν εἰς τὸ ἄγγος ἐν ᾧ ἔφερε τὸν 20
ἕτερον· κοσμήσας δὲ τῷ κόσμῳ παντὶ τοῦ ἑτέρου παιδός,
φέρων εἰς τὸ ἐρημότατον τῶν ὀρῶν τίθησι.

Ὡς δὲ τρίτη ἡμέρα ἐγένετο, ᾔει εἰς πόλιν ὁ βουκόλος,
ἐλθὼν δὲ εἰς τοῦ Ἁρπάγου, ἀποδεικνύναι ἔφη ἕτοιμος
εἶναι τὸν τοῦ παιδίου νέκυν. πέμψας δὲ ὁ Ἅρπαγος 25
τῶν ἑαυτοῦ δορυφόρων τοὺς πιστοτάτους, εἶδέ τε διὰ
τούτων καὶ ἔθαψε τοῦ βουκόλου τὸ παιδίον. τὸν δὲ
Κῦρον παραλαβοῦσα ἔτρεφεν ἡ γυνὴ τοῦ βουκόλου.

B. BOYHOOD OF CYRUS: HOW THE SECRET OF HIS BIRTH IS DISCOVERED

§ 1. *Cyrus plays at being king over his companions.*

Καὶ ὅτε ἦν δεκαετὴς ὁ παῖς, πρᾶγμα τοιόνδε γενόμενον
ἐξέφηνεν αὐτόν. ἔπαιζε μετ᾽ ἄλλων ἡλίκων ἐν ὁδῷ·
καὶ οἱ παῖδες παίζοντες εἵλοντο ἑαυτῶν βασιλέα εἶναι
τοῦτον δὴ τὸν τοῦ βουκόλου ἐπίκλησιν παῖδα. ὁ δὲ τοὺς
μὲν αὐτῶν διέταξεν οἰκίας οἰκοδομεῖν, τοὺς δὲ δορυφό- 5
ρους εἶναι, τὸν δὲ πού τινα αὐτῶν " ὀφθαλμὸν βασιλέως "
εἶναι, ὡς ἑκάστῳ ἔργον προστάττων. εἰς δὴ τούτων τῶν
παίδων συμπαίζων, ὢν Ἀρτεμβάρους παῖς ἀνδρὸς δοκίμου
ἐν τοῖς Μήδοις, οὐκ ἐποίησε τὸ προσταχθὲν ἐκ τοῦ Κύρου.
ἐκέλευσεν οὖν τοὺς ἄλλους παῖδας διαλαβεῖν αὐτόν· πειθομ- 10
ένων δὲ τῶν παίδων, ὁ Κῦρος τὸν παῖδα κάρτα τραχέως
περιέσπε μαστιγῶν· ὁ δέ, ἐπεὶ τάχιστα μεθείθη, ὥς γε
δὴ ἀνάξια ἑαυτοῦ παθών, μᾶλλόν τι περιημέκτει· κατελθὼν
δὲ εἰς πόλιν, πρὸς τὸν πατέρα ἀπῳκτίζετο. ὁ δὲ Ἀρτεμβάρης ὀργῇ, ὡς εἶχεν, ἐλθὼν παρὰ τὸν Ἀστυάγη, καὶ 15
ἅμα ἀγόμενος τὸν παῖδα, ἀνάρσια πράγματα ἔφη πεπονθέναι,

λέγων, " Ὦ βασιλεῦ, ὑπὸ τοῦ σοῦ δούλου, βουκόλου δὲ παιδός, ὧδε περιυβρίσμεθα " (δεικνὺς τοῦ παιδὸς τοὺς ὤμους).

§ 2. *Astyages sends for Cyrus and, suspecting the truth, forces the
herdsman to confess.*

Ἀκούσας δὲ καὶ ἰδὼν ὁ Ἀστυάγης, ἐθέλων τιμωρῆσαι
τῷ παιδὶ τιμῆς τῆς Ἀρτεμβάρους ἕνεκα, μετεπέμπετο
τόν τε βουκόλον καὶ τὸν παῖδα. ἐπεὶ δὲ παρῆσαν ἀμφότεροι, βλέψας πρὸς τὸν Κῦρον ὁ Ἀστυάγης ἔφη, " Σὺ
5 δή, ὢν τοιούτου ἀνδρὸς παῖς, ἐτόλμησας τὸν τοῦδε παῖδα,
ὄντος πρώτου παρ' ἐμοί, αἰκίᾳ τοιᾷδε περιέπειν;"
Ὁ δὲ ἠμείβετο ὧδε, " Ὦ δέσποτα, ἐγὼ ταῦτα τοῦτον
ἐποίησα σὺν δίκῃ. οἱ γὰρ ἐκ τῆς κώμης παῖδες, ὧν καὶ
ὅδε ἦν, παίζοντες ἐστήσαντο ἐμὲ βασιλέα ἑαυτῶν· ἐδόκουν
10 γὰρ αὐτοῖς εἶναι εἰς τοῦτο ἐπιτηδειότατος. οἱ μέν νυν
ἄλλοι παῖδες τὰ ἐπιταττόμενα ἐπετέλουν· οὗτος δὲ
ἀνηκούστει τε καὶ λόγον εἶχεν οὐδένα· εἰς ὃ ἔλαβε τὴν
δίκην. εἰ οὖν δὴ τοῦδε ἕνεκα ἄξιός τινος κακοῦ εἰμί,
ὧδέ τοι πάρειμι."
15 Ταῦτα λέγοντος τοῦ παιδός, τὸν Ἀστυάγη εἰσῄει
ἀνάγνωσις αὐτοῦ· καὶ ὅ τε χαρακτὴρ τοῦ προσώπου
ἐδόκει προσφέρεσθαι εἰς ἑαυτόν, καὶ ἡ ὑπόκρισις ἐλευ-
θερωτάτη εἶναι· ὁ δὲ χρόνος τῆς ἐκθέσεως τῇ ἡλικίᾳ τοῦ
παιδὸς ἐδόκει συμβαίνειν. ἐκπλαγεὶς δὲ τούτοις, ἐπὶ
20 χρόνον ἄφθογγος ἦν. μόγις δὲ δή ποτε ἀνενεχθεὶς εἶπεν,
ἐθέλων ἐκπέμψαι τὸν Ἀρτεμβάρη, ἵνα τὸν βουκόλον μόνον
λαβὼν βασανίσῃ, " Ἀρτέμβαρες, ἐγὼ ταῦτα ποιήσω,
ὥστε σὲ καὶ τὸν παῖδα τὸν σὸν μηδὲν ἐπιμέμφεσθαι."
τὸν μὲν δὴ Ἀρτεμβάρη πέμπει· τὸν δὲ Κῦρον ἦγον
25 εἴσω οἱ θεράποντες, κελεύσαντος τοῦ Ἀστυάγους. ἐπεὶ
δὲ ὑπελέλειπτο ὁ βουκόλος μόνος, τάδε αὐτὸν ἤρετο ὁ
Ἀστυάγης, ὁπόθεν λάβοι τὸν παῖδα, καὶ τίς εἴη ὁ παραδούς.

ὁ δὲ ἐξ ἑαυτοῦ τε ἔφη γεγονέναι, καὶ τὴν τεκοῦσαν αὐτὸν
ἔτι εἶναι παρ' ἑαυτῷ. Ἀστυάγης δὲ οὐκ ἔφη αὐτὸν εὖ
βουλεύεσθαι, ἐπιθυμῶν εἰς ἀνάγκας μεγάλας ἀφικνεῖσθαι· 30
ἅμα τε λέγων ταῦτα, ἐσήμαινε τοῖς δορυφόροις λαμβάνειν
αὐτόν. ὁ δὲ ἀγόμενος εἰς τὰς ἀνάγκας, οὕτω δὴ ἔφαινε
τὸν ὄντα λόγον· καὶ κατέβαινεν εἰς λιτὰς συγγνώμην
ἑαυτῷ κελεύων ἔχειν αὐτόν.

§ 3. *Astyages pardons the herdsman and obtains a confession from
Harpagus, whom he also pretends to pardon.*

Ἀστυάγης δὲ τοῦ μὲν βουκόλου τὴν ἀλήθειαν ἐκφήναντος λόγον ἤδη καὶ ἐλάττω ἐποιεῖτο· Ἁρπάγῳ δὲ καὶ
μεγάλως μεμφόμενος, καλεῖν αὐτὸν τοὺς δορυφόρους
ἐκέλευεν. ὡς δὲ παρῆν ὁ Ἅρπαγος, ἤρετο αὐτὸν ὁ
Ἀστυάγης, " Ἅρπαγε, τίνι δὴ μόρῳ τὸν παῖδα κατε- 5
χρήσω, ὅν σοι παρέδωκα ἐκ θυγατρὸς γεγονότα τῆς ἐμῆς;"
Ὁ δὲ Ἅρπαγος ὡς εἶδε τὸν βουκόλον ἔνδον ὄντα, οὐ
τρέπεται ἐπὶ ψευδῆ ὁδόν, ἵνα μὴ ἐλεγχόμενος ἁλίσκηται,
ἀλλὰ τὸν εὐθὺν ἔφαινε λόγον. Ἀστυάγης δέ, κρύπτων
τὸν χόλον, πρῶτον μέν, καθάπερ ἤκουσεν αὐτὸς πρὸς τοῦ 10
βουκόλου τὸ πρᾶγμα, πάλιν ἀφηγεῖτο τῷ Ἁρπάγῳ· μετὰ
δὲ κατέβαινε λέγων ὡς, " Περίεστί τε ὁ παῖς, καὶ τὸ
γεγονὸς ἔχει καλῶς. τῷ τε γὰρ πεποιημένῳ εἰς τὸν
παῖδα τοῦτον ἔκαμνον μεγάλως, καὶ θυγατρὶ τῇ ἐμῇ
διαβεβλημένος οὐκ ἐν ἐλαφρῷ ἐποιούμην. ὡς οὖν τῆς 15
τύχης εὖ μεθεστηκυίας, τοῦτο μέν, τὸν σεαυτοῦ παῖδα
ἀπόπεμψον παρὰ τὸν παῖδα τὸν νεήλυδα· τοῦτο δέ (σῶστρα
γὰρ τοῦ παιδὸς μέλλω θύειν τοῖς θεοῖς), πάρισθί μοι ἐπὶ
δεῖπνον."
Ἅρπαγος μέν, ὡς ἤκουσε ταῦτα, προσκυνήσας καὶ 20
μεγάλα ποιησάμενος ὅτι τε ἡ ἁμαρτάς οἱ εἰς δέον ἐγεγόνειν, ᾔει εἰς τὰ οἰκία. εἰσελθὼν δὲ τὴν ταχίστην, τὸν

παῖδα τὸν μονογενῆ ἔτη τρία καὶ δέκα γεγονότα ἐκπέμπει,
ἰέναι τε κελεύων εἰς ᾿Αστυάγους καὶ ποιεῖν ὅ τι ἂν ἐκεῖνος
25 κελεύῃ· αὐτὸς δὲ περιχαρὴς ὢν φράζει τῇ γυναικὶ τὰ
συγκυρήσαντα.

§.4. Abominable punishment inflicted upon Harpagus.

᾿Αστυάγης δέ, ὡς ἀφίκετο ὁ ῾Αρπάγου παῖς, σφάξας
αὐτὸν καὶ κατὰ μέλη διελών, τὰ μὲν ὤπτησε, τὰ δὲ ἥψησε
τῶν κρεῶν. ἐπεὶ δὲ ἡ ὥρα ἐγίγνετο τοῦ δείπνου, παρε-
τίθετο ταῦτα τῷ ῾Αρπάγῳ, πλὴν κεφαλῆς καὶ χειρῶν
5 καὶ ποδῶν· ταῦτα δὲ χωρὶς ἔκειτο ἐπὶ κανῷ κατακεκαλυμ-
μένα. ὡς δὲ ὁ ῞Αρπαγος ἐδόκει ἅλις ἔχειν τῆς βορᾶς,
᾿Αστυάγης ἤρετο αὐτὸν εἰ ἡσθείη τι τῇ θοίνῃ· φαμένου
δὲ ῾Αρπάγου καὶ κάρτα ἡσθῆναι, παρέφερόν τινες τὴν
κεφαλὴν τοῦ παιδὸς κατακεκαλυμμένην καὶ τὰς χεῖρας
10 καὶ τοὺς πόδας. ῞Αρπαγον δὲ ἐκέλευον προστάντες
ἀποκαλύπτειν τε καὶ λαβεῖν ὃ βούλεται αὐτῶν. πειθό-
μενος δὲ ὁ ῞Αρπαγος καὶ ἀποκαλύπτων, ὁρᾷ τοῦ παιδὸς
τὰ λείμματα· ἰδὼν δὲ οὔτε ἐξεπλάγη ἐντός τε ἑαυτοῦ
γίγνεται. ἤρετο δὲ αὐτὸν ὁ ᾿Αστυάγης εἰ γιγνώσκοι
15 οὗτινος θηρίου κρέα βεβρώκοι. ὁ δὲ καὶ γιγνώσκειν
ἔφη καὶ ἀρεστὸν εἶναι πᾶν ὃ ἂν βασιλεὺς ἔρδῃ. τούτοις
δὲ ἀμειψάμενος καὶ ἀναλαβὼν τὰ λοιπὰ τῶν κρεῶν, ᾔει
εἰς τὰ οἰκία. ἐντεῦθεν δὲ ἔμελλε, ὡς ἐγὼ δοκῶ, ἀλίσας
θάψειν πάντα.

§ 5. The Magi decide that Astyages need have no more fear of Cyrus; so the boy is sent home safely to his parents in Persia.

῾Αρπάγῳ μὲν ᾿Αστυάγης δίκην ταύτην ἐπέθηκε· Κύρου
δὲ πέρι βουλεύων ἐκάλει τοὺς αὐτοὺς τῶν Μάγων οἳ τὸ
ἐνύπνιον αὐτῷ πρότερον ἔκριναν. ἀφικομένους δὲ ἤρετο
ὁ ᾿Αστυάγης ὅπῃ ἔκριναν τὴν ὄψιν. οἱ δὲ ταὐτὰ εἶπον,

λέγοντες ὡς χρῆν ἂν βασιλεῦσαι τὸν παῖδα, εἰ ἐπέζησε 5
καὶ μὴ ἀπέθανε πρότερον. ὁ δὲ ἠμείβετο αὐτοὺς τοῖσδε,
" Ἔστι τε ὁ παῖς, καὶ περίεστι· καὶ διαιτώμενον αὐτὸν
ἐπ' ἀγροῦ οἱ ἐκ τῆς κώμης παῖδες ἐστήσαντο βασιλέα.
ὁ δὲ πάντα ὅσα περ οἱ ἀληθινοὶ βασιλεῖς ἐτελείωσε
ποιήσας· καὶ γὰρ δορυφόρους καὶ θυρωροὺς καὶ ἀγγε- 10
λιαφόρους καὶ τὰ λοιπὰ πάντα εἶχε. καὶ νῦν εἰς τί ὑμῖν
ταῦτα φαίνεται φέρειν;

Εἶπον οἱ Μάγοι, " Εἰ μὲν περίεστί τε καὶ ἐβασίλευσεν ὁ παῖς μὴ ἐκ προνοίας τινός, θάρσει τε τούτου
ἕνεκα, καὶ θυμὸν ἔχε ἀγαθόν· οὐ γὰρ ἔτι τὸ δεύτερον 15
ἄρξει."

Ἀκούσας ταῦτα ὁ Ἀστυάγης ἐχάρη τε καὶ καλέσας
τὸν Κῦρον ἔλεγεν αὐτῷ τάδε, " Ὦ παῖ, ἐγὼ σὲ δι' ὄψιν
ὀνείρου οὐ τελείαν ἠδίκουν, τῇ δὲ σαυτοῦ μοίρᾳ περίει·
νῦν οὖν ἴθι χαίρων εἰς Πέρσας, πομποὺς δ' ἐγὼ ἅμα πέμψω. 20
ἐλθὼν δ' ἐκεῖ, πατέρα τε καὶ μητέρα εὑρήσεις, οὐ κατὰ
Μιτραδάτην τε τὸν βουκόλον καὶ τὴν γυναῖκα αὐτοῦ."

Ταῦτα εἰπὼν ὁ Ἀστυάγης ἀποπέμπει τὸν Κῦρον.
νοστήσαντα δὲ αὐτὸν εἰς τὰ τοῦ Καμβύσου οἰκία ἐδέξαντο
οἱ τεκόντες, καὶ δεξάμενοι μεγάλως ἠσπάζοντο. 25

C. MANHOOD OF CYRUS

§ 1. *At the instigation of Harpagus, Cyrus induces the Persians
to revolt by a practical demonstration of the advantages they
would enjoy as the dominant race.*

Κύρῳ δὲ ἀνδρουμένῳ καὶ ὄντι τῶν ἡλίκων ἀνδρειοτά-
τῳ καὶ προσφιλεστάτῳ προσέκειτο ὁ Ἄρπαγος, δῶρα
πέμπων, τίσασθαι Ἀστυάγη ἐπιθυμῶν. πρὸ δ' ἔτι
τούτου ὁ Ἄρπαγος, ὄντος τοῦ Ἀστυάγους πικροῦ εἰς
τοὺς Μήδους, συμμίσγων ἑνὶ ἑκάστῳ τῶν πρώτων Μήδων, 5

ἀνέπειθεν ὡς χρὴ Κῦρον προστησαμένους τὸν Ἀστυάγη
παῦσαι τῆς βασιλείας.
Ὁ δὲ Κῦρος ἐφρόντιζεν ᾧτινι τρόπῳ σοφωτάτῳ Πέρσας
ἀναπείσει ἀφίστασθαι. φροντίζων δὲ εὑρίσκει τάδε και-
10 ριώτατα εἶναι. γράψας εἰς βιβλίον ἃ ἐβούλετο, ἁλίαν
τῶν Περσῶν ἐποιήσατο· μετὰ δὲ ἀναπτύξας τὸ βιβλίον
καὶ ἐπιλεγόμενος, ἔφη Ἀστυάγη ἑαυτὸν στρατηγὸν Περσῶν
ἀποδεικνύναι. " Νῦν τε," ἔφη λέγων, " ὦ Πέρσαι,
προαγορεύω ὑμῖν παρεῖναι ἕκαστον ἔχοντα δρέπανον."
15 Κῦρος μὲν ταῦτα προηγόρευσεν. ὡς δὲ παρῆσαν ἅπαντες,
ἐνταῦθα Κῦρος χῶρόν τινα ἀκανθώδη προεῖπεν αὐτοῖς
ἐξημερῶσαι ἐν ἡμέρᾳ. ἐπιτελεσάντων δὲ τῶν Περσῶν
τὸν προκείμενον ἆθλον, προεῖπεν αὐτοῖς εἰς τὴν ὑστεραίαν
παρεῖναι λελουμένους.
20 Ἐν δὲ τούτῳ τά τε αἰπόλια καὶ τὰς ποίμνας καὶ τὰ
βουκόλια πάντα τοῦ πατρὸς συναλίσας εἰς ταὐτὸ ὁ Κῦρος
ἔθυε καὶ παρεσκεύαζεν ὡς δεξόμενος τὸν τῶν Περσῶν
στρατόν. ἀφικομένους δὲ τῇ ὑστεραίᾳ τοὺς Πέρσας
κατακλίνας εἰς λειμῶνα εὐώχει. ἐπεὶ δὲ ἀπὸ δείπνου
25 ἦσαν, ἤρετο αὐτοὺς ὁ Κῦρος πότερον ἃ τῇ προτεραίᾳ
εἶχον ἢ τὰ παρόντα εἴη αὐτοῖς αἱρετώτερα. οἱ δὲ ἔφασαν
πολὺ εἶναι τὸ μέσον, τὴν μὲν γὰρ προτέραν ἡμέραν
πάντα σφίσι κακὰ ἔχειν, τὴν δὲ τότε παροῦσαν πάντα
ἀγαθά.
30 Παραλαβὼν δὲ τοῦτο τὸ ἔπος ὁ Κῦρος παρεγύμνου
τὸν πάντα λόγον, λέγων, " Ἄνδρες Πέρσαι, οὕτως ὑμῖν
ἔχει· βουλομένοις μὲν ὑμῖν ἐμοὶ πείθεσθαι ἔστι τάδε τε
καὶ ἄλλα μυρία ἀγαθά, οὐδένα πόνον δουλοπρεπῆ ἔχουσι·
μὴ βουλομένοις δὲ ἐμοὶ πείθεσθαι εἰσὶν ὑμῖν πόνοι τῷ χθιζῷ
35 παραπλήσιοι ἀναρίθμητοι. νῦν οὖν ἐμοὶ πειθόμενοι γίγ-
νεσθε ἐλεύθεροι, ἀφιστάμενοι ἀπ' Ἀστυάγους ὅτι τάχιστα."

PERSIAN SPEARMAN
Relief of enamelled tiles from Susa

§ 2. *Revolt of the Persians, ending in the accession of Cyrus to the throne.*

Πέρσαι μέν νυν, προστάτου ἐπιλαβόμενοι, ἄσμενοι ἠλευθεροῦντο, καὶ πάλαι δεινὸν ποιούμενοι ὑπὸ Μήδων ἄρχεσθαι. Ἀστυάγης δέ, ὡς ἐπύθετο Κῦρον ταῦτα

CYRUS THE GREAT, DIVINIZED
Persian relief

πράττοντα, πέμψας ἄγγελον ἐκάλει αὐτόν. ὁ δὲ Κῦρος
5 ἐκέλευε τὸν ἄγγελον ἀπαγγέλλειν ὅτι πρότερον ἥξοι παρ'
ἐκεῖνον ἢ Ἀστυάγης αὐτὸς βουλήσεται. ἀκούσας δὲ

ταῦτα ὁ Ἀστυάγης Μήδους τε ὥπλισε πάντας καὶ
στρατηγὸν αὐτῶν, ὡσεὶ θεοβλαβὴς ὤν, Ἅρπαγον ἀπέ-
δειξεν. ὡς δ᾽ οἱ Μῆδοι στρατευσάμενοι τοῖς Πέρσαις
συνέμισγον, οἱ μὲν αὐτῶν ἐμάχοντο, ὅσοι μὴ τοῦ λόγου 10
μετέσχον, οἱ δὲ ηὐτομόλουν πρὸς τοὺς Πέρσας, οἱ δὲ πλεῖστοι
ἠθελοκάκουν τε καὶ ἔφευγον. διαλυθέντος δὲ τοῦ Μηδικοῦ
στρατεύματος αἰσχρῶς, ὡς τάχιστα ἐπύθετο ὁ Ἀστυάγης,
ἔφη ἀπειλῶν τῷ Κύρῳ, " Ἀλλ᾽ οὐδ᾽ ὣς ὁ Κῦρός γε
χαιρήσει." τοσαῦτα εἰπὼν πρῶτον μὲν ἀνεσκολόπισε 15
τοὺς τῶν Μάγων ὀνειροπόλους οἳ ἀνέγνωσαν αὐτὸν μεθεῖναι
τὸν Κῦρον. μετὰ δὲ ὥπλισε τοὺς ὑπολειφθέντας τῶν
Μήδων ἐν τῷ ἄστει νέους τε καὶ πρεσβύτας ἄνδρας. ἐξαγαγὼν δὲ τούτους καὶ συμβαλὼν τοῖς Πέρσαις ἡττήθη·
καὶ αὐτός τε Ἀστυάγης ἐζωγρήθη, καὶ οὓς ἐξήγαγε τῶν 20
Μήδων ἀπέβαλε. Ἀστυάγη δὲ ὁ Κῦρος, κακὸν οὐδὲν
ἄλλο ποιήσας, εἶχε παρ᾽ ἑαυτῷ εἰς ὃ ἐτελεύτησεν.

Οὕτω δὴ Κῦρος γενόμενός τε καὶ τραφεὶς ἐβασίλευσεν.

IX. SOLON AND CROESUS

(a) *Solon, the Athenian statesman and philosopher, visits Croesus,
the rich king of Lydia. He does not regard his wealth as a
criterion for happiness.*

Ἐκδημήσας ὁ Σόλων εἰς Σάρδεις ἀφίκετο παρὰ Κροῖσον.
ἀφικόμενος δὲ ἐξενίζετο ἐν τοῖς βασιλείοις ὑπὸ τοῦ
Κροίσου· μετὰ δέ, ἡμέρᾳ τρίτῃ ἢ τετάρτῃ, κελεύσαντος
Κροίσου, τὸν Σόλωνα θεράποντες περιῆγον κατὰ τοὺς
θησαυρούς, καὶ ἐπεδείκνυσαν πάντα ὄντα μεγάλα τε καὶ 5
ὄλβια. θεασάμενον δὲ αὐτὸν πάντα ἤρετο ὁ Κροῖσος
τάδε, " Ξένε Ἀθηναῖε, παρ᾽ ἡμᾶς περὶ σοῦ λόγος ἀφῖκται
πολύς, καὶ σοφίας ἕνεκα τῆς σῆς καὶ πλάνης· νῦν οὖν
ἵμερος ἐπῆλθέ με ἐπερωτᾶν εἴ τινα ἤδη πάντων εἶδες

CLEOBIS AND BITON

Relief on a sarcophagus at Venice

ὀλβιώτατον." ὁ μὲν ἐλπίζων εἶναι ἀνθρώπων ὀλβιώτατος 10
ταῦτα ἐπηρώτα· Σόλων δέ, οὐδὲν ὑποθωπεύσας ἀλλὰ
τῷ ὄντι χρησάμενος, λέγει, "῏Ω βασιλεῦ, Τέλλον Ἀθη-
ναῖον." ἀποθαυμάσας δὲ Κροῖσος τὸ λεχθὲν ἤρετο
ἐπιστρεφῶς, "Πῶς δὴ κρίνεις Τέλλον εἶναι ὀλβιώτατον;" ὁ δὲ
εἶπε, " Τέλλῳ τοῦτο μὲν παῖδες ἦσαν καλοί τε κἀγαθοί, 15
καὶ εἶδεν ἅπασιν αὐτοῖς τέκνα ἐκγενόμενα, καὶ πάντα
παραμείναντα· τοῦτο δὲ τελευτὴ τοῦ βίου λαμπροτάτη
ἐπεγένετο· γενομένης γὰρ Ἀθηναίοις μάχης πρὸς τοὺς
ἀστυγείτονας ἐν Ἐλευσῖνι, βοηθήσας καὶ τροπὴν ποιήσας
τῶν πολεμίων, ἀπέθανε κάλλιστα. καὶ Ἀθηναῖοι δημοσίᾳ 20
τε ἔθαψαν αὐτὸν ᾗπερ ἔπεσε, καὶ ἐτίμησαν μεγάλως."

(b) *Story of Cleobis and Biton; the gods' best reward.*

Ὡς δὲ τὰ κατὰ τὸν Τέλλον διηγήσατο ὁ Σόλων,
ἐπηρώτα ὁ Κροῖσος τίνα δεύτερον μετ' ἐκεῖνον ἴδοι, δοκῶν
πάνυ δευτερεῖα γοῦν οἴσεσθαι. ὁ δὲ εἶπε, " Κλέοβίν τε
καὶ Βίτωνα· τούτοις γάρ, οὖσι γένος Ἀργείοις, βίος τε
ἀρκῶν ὑπῆν, καὶ πρὸς τούτῳ, ῥώμη σώματος τοιάδε· 5
ἀθλοφόροι τε ἀμφότεροι ὁμοίως ἦσαν, καὶ δὴ καὶ λέγεται
ὅδε ὁ λόγος. οὔσης ἑορτῆς τῇ Ἥρᾳ ἔδει πάντως τὴν
μητέρα αὐτῶν ζεύγει κομισθῆναι εἰς τὸ ἱερόν· οἱ δὲ βόες
ἐκ τοῦ ἀγροῦ οὐ παρεγίνοντο ἐν ὥρα. οἱ δὲ νεανίαι,
ὑποδύντες αὐτοὶ ὑπὸ τὴν ζεύγλην, εἷλκον τὴν ἅμαξαν, 10
ἐπὶ δὲ τῆς ἁμάξης ὠχεῖτο ἡ μήτηρ. σταδίους δὲ πέντε
καὶ τετταράκοντα διακομίσαντες ἀφίκοντο εἰς τὸ ἱερόν·
ταῦτα δὲ ποιήσασιν αὐτοῖς καὶ ὀφθεῖσι ὑπὸ τῆς πανη-
γύρεως τελευτὴ τοῦ βίου ἀρίστη ἐπεγένετο· διέδειξέ τε
ἐν τούτοις ὁ θεὸς ὡς ἄμεινον εἴη ἀνθρώπῳ τεθνάναι μᾶλλον 15
ἢ ζῆν. Ἀργεῖοι μὲν γὰρ περιστάντες ἐμακάριζον τῶν
νεανιῶν τὴν ῥώμην, αἱ δὲ Ἀργεῖαι τὴν μητέρα αὐτῶν
οἵων τέκνων ἐκύρησε· ἡ δὲ μήτηρ περιχαρὴς οὖσα τῷ τε

ἔργῳ καὶ τῇ φήμῃ, στᾶσα ἀντίον τοῦ ἀγάλματος ηὔχετο
20 τὴν θεὸν δοῦναι Κλεοβεί τε καὶ Βίτωνι ὃ ἀνθρώπῳ τυχεῖν
ἄριστόν ἐστι. μετὰ δὲ ταύτην τὴν εὐχήν, ὡς ἔθυσάν
τε καὶ εὐωχήθησαν, κατακοιμηθέντες ἐν αὐτῷ τῷ ἱερῷ οἱ
νεανίαι οὐκέτι ἀνέστησαν, ἀλλ' ἐν τέλει τούτῳ ἔσχοντο.
Ἀργεῖοι δὲ εἰκόνας αὐτῶν ποιησάμενοι ἀνέθεσαν εἰς
25 Δελφούς, ὡς ἀνδρῶν ἀρίστων γενομένων."

(c) *Solon's criterion for happiness, which*
Croesus finds unacceptable.

Σόλων μὲν δὴ εὐδαιμονίας δευτερεῖα ἔνεμε τούτοις·
Κροῖσος δὲ σπερχθεὶς εἶπεν, " Ὦ ξένε Ἀθηναῖε, ἡ δὲ
ἡμετέρα εὐδαιμονία οὕτω τοι ἀπέρριπται εἰς τὸ μηδέν,
ὥστε οὐδὲ ἰδιωτῶν ἀνδρῶν ἀξίους ἡμᾶς ἐποίησας;" ὁ δὲ
5 εἶπεν, " Ὦ Κροῖσε, ἐπιστάμενόν με τὸ θεῖον πᾶν φθονερόν
τε καὶ ταραχῶδες ὃν ἐπερωτᾷς ἀνθρωπείων πραγμάτων
πέρι. ἐμοὶ δὲ σὺ καὶ πλουτεῖν μὲν μέγα φαίνει, καὶ βασιλεὺς πολλῶν εἶναι ἀνθρώπων· εὐδαίμονα δὲ οὔπω σε ἐγὼ
λέγω, πρὶν ἂν τελευτήσαντά σε καλῶς τὸν αἰῶνα πύθωμαι.
10 σκοπεῖν δὲ χρὴ παντὸς χρήματος τὴν τελευτὴν πῇ ἀπο-
βήσεται· πολλοῖς γὰρ δὴ ὑποδείξας ὄλβον ὁ θεὸς προρρίζους
ἀνέτρεψε." ταῦτα λέγων τῷ Κροίσῳ οὔ πως ἐχαρίζετο
ὁ Σόλων· λόγου δὲ αὐτὸν ποιησάμενος οὐδενὸς ἀποπέμπεται
ὁ Κροῖσος, κάρτα δόξας ἀμαθῆ εἶναι, ὃς τὰ παρόντα
15 ἀγαθὰ μεθεὶς τὴν τελευτὴν παντὸς χρήματος ὁρᾶν ἐκέλευε.

(d) *Subsequent misfortunes of Croesus, who at length acknowledges*
the wisdom of Solon's words.

Μετὰ δὲ Σόλωνα οἰχόμενον ἔλαβεν ἐκ θεοῦ νέμεσις
μεγάλη Κροῖσον, ὡς εἰκάσαι, ὅτι ἐνόμισεν ἑαυτὸν εἶναι
ἀνθρώπων ἁπάντων ὀλβιώτατον. οἱ γὰρ Πέρσαι τάς τε
Σάρδεις εἷλον, καὶ αὐτὸν Κροῖσον ἐζώγρησαν, ἄρξαντα
5 ἔτη τεσσαρεσκαίδεκα· λαβόντες δὲ αὐτὸν ἤγαγον παρὰ

Κῦρον. ὁ δὲ συννήσας πυρὰν μεγάλην ἀνεβίβασεν ἐπ᾽
αὐτὴν τὸν Κροῖσόν τε ἐν πέδαις δεδεμένον καὶ δὶς ἑπτὰ
Λυδῶν παρ᾽ αὐτὸν παῖδας. τῷ δὲ Κροίσῳ, ἑστῶτι ἐπὶ
τῆς πυρᾶς, εἰσῆλθε, καίπερ ἐν κακῷ ὄντι τοσούτῳ, τὸ
τοῦ Σόλωνος, ὡς εἴη σὺν θεῷ εἰρημένον, τὸ " μηδένα εἶναι 10
τῶν ζώντων ὄλβιον." ἀνενεγκάμενος δὲ καὶ ἀναστενάξας
ἐκ πολλῆς ἡσυχίας εἰς τρὶς ὠνόμασε Σόλωνα· καὶ ὁ
Κῦρος ἀκούσας ἐκέλευσε τοὺς ἑρμηνέας ἐπέρεσθαι τὸν
Κροῖσον τίνα ἐπικαλοῖτο· καὶ οἱ δὲ προσελθόντες ἐπηρώ-
των. Κροῖσος δὲ τέως μὲν σιγὴν εἶχεν ἐρωτώμενος· 15
μετὰ δὲ ἔλεγεν ὡς ἔλθοι ποτὲ ὁ Σόλων, ὢν Ἀθηναῖος, καὶ
θεασάμενος πάντα τὸν ἑαυτοῦ ὄλβον ἀποφλαυρίσειε· καὶ

GOLD COIN PROBABLY ISSUED BY CROESUS
In the British Museum

πάντα ἑαυτῷ ἀποβεβήκοι ἧπερ ἐκεῖνος εἶπεν, οὐδέν τι
μᾶλλον εἰς ἑαυτὸν λέγων ἢ εἰς ἅπαν τὸ ἀνθρώπινον καὶ
μάλιστα τοὺς παρ᾽ ἑαυτοῖς ὀλβίους δοκοῦντας εἶναι. 20

(e) *Cyrus relents, and, with the assistance of Apollo, Croesus is
saved from the flames.*

Ὁ μὲν Κροῖσος ταῦτα ἀφηγεῖτο, τῆς δὲ πυρᾶς ἤδη
ἡμμένης ἐκάετο τὰ περιέσχατα. καὶ ὁ Κῦρος, ἀκούσας
παρὰ τῶν ἑρμηνέων ἃ Κροῖσος εἶπε, μεταγνούς τε καὶ
ἐννοήσας ὅτι καὶ αὐτὸς ἄνθρωπος ὢν ἄλλον ἄνθρωπον,
γενόμενον ἑαυτοῦ εὐδαιμονίᾳ οὐκ ἐλάττω, ζῶντα πυρὶ 5
διδοίη, ἐκέλευε σβεννύναι τὴν ταχίστην τὸ καόμενον πῦρ,
καὶ καταβιβάζειν Κροῖσόν τε καὶ τοὺς μετὰ Κροίσου. καὶ
οἱ δὲ πειρώμενοι οὐκ ἐδύναντο ἔτι τοῦ πυρὸς ἐπικρατῆσαι.

ἐνταῦθα Κροῖσος, μαθὼν τὴν Κύρου μετάγνωσιν, ἐπε-
10 βοήσατο τὸν Ἀπόλλωνα ἐπικαλούμενος παραστῆναι καὶ
ῥύσασθαι αὐτὸν ἐκ τοῦ παρόντος κακοῦ. ὁ μὲν δακρύων
ἐπεκαλεῖτο τὸν θεόν· ἐκ δὲ αἰθρίας τε καὶ νηνεμίας
συνέδραμεν ἐξαπίνης νέφη, καὶ χειμών τε κατερράγη καὶ
ὗσεν ὕδατι λαβροτάτῳ, κατεσβέσθη τε ἡ πυρά.

X. RESPECT FOR SUPPLIANTS ENFORCED BY AN ORACLE

Ὁ μὲν Πακτύης, δείσας τοὺς Πέρσας, ᾤχετο φεύγων
εἰς Κύμην· ὁ δὲ Μαζάρης ἔπεμπεν εἰς τὴν Κύμην ἀγγέ-
λους, ἐκδιδόναι κελεύων Πακτύην. οἱ δὲ Κυμαῖοι
ἔγνωσαν συμβουλῆς πέρι εἰς θεὸν τὸν ἐν Βραγχίδαις
5 ἀναφέρειν. ἦν γὰρ αὐτόθι μαντεῖον ἐκ παλαιοῦ ἱδρυμένον,
ᾧ Ἴωνές τε πάντες καὶ Αἰολεῖς εἰώθεσαν χρῆσθαι.
πέμψαντες οὖν οἱ Κυμαῖοι θεοπρόπους ἠρώτων ὁποῖόν
τι περὶ Πακτύην ποιοῦντες θεοῖς μέλλοιεν χαριεῖσθαι.
ἐπερωτῶσι δὲ αὐτοῖς ταῦτα χρηστήριον ἐγένετο ἐκδιδόναι
10 Πακτύην τοῖς Πέρσαις.

Ταῦτα δὲ ὡς ἤκουσαν οἱ Κυμαῖοι ὡρμῶντο ἐκδιδόναι·
ὁρμωμένου δὲ τοῦ πλήθους, Ἀριστόδικος, ἀνὴρ τῶν
ἀστῶν δόκιμος, ἔσχε μὴ ποιῆσαι ταῦτα τοὺς Κυμαίους,
ἀπιστῶν τε τῷ χρησμῷ, καὶ δοκῶν τοὺς θεοπρόπους οὐ
15 λέγειν ἀληθῶς· εἰς ὅ, τὸ δεύτερον περὶ Πακτύου ἐπερησό-
μενοι, ἦσαν ἄλλοι θεοπρόποι ὧν καὶ Ἀριστόδικος ἦν.

Ἀφικομένων δὲ αὐτῶν εἰς Βραγχίδας, ἐχρηστηριάζετο
ἐκ πάντων Ἀριστόδικος ἐπερωτῶν τάδε, " Ὦναξ, ἦλθε
παρ᾽ ἡμᾶς ἱκέτης Πακτύης ὁ Λυδός, φεύγων θάνατον
20 βίαιον πρὸς Περσῶν· οἱ δὲ αὐτὸν ἐξαιτοῦνται προεῖναι
Κυμαίους κελεύοντες. ἡμεῖς δέ, δειμαίνοντες τὴν Περσῶν
δύναμιν, τὸν ἱκέτην εἰς τόδε οὐ τετολμήκαμεν ἐκδιδόναι,

CROESUS ON HIS PYRE
Vase in the Louvre

πρὶν ἂν τὸ ἀπὸ σοῦ ἡμῖν δηλωθῇ ἀκριβῶς ὁπότερα
ποιῶμεν."

25 'Ο μὲν ταῦτα ἐπηρώτα· ὁ δὲ θεὸς αὖθις τὸν αὐτὸν
χρησμὸν ἔφαινε, κελεύων ἐκδιδόναι Πακτύην τοῖς Πέρσαις.
πρὸς ταῦτα ὁ 'Αριστόδικος ἐκ προνοίας ἐποίει τάδε·
περιιὼν τὸν νεὼν κύκλῳ ἐξῄρει τοὺς στρουθούς, καὶ
ἄλλα ὅσα ἦν νενεοττευμένα ὀρνίθων γένη ἐν τῷ νεῷ.
30 ποιοῦντος δὲ αὐτοῦ ταῦτα, φωνὴ ἐκ τοῦ ἀδύτου ἐγένετο
λέγουσα τάδε, "'Ανοσιώτατε ἀνθρώπων, τί τάδε τολμᾷς
ποιεῖν; τοὺς ἱκέτας μου ἐκ τοῦ νεὼ κεραΐζεις;" 'Αριστόδικος δὲ οὐκ ἀπορήσας πρὸς ταῦτα εἶπεν, "⁺Ωναξ, αὐτὸς
μὲν οὕτω τοῖς ἱκέταις βοηθεῖς, Κυμαίους δὲ κελεύεις τὸν
35 ἱκέτην ἐκδιδόναι." ὁ δὲ θεὸς αὖθις ἠμείψατο τοῖσδε,
"Ναὶ κελεύω, ἵνα γε ἀσεβήσαντες θᾶττον ἀπόλησθε·
ὡς μὴ τὸ λοιπὸν περὶ ἱκετῶν ἐκδόσεως ἔλθητε ἐπὶ τὸ
χρηστήριον."

XI. Captures of Babylon

A. FIRST CAPTURE, BY CYRUS

*Cyrus captures Babylon by draining off the Euphrates into the
empty basin of a lake.*

'Ο Κῦρος ἤλαυνεν ἐπὶ τὴν Βαβυλῶνα· οἱ δὲ Βαβυλώνιοι
ἐκστρατευσάμενοι ἔμενον αὐτόν. ἐπεὶ δὲ ἐγένετο ἐλαύνων
ἀγχοῦ τῆς πόλεως, συνέβαλόν τε οἱ Βαβυλώνιοι καὶ
ἡττηθέντες τῇ μάχῃ κατειλήθησαν εἰς τὸ ἄστυ, ᾗ εἶχον
5 σιτία ἐτῶν κάρτα πολλῶν.
'Ενταῦθα οὗτοι μὲν λόγον εἶχον τῆς πολιορκίας οὐδένα,
Κῦρος δὲ ἀπορίαις ἐνείχετο. τέλος δὲ ἐποίει τοιόνδε.
τάξας τὴν στρατιὰν ᾗ ὁ ποταμὸς εἰς τὴν πόλιν εἰσβάλλει,
καὶ αὖθις ὄπισθε τῆς πόλεως τάξας ἑτέρους, ᾗ ἐξίησιν ἐκ

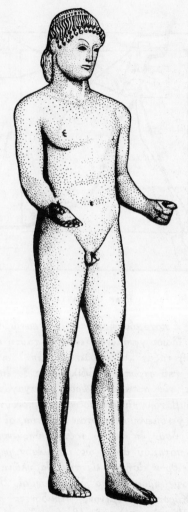

COPY OF THE APOLLO OF BRANCHIDAE
Bronze in the Louvre

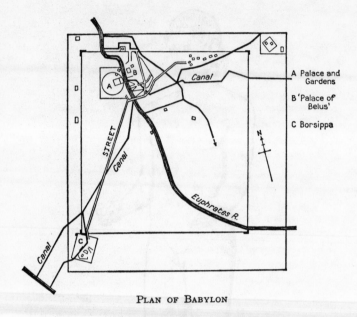

A Palace and
   Gardens

B 'Palace of
   Belus'

C Borsippa

PLAN OF BABYLON

10 τῆς πόλεως ὁ ποταμός, προεῖπε τῷ στρατῷ, ὅταν διαβατὸν
τὸ ῥεῖθρον ἴδωσι γενόμενον, εἰσιέναι ταύτῃ εἰς τὴν πόλιν.
οὕτω τε δὴ τάξας καὶ παραινέσας ἀπήλαυνεν αὐτὸς σὺν
τῷ ἀχρείῳ τοῦ στρατοῦ. ἀφικόμενος δὲ ἐπὶ τὴν λίμνην,
οὖσαν ἕλος, τὸν ποταμὸν διώρυχι εἰσαγαγών, τὸ ἀρχαῖον
15 ῥεῖθρον διαβατὸν εἶναι ἐποίησεν, ὑπονοστήσαντος τοῦ
ποταμοῦ. γενομένου δὲ τούτου τοιούτου, οἱ Πέρσαι οἵπερ
τεταγμένοι ἦσαν ἐπ᾽ αὐτῷ τούτῳ, ὑπονενοστηκότος τοῦ
Εὐφράτου ποταμοῦ ἀνδρὶ ὡς ἐς μέσον μηρὸν μάλιστα,
κατὰ τὸ ῥεῖθρον εἰσῆσαν εἰς τὴν Βαβυλῶνα.
20 Εἰ μέν νυν προεπύθοντο ἢ ἔμαθον οἱ Βαβυλώνιοι τὸ
ἐκ τοῦ Κύρου ποιούμενον, περιιδόντες τοὺς Πέρσας
εἰσελθεῖν εἰς τὴν πόλιν διέφθειραν ἂν κάκιστα· κατα-
κλείσαντες γὰρ πάσας τὰς πυλίδας τὰς εἰς τὸν ποταμὸν

ἀγούσας, καὶ αὐτοὶ ἐπὶ τὰς αἰμασιὰς ἀναβάντες τὰς παρὰ
τὰ τοῦ ποταμοῦ χείλη ἐληλαμένας, ἔλαβον ἂν αὐτοὺς ὡς 25
ἐν κύρτῃ. νῦν δὲ ἐξ ἀπροσδοκήτου αὐτοῖς παρέστησαν οἱ
Πέρσαι. ὑπὸ δὲ μεγέθους τῆς πόλεως, τῶν περὶ τὰ
ἔσχατα τῆς πόλεως ἑαλωκότων, οἱ τὸ μέσον οἰκοῦντες τῆς
Βαβυλῶνος οὐκ ἐμάνθανον ταῦτα, ἀλλά (ἔτυχε γὰρ οὖσα
ἑορτή) ἐχόρευόν τε τοῦτον τὸν χρόνον καὶ ἐν εὐπαθείαις 30
ἦσαν, εἰς ὃ δὴ καὶ τὸ ἀληθὲς ἐπύθοντο.

B. SECOND CAPTURE, BY DARIUS

§ 1. Revolt of the Babylonians from Darius.

Ἀπέστησαν οἱ Βαβυλώνιοι κάρτ' εὖ παρεσκευασμένοι·
ἐπεὶ δὲ ἀπέστησαν ἐποίησαν τοιόνδε· τὰς μητέρας ἐξε-
λόντες, γυναῖκα ἕκαστος μίαν προσεξῃρεῖτο, ἣν ἐβούλετο, ἐκ τῶν ἑαυτοῦ οἰκίων· τὰς δὲ λοιπὰς ἁπάσας
συναγαγόντες ἀπέπνιξαν· τὴν δὲ μίαν ἕκαστος σιτοποιὸν 5
ἐξῃρεῖτο. ἀπέπνιξαν δὲ αὐτὰς ἵνα μὴ σφῶν τὸν σῖτον
ἀναισιμώσωσι.

Πυθόμενος δὲ ταῦτα ὁ Δαρεῖος, καὶ συλλέξας ἅπασαν
τὴν ἑαυτοῦ δύναμιν, ἐστρατεύετο ἐπ' αὐτούς. ἐπελάσας
δὲ ἐπὶ τὴν πόλιν, ἐπολιόρκει τοὺς Βαβυλωνίους φροντί- 10
ζοντας οὐδὲν τῆς πολιορκίας· ἀναβαίνοντες γὰρ ἐπὶ
τοὺς προμαχεῶνας τοῦ τείχους κατωρχοῦντο καὶ κατέ-
σκωπτον Δαρεῖον καὶ τὴν στρατιὰν αὐτοῦ. καί τις αὐτῶν
εἶπε τοῦτο τὸ ἔπος, " Τί κάθησθε ἐνταῦθα, ὦ Πέρσαι,
ἀλλ' οὐκ ἀπαλλάττεσθε; τότε γὰρ αἱρήσετε ἡμᾶς ἐπὴν 15
ἡμίονοι τέκωσι." τοῦτο εἶπε Βαβυλωνίων τις οὐδαμῶς
ἐλπίζων ἂν ἡμίονον τεκεῖν.

Ἑπτὰ δὲ μηνῶν καὶ ἐνιαυτοῦ διεληλυθότος ἤδη, ὁ
Δαρεῖός τε ἤσχαλλε καὶ ἡ στρατιὰ πᾶσα, οὐ δυνατὴ οὖσα
ἑλεῖν τοὺς Βαβυλωνίους. καίτοι πάντα σοφίσματα καὶ 20

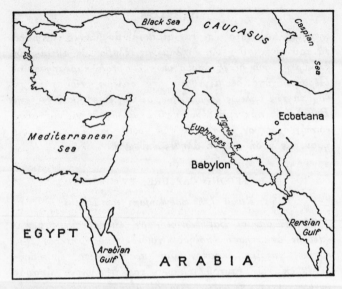

THE TIGRIS AND EUPHRATES

πάσας μηχανὰς ἐπεποιήκειν εἰς αὐτοὺς Δαρεῖος· ἀλλ' οὐδ'
ὡς ἐδύνατο ἑλεῖν αὐτούς, ἄλλοις τε σοφίσμασι πειρασά-
μενος καὶ δὴ καὶ τούτῳ ᾧ Κῦρος εἷλεν αὐτούς· δεινῶς
γὰρ ἦσαν ἐν φυλακαῖς οἱ Βαβυλώνιοι, οὐδὲ αὐτοὺς οἷός τ'
25 ἦν ἑλεῖν.

§ 2. *The Persian Zopyrus, encouraged by an omen, determines to
deceive the Babylonians by feigning desertion, after first
mutilating himself.*

Ἐνταῦθα εἰκοστῷ μηνὶ Ζωπύρῳ τῷ Μεγαβύζου ἐγένετο
τέρας τόδε· τῶν σιτοφόρων ἡμιόνων αὐτοῦ μία ἔτεκεν.
ὡς δὲ ἐξηγγέλθη αὐτῷ, καὶ ὑπὸ ἀπιστίας αὐτὸς ὁ Ζώπυρος
εἶδε τὸ βρέφος, ἀπειπὼν τοῖς ἰδοῦσι μηδενὶ φράζειν τὸ

γεγονός, ἐβουλεύετο. καὶ πρὸς τὰ τοῦ Βαβυλωνίου ῥήματα 5
ἐδόκει Ζωπύρῳ εἶναι ἁλώσιμος ἡ Βαβυλών· σὺν γὰρ
θεῷ ἐκεῖνόν τε εἰπεῖν ἐνόμισε καὶ τὴν ἡμίονον ἑαυτοῦ
τεκεῖν.

Ὡς δὲ αὐτῷ ἐδόκει μόρσιμον εἶναι ἤδη τῇ Βαβυλῶνι
ἁλίσκεσθαι, προσελθὼν Δαρείῳ ἀπεπυνθάνετο εἰ περὶ 10
πολλοῦ ποιεῖται τὴν Βαβυλῶνα ἑλεῖν. πυθόμενος δὲ ὡς
πολλοῦ τιμῷτο, ἐβουλεύετο ὅπως αὐτός τε ἔσται ὁ ἑλὼν
αὐτὴν καὶ ἑαυτοῦ τὸ ἔργον ἔσται. ἄλλως νυν οὐκ ἐφράζετο
δυνατὸς εἶναι ὑποχειρίαν αὐτὴν ποιῆσαι εἰ μὴ ἑαυτὸν
λωβησάμενος αὐτομολήσειεν εἰς αὐτούς. ἐνταῦθα, ἐν 15
ἐλαφρῷ ποιησάμενος, ἑαυτὸν λωβᾶται λώβην ἀνήκεστον·
ἀποτεμὼν γὰρ ἑαυτοῦ τὴν ῥῖνα καὶ τὰ ὦτα, καὶ τὴν
κόμην κακῶς περικείρας, καὶ μαστιγώσας ἑαυτὸν ἦλθε
παρὰ Δαρεῖον.

Δαρεῖος δὲ κάρτα βαρέως ἤνεγκεν ἰδὼν ἄνδρα δοκιμώ- 20
τατον λελωβημένον. ἔκ τε τοῦ θρόνου ἀναπηδήσας
ἀνεβόησέ τε καὶ ἤρετο αὐτὸν ὅστις εἴη ὁ λωβησάμενος.
ὁ δὲ εἶπεν, " Οὐκ ἔστιν οὗτος ἀνήρ (ὅτι μὴ σύ) ᾧ
ἐστι δύναμις τοσαύτη ἐμὲ δὴ ὧδε διαθεῖναι· οὐδέ τις
ἀλλοτρίων, ὦ βασιλεῦ, τάδε εἴργασται, ἀλλ' αὐτὸς ἐγὼ 25
ἐμαυτόν, δεινόν τι ποιούμενος Ἀσσυρίους Πέρσαις
καταγελᾶν."

Ὁ δὲ ἠμείβετο, " Ὦ σχετλιώτατε ἀνδρῶν, ἔργῳ τῷ
αἰσχίστῳ ὄνομα τὸ κάλλιστον ἔθου, φὰς διὰ τοὺς πολιορ-
κουμένους σαυτὸν ἀνηκέστως διαθεῖναι. τί δέ, ὦ μάταιε, 30
λελωβημένου σοῦ θᾶττον οἱ πολέμιοι παραστήσονται;
πῶς οὐκ ἐξέπλευσας τῶν φρενῶν σαυτὸν διαφθείρας;"

Ὁ δὲ εἶπεν, " Εἰ μέν τοι ὑπερέθηκά σοι ἃ ἤμελλον
ποιήσειν, οὐκ ἄν με περιεῖδες· νῦν δὲ ἐπ' ἐμαυτοῦ βαλόμενος ἔπραξα. ἤδη οὖν, ἐὰν μὴ τῶν σῶν δέησῃ, αἱρή- 35
σομεν Βαβυλῶνα.

§ 3. *Zopyrus discloses to Darius the plan by which he hopes to effect the capture of Babylon.*

" 'Εγὼ μὲν γάρ, ὡς ἔχω, αὐτομολήσω εἰς τὸ τεῖχος καὶ φήσω πρὸς αὐτοὺς ὡς ὑπὸ σοῦ τάδε ἔπαθον· καὶ δοκῶ, πείσας αὐτοὺς ταῦτα ἔχειν οὕτω, τεύξεσθαι στρατιᾶς. σὺ δὲ τῇ δεκάτῃ ἡμέρᾳ χιλίους τάξον κατὰ τὰς Σεμι-
5 ράμεως καλουμένας πύλας· αὖθις δὲ τῇ ἑβδόμῃ καὶ δεκάτῃ ἡμέρᾳ ἄλλους μοι τάξον δισχιλίους κατὰ τὰς Νινίων καλουμένας πύλας· μετὰ δὲ ταῦτα διαλιπὼν εἴκοσιν ἡμέρας, ἔπειτα ἄλλους κάθισον ἀγαγὼν κατὰ τὰς Χαλδαίων καλουμένας πύλας τετρακισχιλίους. ἐχόντων
10 δὲ μήτε οἱ πρότεροι ὅπλα μήθ' οὗτοι, πλὴν ἐγχειριδίων. μετὰ δὲ τὴν εἰκοστὴν ἡμέραν εὐθέως τὴν μὲν ἄλλην στρατιὰν κέλευσον πέριξ προσβάλλειν πρὸς τὸ τεῖχος. Πέρσας δέ μοι τάξον κατά τε τὰς Βηλίδας καλουμένας καὶ Κισσίας πύλας. ὡς γὰρ ἐγὼ δοκῶ, ἐμοῦ μεγάλα ἔργα ἀποδειξα-
15 μένου, τά τε ἄλλα ἐπιτρέψονται ἐμοὶ Βαβυλώνιοι καὶ δὴ καὶ τῶν πυλῶν τὰς βαλανάγρας. τὸ δὲ ἐντεῦθεν ἐμοί τε καὶ Πέρσαις μελήσει ἃ δεῖ ποιεῖν."

§ 4. *The Babylonians receive Zopyrus, who pretends that he will reveal to them all Darius' plans of attack. Elated by his apparent successes over the Persian troops, they invest him with the chief command, and he is thus enabled to betray the gates to the Persians.*

Ταῦτα ἐντειλάμενος ᾖει ἐπὶ τὰς πύλας, ἐπιστρεφόμενος ὡς δὴ ἀληθῶς αὐτόμολος. ὁρῶντες δὲ ἀπὸ τῶν πύργων οἱ κατὰ τοῦτο τεταγμένοι κατέτρεχον κάτω, καὶ ὀλίγον τι παρακλίναντες τὴν ἑτέραν πύλην ἠρώτων τίς τε εἴη
5 καὶ οὕτινος δεόμενος ἥκοι. ὁ δὲ αὐτοῖς ἠγόρευεν ὡς εἴη τε Ζώπυρος καὶ αὐτομολοίη εἰς ἐκείνους. ἦγον δὴ αὐτὸν οἱ πυλωροί, ταῦτα ὡς ἤκουσαν, ἐπὶ τὰ κοινὰ τὰ τῶν Βαβυ-

λωνίων, καταστὰς δ᾽ ἐπ᾽ αὐτὰ κατῳκτίζετο, φὰς ὑπὸ
Δαρείου πεπονθέναι ἃ ἐπεπόνθειν ὑφ᾽ ἑαυτοῦ, παθεῖν δὲ
ταῦτα διότι συμβουλεύσειεν αὐτῷ ἀπανιστάναι τὴν στρα- 10
τιάν, ἐπεὶ δὴ οὐδεὶς πόρος φαίνοιτο τῆς ἁλώσεως. " Νῦν
τε," ἔφη λέγων, " ἐγὼ ὑμῖν, ὦ Βαβυλώνιοι, ἥκω μέγιστον
ἀγαθόν, Δαρείῳ δὲ καὶ τῇ στρατιᾷ καὶ Πέρσαις μέγιστον
κακόν· οὐ γὰρ δὴ ἐμέ γε ὧδε λωβησάμενος καταπροΐξεται·
ἐπίσταμαι δὲ αὐτοῦ πάσας τὰς διεξόδους τῶν βουλευ- 15
μάτων."

Τοιαῦτα ἔλεγεν· οἱ δὲ Βαβυλώνιοι ὁρῶντες ἄνδρα
τὸν ἐν Πέρσαις δοκιμώτατον ῥινός τε καὶ ὤτων ἐστερη-
μένον, μάστιγί τε καὶ αἵματι ἀναπεφυρμένον, πάνυ ἐλπί-
σαντες λέγειν αὐτὸν ἀληθῆ καὶ ἥκειν ἑαυτοῖς σύμμαχον, 20
ἐπιτρέπεσθαι ἕτοιμοι ἦσαν πάντα ὧν ἐδεῖτο· ἐδεῖτο δὲ
στρατιᾶς.

Ὁ δὲ ἐπεὶ αὐτῶν τοῦτο παρέλαβεν, ἐποίει ἅπερ Δαρείῳ
συνέθετο· ἐξαγαγὼν γὰρ τῇ δεκάτῃ ἡμέρᾳ τὴν τῶν
Βαβυλωνίων στρατιὰν καὶ κυκλωσάμενος τοὺς χιλίους 25
οὓς πρώτους ἐνετείλατο Δαρείῳ τάξαι, τούτους κατεφόνευσε. μαθόντες δὲ αὐτὸν οἱ Βαβυλώνιοι ὅμοια τοῖς
ἔπεσι τὰ ἔργα παρεχόμενον, πάνυ περιχαρεῖς ὄντες, πᾶν
δὴ ἕτοιμοι ἦσαν ὑπηρετεῖν. ὁ δὲ διαλιπὼν ἡμέρας τὰς
συγκειμένας, αὖθις ἐπιλεξάμενός τινας τῶν Βαβυλωνίων 30
ἐξήγαγε καὶ κατεφόνευσε τῶν Δαρείου στρατιωτῶν τοὺς
δισχιλίους. ἰδόντες δὲ καὶ τοῦτο τὸ ἔργον οἱ Βαβυλώνιοι πάντες Ζώπυρον εἶχον ἐν στόμασιν αἰνοῦντες. ὁ
δὲ αὖθις διαλιπὼν τὰς συγκειμένας ἡμέρας ἐξήγαγεν
εἰς τὸ προειρημένον, καὶ κυκλωσάμενος κατεφόνευσε τοὺς 35
τετρακισχιλίους. ὡς δὲ καὶ τοῦτο κατείργαστο, πάντα
δὴ ἦν ἐν τοῖς Βαβυλωνίοις Ζώπυρος, καὶ στρατάρχης τε
οὗτος καὶ τειχοφύλαξ ἀπεδέδεικτο.

Προσβολὴν δὲ Δαρείου κατὰ τὰ συγκείμενα ποιουμένου

40 πέριξ τὸ τεῖχος, ἐνταῦθα δὴ πάντα τὸν δόλον ὁ Ζώπυρος
ἐξέφαινεν· οἱ μὲν γὰρ Βαβυλώνιοι ἀναβάντες ἐπὶ τὸ
τεῖχος ἠμύνοντο τὴν Δαρείου στρατιὰν προσβάλλουσαν,
ὁ δὲ Ζώπυρος τάς τε Κισσίας καὶ Βηλίδας καλουμένας
πύλας ἀναπετάσας εἰσῆκε τοὺς Πέρσας εἰς τὸ τεῖχος.
45 τῶν δὲ Βαβυλωνίων, οἱ μὲν εἶδον τὸ ποιηθέν, οὗτοι ἔφευγον
εἰς τοῦ Διὸς τοῦ Βήλου τὸ ἱερόν· οἳ δὲ οὐκ εἶδον, ἔμενον
ἐν τῇ ἑαυτοῦ τάξει ἕκαστος, εἰς ὃ δὴ καὶ οὗτοι ἔμαθον
προδεδομένοι.

§ 5. *Punishment inflicted on the Babylonians and honours heaped
upon Zopyrus.*

Βαβυλὼν μέν νυν οὕτω τὸ δεύτερον ᾑρέθη. Δαρεῖος δὲ
ἐπεὶ ἐκράτησε τῶν Βαβυλωνίων, τὸ μὲν τεῖχος περιεῖλε,
καὶ τὰς πύλας πάσας ἀπέσπασε (τὸ γὰρ πρότερον ἑλὼν
Κῦρος τὴν Βαβυλῶνα ἐποίησε τούτων οὐδέτερον). τῶν
5 δὲ ἀνδρῶν τοὺς κορυφαίους μάλιστα εἰς τρισχιλίους ἀνεσκολόπισε, τοῖς δὲ λοιποῖς Βαβυλωνίοις ἀπέδωκε τὴν
πόλιν οἰκεῖν.

Ζωπύρου δὲ ἀγαθουργίαν οὐδεὶς Περσῶν ὑπερεβάλετο
παρὰ Δαρείῳ κριτῇ οὔτε τῶν ὕστερον γενομένων οὔτε τῶν
10 πρότερον, ὅτι μὴ Κῦρος μόνος (τούτῳ γὰρ οὐδεὶς Περσῶν
ἠξίωσέ πω ἑαυτὸν συμβαλεῖν). πολλάκις δὲ Δαρεῖον
λέγεται γνώμην τήνδε ἀποδείξασθαι, ὡς βούλοιτο ἂν
Ζώπυρον εἶναι ἀπαθῆ τῆς αἰκίας μᾶλλον ἢ Βαβυλῶνάς
οἱ εἴκοσι πρὸς τῇ οὔσῃ προσγενέσθαι. ἐτίμησε δὲ αὐτὸν
15 μεγάλως· καὶ γὰρ δῶρα αὐτῷ ἀνὰ πᾶν ἔτος ἐδίδου ἃ
Πέρσαις ἐστὶ τιμιώτατα, καὶ τὴν Βαβυλῶνα αὐτῷ ἔδωκεν
ἀτελῆ νέμεσθαι μέχρι τῆς ἐκείνου ζωῆς, καὶ ἄλλα πολλὰ
ἐπέδωκε.

XII. A Rebuff to Darius for disturbing the Tomb of Nitocris, Queen of Babylon

Νίτωκρις ἡ τῆς Βαβυλῶνος βασίλεια ἀπάτην τοιάνδε
τινὰ ἐμηχανήσατο. ὑπὲρ τῶν μάλιστα λεωφόρων πυλῶν τοῦ
ἄστεως τάφον ἑαυτῇ κατεσκευάσατο μετέωρον, ἐπιπολῆς
αὐτῶν τῶν πυλῶν· ἐνεκόλαψε δὲ εἰς τὸν τάφον γράμματα
λέγοντα τάδε·   5
" Ἢν τις τῶν ἐμοῦ ὕστερον γιγνομένων Βαβυλῶνος
βασιλέων σπανίσῃ χρημάτων, ἀνοίξας τὸν τάφον λαβέτω
ὁπόσα βούλεται χρήματα· μὴ μέντοι γε, μὴ σπανίσας γε,
ἄλλως ἀνοίξῃ· οὐ γὰρ ἄμεινον."
Οὗτος ὁ τάφος ἦν ἀκίνητος μέχρι οὗ εἰς Δαρεῖον   10
περιῆλθεν ἡ βασιλεία. Δαρείῳ δὲ καὶ δεινὸν ἐδόκει εἶναι
ταῖς πύλαις ταύταις μηδὲν χρῆσθαι καί, χρημάτων κει-
μένων καὶ αὐτῶν τῶν χρημάτων ἐπικαλουμένων, μὴ οὐ
λαβεῖν αὐτά. (ταῖς δὲ πύλαις ταύταις οὐδὲν ἐχρῆτο
τοῦδε ἕνεκα, ὅτι ὑπὲρ κεφαλῆς αὐτῷ ἐγίγνετο ἂν ὁ νεκρὸς   15
διεξελαύνοντι.) ἀνοίξας δὲ τὸν τάφον ηὗρε χρήματα μὲν
οὔ, τὸν δὲ νεκρόν, καὶ γράμματα λέγοντα τάδε, " Εἰ μὴ
ἄπληστός τε ἦσθα χρημάτων καὶ αἰσχροκερδής, οὐκ ἂν
νεκρῶν θήκας ἀνέῳγες."

XIII. The Babylonian Wife-Market

*The beautiful women are sold to the highest bidder; the plain or
deformed are given to those who will accept the lowest compensation for a poor match.*

Κατὰ κώμας ἑκάστας ἅπαξ τοῦ ἔτους ἐποιεῖτο τάδε.
ὡς αἱ παρθένοι γίγνοιντο γάμων ὡραῖαι, ταύτας ὅπως
συναγάγοιεν πάσας εἰς ἓν χωρίον εἰσῆγον ἀθρόας· πέριξ δὲ

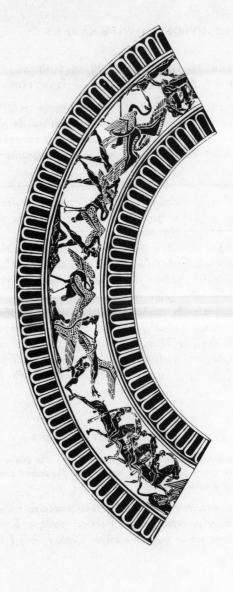

PYGMIES FIGHTING CRANES

From the base of the François Vase, an early sixth-century B.C.
wine bowl (volute *krater*) of the Attic black-figure style, by
the painter Kleitias; Archaeological Museum, Florence
(see pp. 45–48 below).

αὐτὰς ἵστατο ὅμιλος ἀνδρῶν, κῆρυξ δὲ ἀνιστὰς κατὰ μίαν
ἑκάστην ἐπώλει πρῶτον μὲν τὴν εὐειδεστάτην ἐκ πασῶν· 5
ἔπειτα δέ, ὅπως αὕτη εὑροῦσα πολὺ χρυσίον πραθείη,
ἄλλην ἀνεκήρυττεν ἣ μετ᾽ ἐκείνην ἦν εὐειδεστάτη· ἐπω-
λοῦντο δὲ ἐπὶ συνοικήσει. ὅσοι μὲν δὴ εὐδαίμονες τῶν
Βαβυλωνίων ἦσαν ἐπίγαμοι, οὗτοι ὑπερβάλλοντες ἀλλήλους ἐξωνοῦντο τὰς καλλιστευούσας· ὅσοι δὲ τοῦ δήμου 10
ἐπίγαμοι ἦσαν, εἴδους χρηστοῦ οὐ δεόμενοι, χρήματά τε
καὶ αἰσχίονας παρθένους ἐλάμβανον. ὡς γὰρ δὴ διεξέλθοι
ὁ κῆρυξ πωλῶν τὰς εὐειδεστάτας τῶν παρθένων, ἀνίστη
ἂν τὴν ἀμορφεστάτην ἢ ἔμπηρόν τινα, καὶ ἀνεκήρυττεν·
ὅστις δὲ ἐθέλοι ἐλάχιστον χρυσίον λαβὼν συνοικεῖν αὐτῇ, 15
τούτῳ προσέκειτο ἡ παρθένος. καὶ οὕτως αἱ εὔμορφοι
τὰς ἀμόρφους καὶ ἐμπήρους ἐξεδίδοσαν.
Ἐκδοῦναι δὲ τὴν ἑαυτοῦ θυγατέρα ᾧτινι βούλοιτο
ἕκαστος οὐκ ἐξῆν.

XIV. Two Stories of the Alcmaeonid Family

(a) How Alcmaeon was enriched by Croesus.

Οἱ Ἀλκμαιωνίδαι ἦσαν μὲν καὶ πάλαι λαμπροὶ ἐν
ταῖς Ἀθήναις, ἀπὸ δὲ Ἀλκμαίωνος καὶ αὖθις Μεγακλέους
ἐγένοντο καὶ κάρτα λαμπροί. ὁ γὰρ Ἀλκμαίων συμπράκτωρ ἐγίγνετο τοῖς ἐκ Σάρδεων Λυδοῖς παρὰ Κροίσου
ἀφικνουμένοις καὶ συνελάμβανε προθύμως· καὶ Κροῖσος 5
πυθόμενος ταῦτα μεταπέμπεται αὐτὸν εἰς Σάρδεις. ἀφικόμενον δὲ δωρεῖται χρυσῷ τοσούτῳ ὅσον ἂν δύνηται τῷ
ἑαυτοῦ σώματι ἐξενεγκέσθαι εἰσάπαξ.
Ὁ δὲ Ἀλκμαίων ἐνδὺς χιτῶνα μέγαν καὶ κόλπον
βαθὺν καταλιπόμενος τοῦ χιτῶνος, καὶ κοθόρνους οὓς 10
ηὕρισκεν εὐρυτάτους ὄντας ὑποδησάμενος, ἤει εἰς τὸν
θησαυρόν.

Εἰσπεσὼν δὲ εἰς σωρὸν ψήγματος πρῶτον μὲν παρέσαξε
παρὰ τὰς κνήμας ὅσον τοῦ χρυσοῦ ἐχώρουν οἱ κόθορνοι,
15 μετὰ δὲ τὸν κόλπον πάντα πλησάμενος τοῦ χρυσοῦ, καὶ
εἰς τὰς τρίχας τῆς κεφαλῆς διαπάσας τοῦ ψήγματος, καὶ
ἄλλο λαβὼν εἰς τὸ στόμα, ἐξῄει ἐκ τοῦ θησαυροῦ ἕλκων
μὲν μόγις τοὺς κοθόρνους, παντὶ δέ τινι εἰκὼς μᾶλλον ἢ
ἀνθρώπῳ· τό τε γὰρ στόμα ἐβέβυστο καὶ πάντα ἐξ-
20 ώγκωτο. ἰδόντα δὲ τὸν Κροῖσον γέλως εἰσῆλθε, καὶ
αὐτῷ πάντα τε ἐκεῖνα δίδωσι, καὶ προσέτι ἕτερα οὐκ
ἐλάττω ἐκείνων.

(b) *How Megacles, son of Alcmaeon, was chosen by Cleisthenes,
tyrant of Sicyon, as the best match in all Greece for his
daughter.*

Κλεισθένει τῷ Σικυωνίῳ τυράννῳ γίγνεται θυγάτηρ, ᾗ
ὄνομα ἦν Ἀγαρίστη. ταύτην ἠθέλησεν, Ἑλλήνων ἁπάντων ἐξευρὼν τὸν ἄριστον, τούτῳ γυναῖκα προσθεῖναι.
Ὀλυμπίων οὖν ὄντων ὁ Κλεισθένης, νικῶν ἐν αὐτοῖς
5 τεθρίππῳ, κήρυγμα τοῦτο ἐποιήσατο, " Ὅστις Ἑλλήνων
ἑαυτὸν ἀξιοῖ Κλεισθένους γαμβρὸς γενέσθαι, ἡκέτω εἰς
Σικυῶνα, ὡς κυρώσοντος Κλεισθένους τὸν γάμον ἐν
ἐνιαυτῷ."
Ἐνταῦθα ὅσοι τῶν Ἑλλήνων ἦσαν ἑαυτοῖς τε καὶ
10 πάτρᾳ ἐξωγκωμένοι ἐφοίτων μνηστῆρες· ἐκ δὲ Ἀθηνῶν
ἀφίκοντο Μεγακλῆς τε ὁ Ἀλκμαίωνος, τοῦ παρὰ Κροῖσον
ἀφικομένου, καὶ Ἱπποκλείδης Τισάνδρου πλούτῳ καὶ
εἴδει τῶν ἄλλων Ἀθηναίων προφέρων. ἀφικομένων δὲ
τούτων ὁ Κλεισθένης πρῶτον μὲν τὰς πατρας τε αὐτῶν
15 ἀνεπύθετο καὶ γένος ἑκάστου· μετὰ δὲ κατέχων ἐνιαυτὸν
διεπειρᾶτο αὐτῶν τῆς τε ἀνδραγαθίας καὶ τῆς ὀργῆς καὶ
παιδεύσεώς τε καὶ τρόπου· καὶ ἅμα ἐξένιζεν αὐτοὺς
μεγαλοπρεπῶς.

THEMISTOCLES
From a portrait bust of Roman period, thought to be a copy of a
fifth-century B.C. Greek original; Ostia (see pp. 52–61 below).

Καὶ δή που μάλιστα τῶν μνηστήρων ἠρέσκοντο οἱ
20 ἀπ' Ἀθηνῶν ἀφιγμένοι· καὶ τούτων μᾶλλον Ἱπποκλείδης
ὁ Τισάνδρου. ὡς δὲ ἡ κυρία ἡμέρα ἐγίγνετο τῆς κατα-
κλίσεως τοῦ γάμου, θύσας βοῦς ἑκατὸν ὁ Κλεισθένης
εὐώχει αὐτούς τε τοὺς μνηστῆρας καὶ Σικυωνίους πάντας.
ὡς δὲ ἐδείπνησαν, οἱ μνηστῆρες ἔριν εἶχον ἀμφὶ μουσικῇ·
25 προϊούσης δὲ τῆς πόσεως ὁ Ἱπποκλείδης, πολὺ κατέχων
τοὺς ἄλλους, ἐκέλευσε τὸν αὐλητὴν αὐλῆσαι αὐτῷ ἐμμέ-
λειαν, πειθομένου δὲ τοῦ αὐλητοῦ ὠρχήσατο.

FANCY DANCING
From a Greek vase

Καί πως ἑαυτῷ μὲν ἀρεστῶς ὠρχεῖτο· ὁ δὲ Κλεισθένης
ὁρῶν ὅλον τὸ πρᾶγμα ὑπώπτευε. μετὰ δὲ ὁ Ἱπποκλείδης
30 ἐκέλευσέ τινα τράπεζαν εἰσενεγκεῖν, εἰσελθούσης δὲ τῆς
τραπέζης πρῶτον μὲν ἐπ' αὐτῆς ὠρχήσατο Λακωνικὰ καὶ
Ἀττικὰ σχημάτια, ἔπειτα δὲ τὴν κεφαλὴν ἐρείσας ἐπὶ
τὴν τράπεζαν τοῖς σκέλεσιν ἐχειρονόμησε. Κλεισθένης
δέ, τὸ μὲν πρῶτον ὀρχουμένου αὐτοῦ, ἀποστυγῶν γαμβρὸν
35 ἂν γενέσθαι ἑαυτῷ Ἱπποκλείδη διὰ τήν τε ὄρχησιν καὶ
τὴν ἀναίδειαν, κατεῖχεν ἑαυτόν, οὐ βουλόμενος ἐκραγῆναι

εἰς αὐτόν· ὡς δὲ εἶδε τοῖς σκέλεσι χειρονομήσαντα, οὐκέτι
κατέχειν δυνάμενος εἶπεν, " Ὦ παῖ Τισάνδρου, ἀπωρχήσω
γε μὴν τὸν γάμον." ὁ δὲ Ἱπποκλείδης ὑπολαβὼν εἶπεν,
" Οὐ φροντὶς Ἱπποκλείδῃ." 40

Ὁ δὲ Κλεισθένης σιγὴν ποιησάμενος ἔλεξεν εἰς μέσον
τάδε, " Ἄνδρες παιδὸς τῆς ἐμῆς μνηστῆρες, ἐγὼ καὶ
πάντας ὑμᾶς ἐπαινῶ, καὶ πᾶσιν ὑμῖν, εἰ οἷόν τε εἴη,
χαριζοίμην ἄν, μήτε ἕνα ὑμῶν ἐξαίρετον ἀποκρίνων, μήτε
τοὺς λοιποὺς ἀποδοκιμάζων. ἀλλ', οὐ γὰρ οἷός τ' εἰμὶ 45

FLUTE PLAYING
From a Greek vase

μιᾶς περὶ παρθένου βουλεύων πᾶσι κατὰ νοῦν ποιεῖν,
τοῖς μὲν ὑμῶν ἀπελαυνομένοις τοῦδε τοῦ γάμου τάλαντον
ἀργυρίου ἑκάστῳ δωρεὰν δίδωμι, τῷ δὲ Μεγακλεῖ τῷ
Ἀλκμαίωνος ἐγγυῶ παῖδα τὴν ἐμὴν Ἀγαρίστην."

XV. EXPLORATION OF AFRICA

A. THE PYGMIES AND THE SOURCE OF THE NILE

Μέχρι μὲν τεττάρων μηνῶν πλοῦ καὶ ὁδοῦ γιγνώ-
σκεται ὁ Νεῖλος, πάρεξ τοῦ ἐν Αἰγύπτῳ ῥεύματος. ῥεῖ

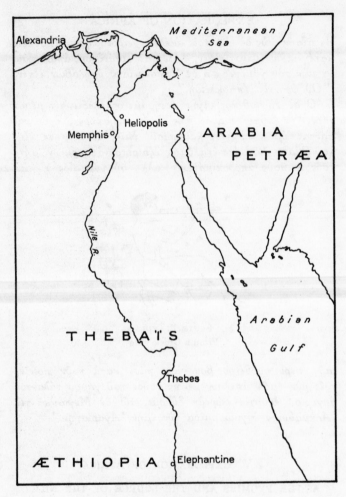

THE COURSE OF THE NILE

δ' ἀφ' ἑσπέρας τε καὶ ἡλίου δυσμῶν. τὸ δ' ἀπὸ τοῦδε
οὐδεὶς ἔχει σαφῶς φράσαι· ἔρημος γάρ ἐστιν ἡ χώρα
αὕτη ὑπὸ καύματος. ἀλλὰ τάδε μὲν ἤκουσα ἀνδρῶν 5
Κυρηναίων φαμένων ἐλθεῖν τε ἐπὶ τὸ "Αμμωνος χρηστήριον καὶ ἀφικέσθαι εἰς λόγους 'Ετεάρχῳ τῷ 'Αμμωνίων
βασιλεῖ· καί πως ἐκ λόγων ἄλλων ἀφίκοντο εἰς λέσχην
περὶ τοῦ Νείλου, ὡς οὐδεὶς οἶδε τὰς πηγὰς αὐτοῦ. ὁ δὲ
'Ετέαρχος ἔφη ἐλθεῖν ποτε παρ' ἑαυτὸν Νασαμῶνας 10
ἄνδρας, οἵ, ἐρωτώμενοι εἴ τι ἔχουσι πλέον λέγειν περὶ τῶν
ἐρήμων τῆς Λιβύης, ἔφασαν παρ' ἑαυτοῖς γενέσθαι ἀνδρῶν

PYGMY AND CRANES
From an Attic vase

δυναστῶν παῖδας ὑβριστάς, οἳ ἄλλα τε μηχανῶντο ἀνδρω-
θέντες περιττὰ καὶ δὴ καὶ ἀποκληρώσειαν πέντε ἑαυτῶν
ὀψομένους τὰ ἔρημα τῆς Λιβύης. τῆς γὰρ Λιβύης τὰ 15
μὲν κατὰ τὴν βορείαν θάλατταν, ἀπ' Αἰγύπτου ἀρξάμενοι
μέχρι Σολόεντος ἄκρας, ἣ τελευτᾷ τῆς Λιβύης, οἰκοῦσι
Λίβυες καὶ Λιβύων ἔθνη πολλά, πλὴν ὅσον Ἕλληνες καὶ
Φοίνικες ἔχουσι· τὰ δὲ καθύπερθε τούτων θηριώδης
ἐστὶν ἡ Λιβύη· τὰ δὲ καθύπερθε τῆς θηριώδους ψάμμος τέ 20
ἐστι καὶ ἄνυδρος δεινῶς καὶ ἔρημος πάντων.
    Οἱ οὖν νεανίαι, ὡς ἔφασαν οἱ Νασαμῶνες, ἀποπεμ-
πόμενοι ὑπὸ τῶν ἡλίκων, ὕδατί τε καὶ σιτίοις εὖ ἐξηρτυ-
μένοι, ἦσαν πρῶτον μὲν διὰ τῆς οἰκουμένης· ταύτην δὲ

25 διεξελθόντες εἰς τὴν θηριώδη ἀφίκοντο, ἐκ δὲ ταύτης
τὴν ἔρημον διεξῆσαν, τὴν ὁδὸν ποιούμενοι πρὸς ζέφυρον
ἄνεμον. διεξελθόντες δὲ χῶρον πολὺν ψαμμώδη καὶ ἐν
πολλαῖς ἡμέραις, εἶδον δή ποτε δένδρα ἐν πεδίῳ πεφυκότα,
καὶ προσελθόντες ἥπτοντο τοῦ ἐπόντος ἐπὶ τῶν δενδρῶν
30 καρποῦ· ἁπτομένοις δὲ αὐτοῖς ἐπῆλθον ἄνδρες μικροί,
μετρίων ἐλάττονες ἀνδρῶν, λαβόντες δὲ ἦγον αὐτοὺς
δι' ἑλῶν μεγίστων, καὶ διεξελθόντες ταῦτα ἀφίκοντο εἰς
πόλιν ἐν ᾗ πάντες ἦσαν ἴσοι τοῖς ἄγουσι τὸ μέγεθος,
χρῶμα δὲ μέλανες. παρὰ δὲ τὴν πόλιν ἔρρει ποταμὸς
35 μέγας, ἔρρει δ' ἀφ' ἑσπέρας πρὸς ἥλιον ἀνατέλλοντα,
ἐφαίνοντο δὲ ἐν αὐτῷ κροκόδειλοι.

Ὁ μὲν δὴ τοῦ Ἀμμωνίου Ἐτεάρχου λόγος εἰς τοῦτό
μοι δεδηλώσθω, πλὴν ὅτι ἀπονοστῆσαί τε ἔφη τοὺς
Νασαμῶνας, ὡς οἱ Κυρηναῖοι ἔλεγον, καὶ τοὺς ἀνθρώπους
40 εἰς οὓς οὗτοι ἀφίκοντο γόητας εἶναι ἅπαντας. τὸν δὲ δὴ
ποταμὸν τοῦτον Ἐτέαρχος συνεβάλλετο εἶναι τὸν Νεῖλον.

B. THE ETHIOPIANS

§ 1. *Cambyses, king of Persia, sends men to spy on the Ethiopians,
in preparation for an expedition against them; description
of the so-called ' table of the sun.'*

Ἐβουλεύσατό ποτε ὁ Καμβύσης στρατείαν ἐπὶ τοὺς
μακροβίους Αἰθίοπας οἰκουμένους Λιβύης ἐπὶ τῇ νοτίᾳ
θαλάττῃ. ἔδοξε δὲ αὐτῷ πρῶτον κατόπτας ἀποστέλλειν,
ὀψομένους τε τὴν ἐν τούτοις τοῖς Αἰθίοψι λεγομένην
5 εἶναι ἡλίου τράπεζαν εἰ ἔστιν ἀληθῶς, καὶ πρὸς ταύτῃ
τὰ ἄλλα κατοψομένους, δῶρα δὲ τῷ λόγῳ φέροντας τῷ
βασιλεῖ αὐτῶν.

Ἡ δὲ τράπεζα τοῦ ἡλίου τοιάδε τις λέγεται εἶναι.
λειμών ἐστιν ἐν τῷ προαστείῳ ἐπίπλεως κρεῶν ἑφθῶν

πάντων τῶν τετραπόδων, εἰς ὃν τὰς μὲν νύκτας τιθέασι τὰ 10
κρέα οἱ ἐν τέλει ὄντες, τὰς δὲ ἡμέρας δαίνυται προσιὼν
ὁ βουλόμενος. οἱ δὲ ἐπιχώριοί φασι ταῦτα τὴν γῆν
αὐτὴν ἀναδιδόναι ἑκάστοτε.

Ἡ μὲν δὴ τράπεζα τοῦ ἡλίου καλουμένη λέγεται εἶναι
τοιάδε. Καμβύσῃ δὲ ὡς ἔδοξε πέμπειν τοὺς κατασκόπους, 15
αὐτίκα μετεπέμπετο ἐξ Ἐλεφαντίνης πόλεως τῶν Ἰχθυοφάγων ἀνδρῶν τινας ἐπισταμένους τὴν Αἰθιοπίδα γλῶτ-
ταν. ἐπεὶ δὲ ἀφίκοντο, ἔπεμπεν αὐτοὺς εἰς τοὺς Αἰθίοπας,
ἐντειλάμενος ἃ λέγειν χρῆν, δῶρα φέροντας πορφυροῦν
τε εἷμα καὶ χρυσοῦν στρεπτὸν περιαυχένιον καὶ ψέλια 20
καὶ μύρου ἀλάβαστρον καὶ φοινικείου οἴνου κάδον.

Οἱ δὲ Αἰθίοπες οὗτοι λέγονται εἶναι μέγιστοι καὶ
κάλλιστοι ἀνθρώπων πάντων· νόμοις δὲ καὶ ἄλλοις
χρῶνται κεχωρισμένοις τῶν ἄλλων ἀνθρώπων καὶ δὴ καὶ
κατὰ τὴν βασιλείαν τοιῷδε· ὃν ἂν τῶν ἀστῶν κρίνωσι 25
μέγιστόν τε εἶναι καὶ κατὰ τὸ μέγεθος ἔχειν τὴν ἰσχύν,
τοῦτον ἀξιοῦσι βασιλεύειν.

Εἰς τούτους δὴ οὖν τοὺς ἄνδρας ὡς ἀφίκοντο οἱ Ἰχθυο-
φάγοι, διδόντες τὰ δῶρα τῷ βασιλεῖ αὐτῶν ἔλεγον τάδε,
" Βασιλεὺς ὁ Περσῶν Καμβύσης βουλόμενος φίλος καὶ 30
ξένος σοι γενέσθαι ἡμᾶς τε ἀπέπεμψεν, εἰς λόγους ἐλθεῖν
κελεύων, καὶ δῶρα ταῦτά σοι δίδωσι, οἷς καὶ αὐτὸς μάλιστα
ἥδεται χρώμενος."

Ὁ δὲ Αἰθίοψ μαθὼν ὅτι κατόπται ἥκοιεν λέγει πρὸς
αὐτοὺς τοιάδε, " Οὔτε ὁ Περσῶν βασιλεὺς δῶρα ὑμᾶς 35
ἔπεμψε φέροντας βουλόμενος ἐμοὶ ξένος γενέσθαι, οὔτε
ὑμεῖς λέγετε ἀληθῆ (ἥκετε γὰρ κατόπται τῆς ἐμῆς
ἀρχῆς), οὔτε ἐκεῖνος ἀνήρ ἐστι δίκαιος· εἰ γὰρ ἦν δίκαιος,
οὔτ' ἂν ἐπεθύμησε χώρας ἄλλης ἢ τῆς ἑαυτοῦ, οὔτ' ἂν
εἰς δουλοσύνην ἀνθρώπους ἦγεν ὑφ' ὧν οὐδὲν ἠδίκηται. 40
νῦν δὲ αὐτῷ τόξον τόδε διδόντες τάδε ἔπη λέγετε, 'Βασι-

λεὺς ὁ Αἰθιόπων συμβουλεύει τῷ Περσῶν βασιλεῖ τότε
ἐπ᾽ Αἰθίοπας τοὺς μακροβίους στρατεύεσθαι ἐπὴν οὕτως
εὐπετῶς Πέρσαι ἕλκωσι τὰ τόξα ὄντα μεγέθει τοσαῦτα·
45 μέχρι δὲ τούτου θεοῖς εἰδέναι χάριν, οἳ οὐκ ἐπὶ νοῦν
τρέπουσιν Αἰθίοψι γῆν ἄλλην προσκτᾶσθαι τῇ ἑαυτῶν.᾽ ''
    Ταῦτα δὲ εἰπὼν καὶ ἀνεὶς τὸ τόξον παρέδωκε τοῖς
ἥκουσι.

§ 2. *The Ethiopian king despises the dyed garment, the perfume,
and the gold ornaments presented to him by the Persians, but
is delighted with their wine, which he declares to be the
redeeming feature in Persian diet.*

    Λαβὼν δὲ τὸ εἷμα τὸ πορφυροῦν ἤρετο ὅ τι εἴη καὶ
ὅπως πεποιημένον· εἰπόντων δὲ τῶν Ἰχθυοφάγων τὴν
ἀλήθειαν περὶ τῆς πορφύρας καὶ τῆς βαφῆς, δολεροὺς
μὲν τοὺς ἀνθρώπους ἔφη εἶναι, δολερὰ δὲ αὐτῶν τὰ
5 εἵματα. δεύτερον δὲ περὶ τοῦ χρυσοῦ περιαυχενίου
ἤρετο καὶ περὶ τῶν ψελίων· ἐξηγουμένων δὲ τῶν Ἰχθυοφάγων, γελάσας ὁ βασιλεὺς καὶ νομίσας αὐτὰ εἶναι
πέδας εἶπεν ὡς παρ᾽ ἑαυτοῖς εἰσι ῥωμαλεώτεραι τούτων
πέδαι. τρίτον δὲ ἤρετο περὶ τοῦ μύρου· εἰπόντων δὲ
10 αὐτῶν περὶ τῆς ποιήσεως καὶ ἀλείψεως, τὸν αὐτὸν λόγον
ὃν καὶ περὶ τοῦ εἵματος εἶπεν. ὡς δὲ εἰς τὸν οἶνον ἀφίκετο
καὶ ἐπύθετο αὐτοῦ τὴν ποίησιν, ὑπερησθεὶς τῷ πώματι
ἐπήρετο ὁ βασιλεὺς ὅ τι σιτοῦνται οἱ Πέρσαι καὶ ὁπόσον
χρόνον μακρότατον ἀνὴρ Πέρσης ζῇ. οἱ δὲ σιτεῖσθαι
15 μὲν τὸν ἄρτον ἔφασαν, ἐξηγησάμενοι τῶν πυρῶν τὴν
φύσιν, ὀγδοήκοντα δὲ ἔτη ζωῆς πλήρωμα μακρότατον
ἀνδρὶ προκεῖσθαι. πρὸς ταῦτα ὁ Αἰθίοψ ἔφη οὐδὲν
θαυμάζειν εἰ σιτούμενοι κόπρον ἔτη ὀλίγα ζῶσιν· οὐδὲ
γὰρ ἂν τοσαῦτα ἔφη δύνασθαι ζῆν αὐτούς, εἰ μὴ τῷ
20 πώματι ἀνέφερον (φράζων τὸν οἶνον)· τούτῳ γὰρ ἑαυτοὺς
ὑπὸ Περσῶν ἡττᾶσθαι.

§ 3. *Long life of the Ethiopians; their diet and the miraculous power of a certain fountain.*

'Αντερομένων δὲ τὸν βασιλέα τῶν 'Ιχθυοφάγων περὶ τῆς ζωῆς καὶ διαίτης, ἔφη ἔτη μὲν εἰς εἴκοσι καὶ ἑκατὸν τοὺς πολλοὺς αὐτῶν ἀφικνεῖσθαι, ὑπερβάλλειν δέ τινας καὶ ταῦτα, σίτησιν δὲ εἶναι κρέα ἑφθὰ καὶ πῶμα γάλα. θαῦμα δὲ ποιουμένων τῶν κατασκόπων περὶ τῶν ἐτῶν, 5 ἐπὶ κρήνην αὐτοῖς ἡγήσατο ἀφ' ἧς λουόμενοι λιπαρώτεροι ἐγίγνοντο, καθάπερ εἰ ἐλαίου ἡ κρήνη εἴη, ὦζε δ' ἀπ' αὐτῆς ὡς εἰ ἴων. ἀσθενὲς δὲ τὸ ὕδωρ τῆς κρήνης ταύτης οὕτω δή τι ἔλεγον εἶναι οἱ κατάσκοποι ὥστε μηδὲν οἷόν τ' εἶναι ἐπ' αὐτοῦ ἐπιπλεῖν, μήτε ξύλον μήτε ὅσα ξύλου 10 ἐστὶν ἐλαφρότερα, ἀλλὰ πάντα χωρεῖν εἰς βυθόν. καὶ διὰ τὸ ὕδωρ τοῦτο, εἴ ἐστιν ἀληθῶς οἷόν τι λέγεται, μακρόβιοι ἂν εἶεν, εἰς πάντα χρώμενοι.

'Απὸ τῆς κρήνης δὲ ἀπαλλαχθέντων αὐτῶν, ἤγαγεν ὁ βασιλεὺς εἰς τὸ δεσμωτήριον, ἔνθα οἱ πάντες ἐν πέδαις 15 χρυσαῖς ἐδέδεντο. ἔστι δὲ ἐν τούτοις τοῖς Αἰθίοψι ὁ χαλκὸς πάντων σπανιώτατον καὶ τιμιώτατον. θεασάμενοι δὲ τὸ δεσμωτήριον ἐθεάσαντο καὶ τὴν τοῦ ἡλίου λεγομένην τράπεζαν. θεασάμενοι δὲ πάντα ἀπαλλάττονται ὀπίσω.

§ 4. *Frenzied and disastrous expedition of Cambyses against the Ethiopians.*

'Απαγγειλάντων δὲ τῶν κατασκόπων ταῦτα, αὐτίκα ὁ Καμβύσης ὀργὴν ποιησάμενος ἐστρατεύετο ἐπὶ τοὺς Αἰθίοπας, οὔτε παρασκευὴν σίτου οὐδεμίαν παραγγείλας οὔτε λόγον ἑαυτῷ δοὺς ὅτι εἰς τὰ ἔσχατα γῆς ἤμελλε στρατεύσεσθαι· οἷα δὲ ἐμμανής τε ὢν καὶ οὐ φρενήρης, ὡς 5 ἤκουσε τῶν 'Ιχθυοφάγων, ἐστρατεύετο πάντα τὸν πεζὸν ἅμα ἀγόμενος. πρὶν δὲ τῆς ὁδοῦ τὸ πέμπτον μέρος διεληλυθέναι τὴν στρατιάν, αὐτίκα τὰ σιτία ἐπελελοίπειν

αὐτούς, μετὰ δὲ τὰ σιτία καὶ τὰ ὑποζύγια ἐπέλιπε κατεσ-
10 θιόμενα. εἰ μέν νυν μαθὼν ταῦτα ὁ Καμβύσης ἐγνωσιμάχει καὶ ἀπῆγεν ὀπίσω τὸν· στρατόν, ἐπὶ τῇ ἀρχῆθεν
γενομένῃ ἁμαρτάδι ἦν ἂν ἀνὴρ σοφός· νῦν δὲ οὐδένα
λόγον ποιούμενος ἤει ἀεὶ εἰς τὸ πρόσω. οἱ δὲ στρατιῶται,
ἕως μέν τι εἶχον ἐκ τῆς γῆς λαμβάνειν, ποιηφαγοῦντες
15 διέζων· ἐπεὶ δὲ εἰς τὴν ψάμμον ἀφίκοντο, δεινὸν ἔργον
αὐτῶν τινες εἰργάσαντο· ἐκ δεκάδος γὰρ ἕνα ἑαυτῶν
ἀποκληρώσαντες κατέφαγον.

Πυθόμενος δὲ ταῦτα ὁ Καμβύσης, δείσας τὴν ἀλληλο-
φαγίαν, ἀφεὶς τὸν ἐπ' Αἰθίοπας στόλον ὀπίσω ἐπορεύετο,
20 καὶ ἀφικνεῖται εἰς Θήβας πολλοὺς ἀπολέσας τοῦ στρατοῦ.

XVI. The Battle of Salamis, 480 b.c.

[Ten years after the defeat of the Persians at Marathon in 490 B.C.
Xerxes, who came to the throne in 485, executed another invasion of Greece on an enormous scale by both land and sea.
His land forces marched around by the northern coasts of the
Aegean Sea and down into Greece by way of Thessaly, while the
fleet accompanied them as closely as possible along the coast.
No real opposition was encountered until they came to the
Pass of Thermopylae, where the Spartans made a heroic
stand. But the Spartans were betrayed and cut to pieces, and
the Persians were thus able to overrun Boeotia and Attica
without opposition.

Simultaneously with the fighting at Thermopylae, naval
engagements had taken place at near-by Artemisium, where
the Greek fleet had first taken up its position. Although the
result of these battles was indecisive, the Greeks nevertheless
determined to retire southward, mainly on account of the
defeat of their land forces at Thermopylae. The island of
Salamis was chosen as their next station, chiefly to enable the
Athenian fleet to transport their families and movable property to that place of refuge. Meanwhile the Persian army

*occupied Athens and captured the Acropolis, where a few
defenders had made a stand, while the fleet followed the Greek
navy and took up a position opposite it off the cost of Attica.
At this point the text begins.*]

(a) *On hearing of the capture of Athens, the Greek naval com-
manders, seized with a panic, determine to abandon their
position at Salamis and retire to the Isthmus of Corinth.
An Athenian points out to Themistocles the fatal consequences
that this would involve to the whole Greek cause.*

Οἱ δὲ ἐν Σαλαμῖνι Ἕλληνες, ὡς αὐτοῖς ἐξηγγέλθη ὡς
ἔσχε τὰ περὶ τὴν Ἀθηνῶν ἀκρόπολιν, εἰς τοσοῦτον
θόρυβον ἀφίκοντο ὥστε ἔνιοι τῶν στρατηγῶν εἴς τε τὰς
ναῦς εἰσέπιπτον καὶ ἱστία ἤραντο ὡς ἀποθευσόμενοι· τοῖς
τε ὑπολειπομένοις αὐτῶν ἐκυρώθη πρὸ τοῦ Ἰσθμοῦ 5
ναυμαχεῖν. νύξ τε ἐγίγνετο καὶ οἱ δέ, διαλυθέντες ἐκ τοῦ
συνεδρίου, εἰσέβαινον εἰς τὰς ναῦς.
Ἐνταῦθα δὴ Θεμιστοκλέα ἀφικόμενον ἐπὶ τὴν ναῦν
ἤρετο Μνησίφιλος, ἀνὴρ Ἀθηναῖος, ὅ τι εἴη βεβουλευμένον. πυθόμενος δὲ πρὸς αὐτοῦ ὡς εἴη δεδογμένον 10
ἀνάγειν τὰς ναῦς πρὸς τὸν Ἰσθμὸν καὶ πρὸ τῆς Πελοποννήσου ναυμαχεῖν, εἶπεν, " Οὗτοι ἄρα, ἐὰν ἀπαίρωσι
τὰς ναῦς ἀπὸ Σαλαμῖνος, περὶ οὐδεμιᾶς ἔτι πατρίδος
ναυμαχήσεις· κατὰ γὰρ πόλεις ἕκαστοι τρέψονται, καὶ
οὔτε αὐτοὺς Εὐρυβιάδης κατέχειν δυνήσεται οὔτε τις 15
ἀνθρώπων ἄλλος· ἀπολεῖταί τε ἡ Ἑλλὰς ἀβουλίαις.
ἀλλ' εἴ τις ἔστι μηχανή, ἴθι καὶ πειρῶ διαχέαι τὰ βεβου-
λευμένα, ἐάν πως δύνῃ ἀναγνῶσαι Εὐρυβιάδην μετα-
βουλεύσασθαι ὥστε αὐτοῦ μένειν."

(b) *Urged by Themistocles, Eurybiades recalls the meeting and
Themistocles presents the plan of action.*

Κάρτα δὴ τῷ Θεμιστοκλεῖ ἤρεσεν ἡ ὑποθήκη, καὶ
οὐδὲν πρὸς ταῦτα ἀμειψάμενος ᾔει ἐπὶ τὴν ναῦν τὴν

Εὐρυβιάδου. ἀφικόμενος δὲ ἔφη ἐθέλειν αὐτῷ κοινόν τι
πρᾶγμα συμμῖξαι· ὁ δ' αὐτὸν εἰς τὴν ναῦν ἐκέλευεν
5 εἰσβάντα λέγειν, εἴ τι ἐθέλει.

Ἐνταῦθα ὁ Θεμιστοκλῆς παριζόμενος αὐτῷ καταλέγει
ἐκεῖνά τε πάντα ἃ ἤκουσε Μνησιφίλου καὶ ἄλλα πολλὰ
προστιθείς, εἰς ὃ ἀνέγνωσεν ἔκ τε τῆς νεὼς ἐκβῆναι,
συλλέξαι τε τοὺς στρατηγοὺς εἰς τὸ συνέδριον.

10 Ὡς δὲ ἄρα συνελέχθησαν, πρὶν τὸν Εὐρυβιάδην προ-
θεῖναι τὸν λόγον ὧν ἔνεκα συνήγαγε τοὺς στρατηγούς,
πόλλ' ἔλεγεν ὁ Θεμιστοκλῆς οἷα κάρτα δεόμενος. λέγοντος δὲ αὐτοῦ, ὁ Κορίνθιος στρατηγὸς Ἀδείμαντος εἶπεν,
"Ὦ Θεμιστόκλεις, ἐν τοῖς ἀγῶσιν οἱ προεξανιστάμενοι
15 ῥαπίζονται."

Ὁ δὲ ἀπολυόμενος ἔφη, " Οἱ δέ γε ἐγκαταλειπόμενοι οὐ
στεφανοῦνται."

(c) Speech of Themistocles on the advantages of remaining at
Salamis.

Τότε μὲν ἠπίως πρὸς τὸν Κορίνθιον ἠμείψατο· πρὸς δὲ
τὸν Εὐρυβιάδην ἔλεγε τάδε·

"Ἐν σοὶ νῦν ἐστι σῶσαι τὴν Ἑλλάδα, ἐὰν ἐμοὶ πειθό-
μενος ναυμαχίαν αὐτοῦ μένων ποιῇ, μηδὲ ἀναζεύξῃς
5 πρὸς τὸν Ἰσθμὸν τὰς ναῦς. πρῶτον μὲν γὰρ ἐν στενῷ
συμβάλλοντες ναυσὶν ὀλίγαις πρὸς πολλάς, ἢν τὰ εἰκότα
ἐκ τοῦ πολέμου ἐκβαίνῃ, πολὺ κρατήσομεν· τὸ γὰρ ἐν
στενῷ ναυμαχεῖν πρὸς ἡμῶν ἐστιν, ἐν εὐρυχωρίᾳ δὲ
πρὸς ἐκείνων. αὖθις δὲ Σαλαμὶς περιγίγνεται, εἰς ἣν
10 ἡμῖν ὑπέκκειται τέκνα τε καὶ γυναῖκες. καὶ μὴν ὁμοίως
αὐτοῦ τε μένων καὶ πρὸς τῷ Ἰσθμῷ προναυμαχήσεις τῆς
Πελοποννήσου, οὐδ' αὐτούς, εἴπερ εὖ φρονεῖς, ἄξεις ἐπὶ
τὴν Πελοπόννησον. ἢν δέ γε ἃ ἐγὼ ἐλπίζω γένηται
καὶ νικήσωμεν ταῖς ναυσίν, οὔτε ὑμῖν εἰς τὸν Ἰσθμὸν

παρέσονται οἱ βάρβαροι, οὔτε προβήσονται ἑκαστέρω 15
τῆς Ἀττικῆς· ἀπίασί τε οὐδενὶ κόσμῳ."

(d) *Attacked by Adeimantus, Themistocles declares, as a con-*
clusive argument in favour of staying at Salamis, that otherwise
the whole Athenian fleet and people will sail off and found a
new home for themselves in Italy. Eurybiades and the rest are
thus persuaded to remain.

Ταῦτα λέγοντος Θεμιστοκλέους αὖθις ὁ Κορίνθιος
Ἀδείμαντος ἐπεφέρετο, σιγᾶν τε κελεύων αὐτὸν ᾧ μή
ἐστι πατρίς, καὶ Εὐρυβιάδην οὐκ ἐῶν ἐπιψηφίζειν ἀπόλει
ἀνδρί. (ταῦτα δὲ εἶπεν ὅτι ἡλώκεσάν τε καὶ κατείχοντο
αἱ Ἀθῆναι.)   5
Τότε δὴ ὁ Θεμιστοκλῆς ἐκεῖνόν τε καὶ τοὺς Κορινθίους
πολλά τε καὶ κακὰ ἔλεγεν, ἐδήλου τε λόγῳ ὡς ἑαυτοῖς
εἴη καὶ πόλις καὶ γῆ μείζων ἤ περ ἐκείνοις, ἕως ἂν
διακόσιαι νῆες ἑαυτοῖς ὦσι πεπληρωμέναι· οὐδαμοὺς
γὰρ ἔφη Ἑλλήνων αὐτοὺς ἐπιόντας ἀποκρούσεσθαι.   10
Σημαίνων δὲ ταῦτα, τῷ λόγῳ διέβαινεν εἰς Εὐρυβιάδην,
λέγων μᾶλλον ἐπιστρεφῶς, "Σὺ εἰ μενεῖς αὐτοῦ, καὶ
μένων ἀνὴρ ἀγαθὸς ἔσει, — εἰ δὲ μή, ἀνατρέψεις τὴν
Ἑλλάδα. ἀλλ' ἐμοὶ πείθου· εἰ δὲ μὴ ταῦτα ποιήσεις,
ἡμεῖς μέν, ὡς ἔχομεν, ἀναλαβόντες τοὺς οἰκέτας κομιού- 15
μεθα εἰς Σῖριν τὴν ἐν Ἰταλίᾳ (ἥπερ ἡμετέρα τέ ἐστιν
ἐκ παλαιοῦ, καὶ τὰ λόγια λέγει ὅτι ὑφ' ἡμῶν δεῖ αὐτὴν
κτισθῆναι)· ὑμεῖς δὲ συμμάχων τοιῶνδε μονωθέντες
μεμνήσεσθε τῶν ἐμῶν λόγων."
Ταῦτα δὲ Θεμιστοκλέους λέγοντος ἀνεδιδάσκετο Εὐρυ- 20
βιάδης· ἀπολιπόντων γὰρ Ἀθηναίων, οὐκέτι ἂν ἐγίγνοντο
ἀξιόμαχοι οἱ λοιποί. ταύτην δὲ τὴν γνώμην αἱρεῖται
αὐτοῦ μένοντας διαναυμαχεῖν.

(e) *Alarmed at the proximity of the Persian fleet, the resolution*
of the Greeks is again shaken. Themistocles, however, compels

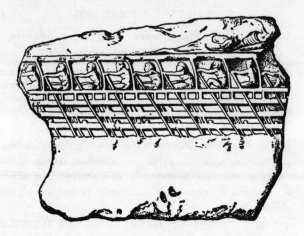

RELIEF AT ATHENS SHOWING THE WAIST
OF A TRIREME

*them to stay by a stratagem: he secretly sends a messenger to
the Persians, feigning treachery, and persuades them to cut
off the retreat of the Greek fleet during the night.*

Οἱ δὲ Πέρσαι ἀνῆγον τὰς ναῦς ἐπὶ τὴν Σαλαμῖνα
καὶ παρεκρίθησαν διαταχθέντες καθ' ἡσυχίαν· καὶ ναυμαχεῖν παρεσκευάζοντο εἰς τὴν ὑστεραίαν. τοὺς δὲ Ἕλλη-
νας εἶχε δέος τε καὶ ὀρρωδία, οὐχ οὕτω περὶ ἑαυτοῖς
5 δειμαίνοντες ὡς περὶ τῇ Πελοποννήσῳ. αὖθις δὲ σύλλογος
ἐγίγνετο, καὶ οἱ μὲν ἔλεγον ὡς εἰς τὴν Πελοπόννησον χρεὼν
εἴη ἀποπλεῖν καὶ περὶ ἐκείνης κινδυνεύειν, μηδὲ πρὸ
χώρας δοριαλώτου μένοντας μάχεσθαι, οἱ δὲ Ἀθηναῖοι
καὶ Αἰγινῆται καὶ Μεγαρεῖς ὡς χρείη αὐτοῦ μένοντας
10 ἀμύνεσθαι.

Ἐνταῦθα Θεμιστοκλῆς ὡς ἡττᾶτο τῇ γνώμῃ ὑπὸ
τῶν Πελοποννησίων, λαθὼν ἐξέρχεται ἐκ τοῦ συνεδρίου,
ἐξελθὼν δὲ πέμπει εἰς τὸ στρατόπεδον τὸ Μήδων ἄνδρα

πλοίῳ, ἐντειλάμενος ἃ λέγειν χρή, ᾧ ὄνομα μὲν ἦν Σίκιννος, οἰκέτης δὲ καὶ παιδαγωγὸς ἦν τῶν Θεμιστοκλέους 15
παίδων. ἀφικόμενος δὲ οὗτος ἔλεγε πρὸς τοὺς τῶν
βαρβάρων στρατηγοὺς τάδε, '' "Επεμψέ με στρατηγὸς
ὁ 'Αθηναίων λάθρᾳ τῶν ἄλλων 'Ελλήνων (τυγχάνει
γὰρ βουλόμενος μᾶλλον τὰ ὑμέτερα καθύπερθε γίγνεσθαι
ἢ τὰ τῶν 'Ελλήνων πράγματα), φράσοντα ὅτι οἱ "Ελληνες 20
δρασμὸν βουλεύονται κατορρωδηκότες· καὶ νῦν παρέχει
κάλλιστον ὑμᾶς ἔργων ἀπάντων ἐξεργάσασθαι, ἢν μὴ
περιίδητε διαδράντας αὐτούς· οὔτε γὰρ ἀλλήλοις ὁμο-
φρονοῦσιν οὔτε ἀντιστήσονται ὑμῖν, πρὸς ἑαυτούς τε
ὄψεσθε ναυμαχοῦντας τοὺς τὰ ὑμέτερα φρονοῦντας καὶ 25
τοὺς μή.''

'Ο μὲν ταῦτα αὐτοῖς σημήνας ἐκποδὼν ἀπηλλάττετο·
τοῖς δὲ ὡς πιστὰ ἐγένετο τὰ ἀγγελθέντα, ἐπειδὴ ἐγίγνοντο
μέσαι νύκτες ἀνῆγον τὸ ἀφ' ἑσπέρας κέρας κυκλούμενοι
πρὸς τὴν Σαλαμῖνα, κατεῖχόν τε μέχρι Μουνυχίας πάντα 30
τὸν πορθμὸν ταῖς ναυσί. τῶνδε δὲ ἕνεκα ἀνῆγον τὰς
ναῦς ἵνα δὴ τοῖς "Ελλησι μηδὲ φυγεῖν ἐξείη, ἀλλ' ἀπο-
ληφθέντες ἐν τῇ Σαλαμῖνι δοῖεν τίσιν τῶν ἐπ' 'Αρτεμισίῳ
ἀγωνισμάτων.

*(f) The Persian movements are reported to Themistocles by
Aristeides.*

Τῶν δὲ ἐν Σαλαμῖνι στρατηγῶν ἐγίγνετο ὠθισμὸς
λόγων πολύς· ἦσαν δὲ οὔπω ὅτι περιεκυκλοῦντο ἑαυτοὺς
ταῖς ναυσὶν οἱ βάρβαροι. συνεστηκότων δὲ τῶν στρατηγῶν, ἐξ Αἰγίνης διέβη 'Αριστείδης ὁ Λυσιμάχου,
ἀνὴρ 'Αθηναῖος μὲν ἐξωστρακισμένος δὲ ὑπὸ τοῦ δήμου, 5
ὃν ἐγὼ νενόμικα, πυνθανόμενος αὐτοῦ τὸν τρόπον, ἄριστον
ἄνδρα γενέσθαι ἐν 'Αθήναις καὶ δικαιότατον.

Οὗτος ὁ ἀνὴρ στὰς ἐπὶ τὸ συνέδριον ἐξεκαλεῖτο Θεμιστοκλέα, ὄντα μὲν ἑαυτῷ οὐ φίλον, ἐχθρὸν δὲ τὰ μάλιστα·

10 ὑπὸ δὲ μεγέθους τῶν παρόντων κακῶν λήθην ἐκείνων
ποιούμενος ἐξεκαλεῖτο, ἐθέλων αὐτῷ συμμῖξαι. προηκη-
κόει δὲ ὅτι σπεύδοιεν οἱ ἀπὸ Πελοποννήσου ἀνάγειν τὰς
ναῦς πρὸς τὸν Ἰσθμόν.

Ὡς δὲ ἐξῆλθε Θεμιστοκλῆς, ἔλεγεν Ἀριστείδης τάδε,
15 "Ἡμᾶς στασιάζειν χρεών ἐστιν ἔν τε τῷ ἄλλῳ καιρῷ
καὶ δὴ καὶ ἐν τῷδε περὶ τοῦ ὁπότερος ἡμῶν πλείω ἀγαθὰ
τὴν πατρίδα ἐργάσεται. λέγω δέ τοι ὅτι ἴσον ἐστὶ
πολλά τε καὶ ὀλίγα λέγειν περὶ ἀπόπλου τοῦ ἐντεῦθεν.
ἐγὼ γὰρ αὐτόπτης τοι γενόμενος λέγω ὅτι νῦν, οὐδ'
20 ἢν ἐθέλωσι Κορίνθιοί τε καὶ αὐτὸς Εὐρυβιάδης, οἷοί
τε ἔσονται ἐκπλεῦσαι· περιεχόμεθα γὰρ ὑπὸ τῶν πολεμίων κύκλῳ. ἀλλ' εἰσελθὼν ταῦτα αὐτοῖς σήμηνον."

(g) *At Themistocles' request, Aristeides announces the news in
person to the council; but they remain incredulous until the
report is confirmed by some deserters.*

Ὁ δὲ ἠμείβετο τοῖσδε, "Κάρτα τε χρηστὰ διακελεύει
καὶ εὖ ἤγγειλας· ἃ γὰρ ἐγὼ ἐδεόμην γενέσθαι αὐτὸς
αὐτόπτης γενόμενος ἥκεις. ἴσθι γὰρ ἐξ ἐμοῦ τὰ ποιού-
μενα ὑπὸ Μήδων· ἔδει γάρ, ὅτε οὐχ ἑκόντες ἤθελον εἰς
5 μάχην καθίστασθαι οἱ Ἕλληνες, ἄκοντας παραστήσασθαι.
σὺ δὲ ἐπείπερ ἥκεις χρηστὰ ἀπαγγέλλων, αὐτὸς αὐτοῖς
ἄγγειλον· ἢν γὰρ ἐγὼ αὐτὰ λέγω δόξω πλάσας λέγειν.
ἐπὴν δὲ σημήνῃς, ἢν μὲν πείθωνται, ταῦτα δὴ τὰ κάλλιστα
ἔσται· ἢν δὲ αὐτοῖς μὴ πιστὰ γένηται ταῦτα, ὅμοιον
10 ἡμῖν ἔσται· οὐ γὰρ ἔτι διαδράσονται, εἴπερ περιεχόμεθα
πανταχόθεν, ὡς σὺ λέγεις."

Ταῦτα ἔλεγε παρελθὼν ὁ Ἀριστείδης, φάμενος ἐξ
Αἰγίνης τε ἥκειν, καὶ μόγις ἐκπλεῦσαι λαθὼν τοὺς
ἐφορμοῦντας· περιέχεσθαι γὰρ πᾶν τὸ στρατόπεδον τὸ
15 Ἑλληνικὸν ὑπὸ τῶν νεῶν τῶν Ξέρξου. καὶ ὁ μὲν

ταῦτα εἰπὼν μεθειστήκει, τῶν δὲ αὖθις ἐγίγνετο λόγων
ἀμφισβασία· οἱ γὰρ πλέονες τῶν στρατηγῶν οὐκ ἐπεί-
θοντο τὰ ἐξαγγελθέντα. ἀπιστούντων δὲ τούτων ἧκε
τριήρης ἀνδρῶν Τηνίων αὐτομολοῦσα, ἧς ἧρχεν ἀνὴρ
Παναίτιος ὁ Σωσιμένους, ἧπερ δὴ ἔφερε τὴν ἀλήθειαν 20
πᾶσαν.

(h) How the battle began.

Τοῖς δὲ Ἕλλησιν ὡς πιστὰ δὴ τὰ λεγόμενα ἦν, παρεσκευάζοντο ὡς ναυμαχήσοντες. ἐνταῦθα ἀνῆγον τὰς ναῦς
ἁπάσας Ἕλληνες, ἀναγομένοις δὲ αὐτοῖς ἐπέκειντο οἱ
βάρβαροι. οἱ μὲν δὴ ἄλλοι Ἕλληνες ἐπὶ πρύμναν ἀνεκρούοντο καὶ ὤκελλον τὰς ναῦς· Ἀμεινίας δὲ Παλληνεὺς 5
ἀνὴρ Ἀθηναῖος ἐξαναχθεὶς νηὶ ἐμβάλλει· συμπλακείσης
δὲ τῆς νεώς, οὕτω δὴ οἱ ἄλλοι Ἀμεινίᾳ βοηθοῦντες
συνέμισγον. λέγεται δὲ καὶ τάδε, ὡς φάσμα γυναικὸς
ἐφάνη, φανεῖσα δὲ διεκελεύσατο ὥστε καὶ ἅπαν ἀκοῦσαι
τὸ τῶν Ἑλλήνων στρατόπεδον, ὀνειδίσασα πρότερον 10
τάδε, "Ὦ δαιμόνιοι, μέχρι πόσου ἔτι πρύμναν ἀνακρούεσθε;"

(i) Total defeat of the Persian navy.

Κατὰ μὲν δὴ Ἀθηναίους ἐτάχθησαν Φοίνικες (οὗτοι
γὰρ εἶχον τὸ πρὸς Ἐλευσῖνός τε καὶ ἑσπέρας κέρας),
κατὰ δὲ Λακεδαιμονίους Ἴωνες· οὗτοι δὲ εἶχον τὸ πρὸς
τὴν ἔω τε καὶ τὸν Πειραιέα.

Τὸ δὲ πλῆθος τῶν νεῶν ἐν τῇ Σαλαμῖνι ἐκεραΐζετο, 5
αἱ μὲν ὑπ' Ἀθηναίων διαφθειρόμεναι, αἱ δὲ ὑπ' Αἰγι-
νητῶν. τῶν μὲν γὰρ Ἑλλήνων σὺν κόσμῳ ναυμα-
χούντων κατὰ τάξιν, τῶν δὲ βαρβάρων οὔτε τεταγμένων ἔτι, οὔτε σὺν νῷ ποιούντων οὐδέν, ἤμελλε τοιοῦτο
αὐτοῖς συνοίσεσθαι οἷόν περ ἀπέβη. καίτοι ἦσάν γε 10
ταύτην τὴν ἡμέραν μακρῷ ἀμείνονες ἢ πρὸς Εὐβοίᾳ,

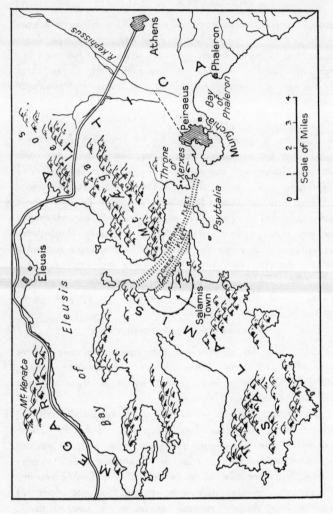

BATTLE OF SALAMIS, 480 B.C.

πᾶς τις προθυμούμενος καὶ δειμαίνων Ξέρξην· ἐδόκει
τε ἕκαστος ἑαυτὸν θεάσεσθαι βασιλέα.

(j) *Losses of the Persians in ships and men.*

Ἐν δὲ τῷ πόνῳ τούτῳ ἀπέθανε μὲν ὁ στρατηγὸς
Ἀριαβίγνης ὁ Δαρείου, Ξέρξου ὢν ἀδελφός, ἀπέθανον
δὲ ἄλλοι πολλοί τε καὶ ὀνομαστοὶ Περσῶν τε καὶ Μήδων
καὶ τῶν ἄλλων συμμάχων, ὀλίγοι δέ τινες Ἑλλήνων·
ἅτε γὰρ νεῖν ἐπιστάμενοι, εἰς τὴν Σαλαμῖνα διένεον, εἴ 5
τισιν αἱ νῆες διεφθείροντο· τῶν δὲ βαρβάρων οἱ πολλοὶ
ἐν τῇ θαλάττῃ διεφθάρησαν, νεῖν οὐκ ἐπιστάμενοι. ἐπεὶ
δὲ αἱ πρῶται νῆες εἰς φυγὴν ἐτράποντο, ἐνταῦθα αἱ
πλεῖσται διεφθείροντο· οἱ γὰρ ὄπισθε τεταγμένοι, εἰς
τὸ πρόσθεν παριέναι ταῖς ναυσὶ πειρώμενοι ὡς ἀποδειξό- 10
μενοι ἔργον τι καὶ αὐτοὶ βασιλεῖ, ταῖς ἄλλαις ναυσὶ ταῖς
φευγούσαις περιέπιπτον.

Τῶν δὲ βαρβάρων εἰς φυγὴν τραπομένων καὶ ἐκ-
πλεόντων πρὸς τὸ Φάληρον, Αἰγινῆται ὑποστάντες ἐν
τῷ πορθμῷ ἔργα ἀπεδείξαντο λόγου ἄξια· οἱ μὲν γὰρ 15
Ἀθηναῖοι ἐν τῷ θορύβῳ ἐκεράϊζον τάς τε ἀνθισταμένας
καὶ τὰς φευγούσας τῶν νεῶν, οἱ δὲ Αἰγινῆται τὰς ἐκ-
πλεούσας· ὅπως δέ τινες τοὺς Ἀθηναίους διαφύγοιεν,
φερόμενοι εἰσέπιπτον εἰς τοὺς Αἰγινήτας. οἱ δὲ βάρβαροι ὧν αἱ νῆες περιεγένοντο φεύγοντες ἀφίκοντο εἰς 20
Φάληρον ὑπὸ τὸν πεζὸν στρατόν.

XVII. How Gold is procured in India from Ant-hills

Ἐν τῇ τῶν Ἰνδῶν χώρᾳ ἔστιν ἐρημία διὰ τὴν ψάμμον·
ἐν δὴ οὖν τῇ ἐρημίᾳ ταύτῃ καὶ τῇ ψάμμῳ γίγνονται
μύρμηκες μέγεθος ἔχοντες κυνῶν μὲν ἔλαττον ἀλω-

πέκων δὲ μεῖζον· εἰσὶ γάρ τινες αὐτῶν καὶ παρὰ βασι-
5 λεῖ τῷ Περσῶν ἐντεῦθεν θηρευθέντες. οὗτοι οὖν οἱ
μύρμηκες ποιούμενοι οἴκησιν ὑπὸ γῆν ἀναφοροῦσι τὴν
ψάμμον καθάπερ οἱ ἐν τοῖς Ἕλλησι μύρμηκες, εἰσὶ δὲ
καὶ αὐτοὶ εἶδος ὁμοιότατοι. ἡ δὲ ψάμμος ἡ ἀναφερομένη
ἐστὶ χρυσῖτις· ἐπὶ δὲ ταύτην τὴν ψάμμον στέλλονται εἰς
10 τὴν ἔρημον οἱ Ἰνδοί, ζευξάμενος ἕκαστος καμήλους τρεῖς,
σειραφόρον μὲν ἑκατέρωθεν ἄρσενα παρέλκειν, θήλειαν
δὲ εἰς μέσον. ἐπὶ ταύτην δὴ αὐτὸς ἀναβαίνει, ἐπιτηδεύ-
ασς ὅπως ἀπὸ τέκνων ὡς νεωτάτων ἀποσπάσας ζεύξει
αἱ γὰρ κάμηλοι ἵππων οὐχ ἥττονες εἰς ταχυτῆτά εἰσι,
15 χωρὶς δὲ ἄχθη πολὺ δυνατώτεραι φέρειν.

Οἱ δὲ δὴ Ἰνδοὶ τρόπῳ τοιούτῳ καὶ ζεύξει τοιαύτῃ
χρώμενοι ἐλαύνουσιν ἐπὶ τὸν χρυσὸν λελογισμένως ὅπως
καυμάτων τῶν θερμοτάτων ὄντων ἔσονται ἐν τῇ ἁρπαγῇ·
ὑπὸ γὰρ τοῦ καύματος οἱ μύρμηκες ἀφανεῖς γίγνονται
20 ὑπὸ γῆν. ἐπὴν δὲ ἔλθωσιν εἰς τὸν χῶρον οἱ Ἰνδοὶ ἔχοντες
θυλάκια, ἐμπλήσαντες ταῦτα τῆς ψάμμου τὴν ταχίστην
ἐλαύνουσιν ὀπίσω· αὐτίκα γὰρ οἱ μύρμηκες ὀσμῇ, ὡς δὴ
λέγεται ὑπὸ Περσῶν, μαθόντες διώκουσι. εἰσὶ δὲ ταχυτῆτα οὐδενὶ ἑτέρῳ ὅμοιοι, οὕτως ὥστε εἰ μὴ προυλάμβανον
25 οἱ Ἰνδοὶ τῆς ὁδοῦ οὐδεὶς ἂν αὐτῶν ἀπεσώζετο. οἱ μέν
νυν ἄρσενες τῶν καμήλων, εἰσὶ γὰρ ἥττονες τρέχειν τῶν
θηλειῶν, παραλύονται ἐφελκόμενοι, οὐχ ὁμοῦ ἀμφότεροι·
αἱ δὲ θήλειαι ἀναμιμνησκόμεναι ὧν ἔλιπον τέκνων ἐνδι-
δόασι μαλακὸν οὐδέν.

XVIII. CURIOSITIES OF ARABIA

(a) *The spices of Arabia and the methods by which they are gathered.*

Ἐν τῇ Ἀραβίᾳ μόνῃ χωρῶν πασῶν λιβανωτός τέ
ἐστι φυόμενος καὶ σμύρνα καὶ κασία καὶ κινάμωμον καὶ

λήδανον. ταῦτα πάντα πλὴν τῆς σμύρνης δυσπετῶς κτῶνται οἱ Ἀράβιοι.

Τὸν μέν γε λιβανωτὸν συλλέγουσι τὴν στύρακα θυμιῶν- 5
τες· τὰ γὰρ δένδρα ταῦτα τὰ λιβανωτοφόρα ὄφεις ὑπόπτεροι, μικροὶ τὸ μέγεθος ποικίλοι τὸ εἶδος, φυλάττουσι, πλήθει πολλοὶ περὶ δένδρον ἕκαστον. οὐδενὶ δὲ ἄλλῳ ἀπελαύνονται ἀπὸ τῶν δένδρων ἢ τῷ τῆς στύρακος καπνῷ. 10

Τὴν δὲ κασίαν κτῶνται Ἀράβιοι ὧδε· ἐπὴν καταδήσωνται βύρσαις καὶ δέρμασιν ἄλλοις πᾶν τὸ σῶμα καὶ τὸ πρόσωπον πλὴν αὐτῶν τῶν ὀφθαλμῶν, ἔρχονται ἐπὶ τὴν κασίαν· ἡ δὲ ἐν λίμνῃ φύεται οὐ βαθείᾳ, περὶ δὲ αὐτὴν καὶ ἐν αὐτῇ αὐλίζεταί που θηρία πτερωτά, 15
ταῖς νυκτερίσι προσείκελα μάλιστα, καὶ τέτριγε δεινόν, καὶ εἰς ἀλκήν ἐστιν ἄλκιμα· ἃ δεῖ ἀπαμύνειν ἀπὸ τῶν ὀφθαλμῶν δρέποντας τὴν κασίαν.

Τὸ δὲ δὴ κινάμωμον ἔτι τούτων θαυμαστότερον συλλέγουσιν. ὅπου μὲν γὰρ γίγνεται καὶ ἥτις αὐτὸ γῆ ἡ 20
τρέφουσά ἐστιν οὐκ ἔχουσιν εἰπεῖν, ὄρνιθας δὲ λέγουσι μεγάλας φορεῖν ταῦτα τὰ κάρφη ἃ ἡμεῖς, ἀπὸ Φοινίκων μαθόντες, κινάμωμον καλοῦμεν. φοροῦσι δὲ αἱ ὄρνιθες εἰς νεοττιὰς προσπεπλασμένας ἐκ πηλοῦ πρὸς ἀποκρήμνοις ὄρεσιν, ἔνθα πρόσβασις ἀνθρώπῳ οὐδεμία 25
ἔστιν. πρὸς οὖν δὴ ταῦτα οἱ Ἀράβιοι σοφίζουσι τάδε. βοῶν τε καὶ ὄνων καὶ τῶν ἄλλων ὑποζυγίων τὰ μέλη διατεμόντας ὡς μέγιστα, κομίζουσιν εἰς ταῦτα τὰ χωρία, καὶ θέντες ἀγχοῦ τῶν νεοττιῶν ἀπαλλάττονται ἑκὰς αὐτῶν. αἱ δὲ ὄρνιθες καταπετόμεναι τὰ μέλη τῶν 30
ὑποζυγίων ἀναφοροῦσιν ἐπὶ τὰς νεοττιάς· αἱ δὲ οὐ δυνάμεναι ἴσχειν καταρρήγνυνται ἐπὶ γῆν· οἱ δὲ ἐπιόντες συλλέγουσι τὸν κινάμωμον.

(b) *Unusual size of the tails of Arabian sheep.*

Δύο δὲ γένη οἰῶν αὐτοῖς ἐστι θαύματος ἄξια, ἃ οὐδαμοῦ ἑτέρωθι ἔστι. τὸ μὲν γὰρ αὐτῶν ἕτερον ἔχει τὰς
οὐρὰς μακράς, τριῶν πήχεων οὐκ ἐλάττονας· ἃς εἴ τις
ἐφείη αὐτοῖς ἐφέλκειν, ἕλκη ἂν ἔχοιεν ἀνατριβομένων
5 πρὸς τῇ γῇ τῶν οὐρῶν· νῦν δὲ ἅπας τις τῶν ποιμένων
ἐπίσταται ξυλουργεῖν εἰς τοσοῦτο· ἁμαξίδας γὰρ ποιοῦντες
ὑποδοῦσιν αὐτὰς ταῖς οὐραῖς. τὸ δὲ ἕτερον γένος τῶν
οἰῶν τὰς οὐρὰς πλατείας φοροῦσι καὶ ἐπὶ πῆχυν πλάτος.

XIX. SCYTHIAN PROPHETS

(a) *How they attribute any illness of the king to the perjury of one
of his subjects, who is accordingly beheaded.*

Μάντεις δὲ Σκυθῶν εἰσὶ πολλοί, οἳ μαντεύονται ῥάβδοις
ἰτεΐναις πολλαῖς ὧδε· ἐπὴν φακέλους ῥάβδων μεγάλους
ἐνέγκωνται, θέντες χαμαί, διεξελίττουσιν αὐτούς, καὶ
ἐπὶ μίαν ἑκάστην ῥάβδον τιθέντες θεσπίζουσι· ἅμα τε
5 λέγοντες ταῦτα συνειλοῦσι τὰς ῥάβδους ὀπίσω, καὶ αὖθις
κατὰ μίαν συντιθέασιν. αὕτη μὲν αὐτοῖς ἡ μαντικὴ
πατρῴα ἐστίν.

Ἐπὴν δὲ βασιλεὺς ὁ Σκυθῶν κάμῃ, μεταπέμπεται
ἄνδρας τρεῖς τοὺς εὐδοκιμοῦντας μάλιστα τῶν μάντεων,
10 οἳ τρόπῳ τῷ εἰρημένῳ μαντεύονται· καὶ λέγουσιν οὗτοι
ὡς τὸ ἐπίπαν μάλιστα τάδε, ὡς τὰς βασιλείας ἑστίας
ἐπιώρκηκέ τις, λέγοντες τῶν ἀστῶν ὃν ἂν δὴ λέγωσι.
(τὰς δὲ βασιλείας ἑστίας νόμος Σκύθαις ἐστὶν ὀμνύναι
τότε ἐπὴν τὸν μέγιστον ὅρκον ἐθέλωσιν ὀμνύναι.) αὐτίκα
15 δὲ διειλημμένος ἄγεται οὗτος ὃν ἂν δὴ φῶσιν ἐπιορκῆσαι·
ἀφιγμένον δὲ ἐλέγχουσιν οἱ μάντεις ὡς ἐπιορκήσας
φαίνεται ἐν τῇ μαντικῇ τὰς βασιλείας ἑστίας, καὶ διὰ

ταῦτα ἀλγεῖ ὁ βασιλεύς. ὁ δὲ ἀρνεῖται, οὐ φάμενος ἐπιορκῆσαι, καὶ δεινολογεῖται.

'Αρνουμένου δὲ τούτου, ὁ βασιλεὺς μεταπέμπεται 20
ἄλλους διπλασίους μάντεις· καὶ ἐὰν μὲν καὶ οὗτοι,
εἰσορῶντες εἰς τὴν μαντικήν, καταδήσωσιν ἐπιορκῆσαι,
ἐκείνου εὐθέως τὴν κεφαλὴν ἀποτέμνουσι καὶ τὰ χρήματα αὐτοῦ διαλαγχάνουσιν οἱ πρῶτοι τῶν μάντεων·
ἐὰν δὲ οἱ ἐπελθόντες μάντεις ἀπολύσωσιν, ἄλλοι πάρ- 25
εισι μάντεις, καὶ μάλα ἄλλοι. ἐὰν οὖν οἱ πλέονες τὸν
ἄνθρωπον ἀπολύσωσι, δέδοκται τοῖς πρώτοις τῶν μάντεων
αὐτοῖς ἀπόλλυσθαι.

(b) *How the prophets themselves are put to death when mistaken.*

'Απολλῦσι δῆτα αὐτοὺς τρόπῳ τοιῷδε· ἐπὴν ἅμαξαν
φρυγάνων πλήσωσι καὶ ὑποζεύξωσι βοῦς, ἐμποδίσαντες
τοὺς μάντεις καὶ χεῖρας ὀπίσω δήσαντες καὶ στομώ-
σαντες, κατειργνῦσιν εἰς μέσα τὰ φρύγανα· ὑποπρή-
σαντες δὲ αὐτὰ ἀφιᾶσι φοβήσαντες τοὺς βοῦς. πολλοὶ 5
μὲν δὴ βόες συγκατακάονται τοῖς μάντισι, πολλοὶ δὲ
περικεκαυμένοι ἀποφεύγουσιν ἐπὴν αὐτῶν ὁ ῥυμὸς κατα-
καυθῇ.

Κατακάουσι δὲ τρόπῳ τῷ εἰρημένῳ καὶ δι' ἄλλας
αἰτίας τοὺς μάντεις, ψευδομάντεις καλοῦντες. οὓς δ' 10
ἂν ἀποκτείνῃ βασιλεύς, τούτων οὐδὲ τοὺς παῖδας λείπει,
ἀλλὰ πάντα τὰ ἄρσενα κτείνει, τὰ δὲ θήλεα οὐκ ἀδικεῖ.

XX. THE POWER OF CUSTOM

῞Εκαστοι νομίζουσι πολύ τι καλλίστους τοὺς ἑαυτῶν
νόμους. τοῦτο δὲ πολλοῖς τε ἄλλοις τεκμηρίοις πάρεστι σταθμώσασθαι καὶ δὴ καὶ τῷδε.

Δαρεῖος ἐπὶ τῆς ἑαυτοῦ ἀρχῆς καλέσας ῞Ελληνάς

5 τινας ἤρετο ἐφ᾽ ὁπόσῳ ἂν χρήματι βούλοιντο τοὺς πατέρας
ἀποθνήσκοντας κατασιτεῖσθαι· οἱ δὲ ἐπ᾽ οὐδενὶ ἔφασαν
ἔρδειν ἂν τοῦτο. Δαρεῖος δὲ μετὰ ταῦτα καλέσας Ἰνδῶν
τοὺς καλουμένους Καλλατίας, οἳ τοὺς γονέας κατεσ-
θίουσιν, ἤρετο (παρόντων τῶν Ἑλλήνων καὶ δι᾽ ἑρμηνέως
10 μανθανόντων τὰ λεγόμενα) ἐπὶ τίνι χρήματι δέξαιντ᾽ ἂν
τελευτῶντας τοὺς πατέρας κατακάειν πυρί· οἱ δέ, ἀνα-
βοήσαντες μέγα, εὐφημεῖν αὐτὸν ἐκέλευον.

GREEK KILLING PERSIAN
From an Attic vase in the red-figure style, mid fifth century B.C.

NOTES

I. Games invented by the Lydians

1. φασὶν οἱ Λυδοί κ.τ.λ. As a matter of fact, most of the games mentioned were of much greater antiquity than is implied, but Herodotus very properly abstains from spoiling a good story by disputing the accuracy of its details.

3. ἐπὶ Ἄτυος τοῦ Μάνου, sc. υἱοῦ, 'in the time of Atys, son of Manes.' A noun qualified by an adjective or adjectival substitute is frequently represented by its article alone, the noun being understood from the context. The adjectival substitute in this instance is the possessive genitive Μάνου. When the neuter article is employed in this usage, no definite noun is to be supplied (e.g.: τὸ τοῦ Σόλωνος, p. 27, ll. 9, 10; τὸ ἀπὸ σοῦ, p. 30, l. 23; τὰ περὶ τὴν ... ἀκρόπολιν, p. 53, a, l. 2).

4. ἀνὰ τὴν Λυδίαν πᾶσαν, 'throughout all of Lydia,' an example of the so-called 'distributive' use of ἀνά, which occurs frequently in expressions of time and place. Cf. ἀνὰ πᾶν ἔτος (p. 38, l. 15), 'every year' (lit., 'throughout every year ').

5. τέως μὲν διῆγον λιπαροῦντες, 'for a while they lived (through this) patiently ' (lit., ' enduring ' or ' holding out '), i.e., they endured this hardship as best they could.

Μετά appears frequently as an adverb in Herodotus. It is usually followed by δέ. Cf. p. 7, a, l. 4; p. 12, ll. 8, 9; p. 17, ll. 11, 12; p. 20, l. 11; p. 23, l. 17, et al.

6. ἄλλος δὲ ἄλλο ἐπεμηχανᾶτο, ' one man devised one remedy, another devised another,' or, ' different people devised different remedies.' The conciseness of the Greek, with its double meaning for each use of ἄλλος, cannot be duplicated in English. (Cf. the Latin alius aliud fecit.)

7. κύβων, dice with markings on six sides.

ἀστραγάλων, dice (originally of knucklebones) having markings on four sides only. The two unmarked sides were rounded.

8. πεττῶν, oval-shaped stones for playing a game that resembled draughts or chess. The game is said to have been known in Egypt as early as 2,000 B.C. It was popular among the Greeks, and Pindar, a celebrated poet who composed choral songs, represents the heroes in Elysium as amusing themselves with this game.

10. πρὸς τὸν λιμόν, lit., 'against their hunger,' i.e., 'to stave off their hunger.'

11. τὴν μὲν ἑτέραν τῶν ἡμερῶν κ.τ.λ., 'they played one day... and ate the next,' or, 'they played and ate on alternate days.' Τὴν ἑτέραν τῶν ἡμερῶν πᾶσαν is the equivalent of our 'every other day.'

II. THE OLDEST RACE ON EARTH

4. ἀπὸ τούτου, to be taken with ἐπειδή, 'from the time that Psammetichus. . . .'

5. προτέρους, actually a comparative without positive form, hence the genitive of comparison in ἑαυτῶν. The positive stem from which πρότερος is derived may be seen in the preposition πρό.

6, 7. οὐκ . . . οὐδένα, 'couldn't find any.' When the second of two negatives in the same clause is a compound, the negation is strengthened, not cancelled. Cf. ll. 9, 10 below, μηδένα . . . μηδεμίαν.

7. Τούτου anticipates the clause οἳ γένοιντο κ.τ.λ.

11. ἐφ' ἑαυτῶν, 'by themselves.' 'Επί with the genitive is frequently used to indicate 'place where'; hence with a personal noun or pronoun it may mean 'in the presence of'; thus ἐφ' ἑαυτῶν (lit., 'in their own presence') acquires the meaning of 'alone,' 'by themselves.'

12. πλήσαντα δὲ τοῦ γάλακτος, 'having filled (them) with the milk.' Verbs of fullness and want are commonly followed by a genitive of the material.

15. ἀπαλλαχθέντων τῶν ἀσήμων κνυζημάτων, 'apart from meaningless babblings'; lit., 'meaningless babblings having been set aside.'

20. πολὺ ἦν, i.e., was frequently repeated.

24, 25. ηὕρισκε . . . τὸν ἄρτον, sc. βέκος, 'found that the

Phrygians called bread "βέκος." ' Εὑρίσκω may take a participle in indirect discourse because in this use it has the force of a verb of perception.

26. πρεσβυτέρους. Note that the positive from which th' comparative adjective is formed is the substantive πρέσβ ;. Cf. note on προτέρους, p. 68, l. 5.

III. CROCODILES IN EGYPT

4. ἑκάτεροι. The plural indicates each set, or group, of p ( )le.

11. ἄγραι, ' methods of catching,' for which ἁλώσεις ι 'ht be used in Attic prose. In the Attic writers ἄγρα is r t ier ' the act of catching ' or ' the chase.'

14. δελεάσῃ . . . περὶ ἄγκιστρον, ' puts on a hook as ' a t.' The more common meaning of δελεάζω is ' entice by l a t,' then ' entice ' or ' allure ' generally.

Ἄγκιστρον, an old word for ' hook,' is retained in Attic)n ly in the special sense of the hook of a spindle.

17. κατὰ τὴν φωνήν, lit., ' down to the sound,' i.e., ' in tl e direction of the sound.'

18. οἱ δέ. When followed by μέν or δέ, the article ret; ir.s the original demonstrative force which it had in early Gr. el. In such cases it is frequently the equivalent of an Eng ish personal pronoun, ' he, she, it,' etc. Ὁ δέ without preced n|; ὁ μέν is used to indicate a change of subject. Thus οἱ δέ in the present passage refers to the hunters.

19. κατέπλασεν, for the present, καταπλάττει. This use of the aorist is called gnomic, because it is commonly employed in general precepts or proverbs (γνῶμαι). It expresses the fact that an action has always taken place in the past under certain circumstances and continues to do so in the present. In English we consider the present nature of the action or condition, and so use a present tense, whereas the Greeks fixed their attention on the past instances and employed the aorist.

IV. STORY OF MYCERINUS

1. τοῦ πατρός, Cheops, who built the first of the three pyramids (the one known as the Great Pyramid) at Giza in

Egypt. He closed the temples, abolished the sacrifices, and forced the people to give up their own occupations in order to devote themselves exclusively to the building of the pyramid. His reign lasted fifty years.

ὁ δέ, i.e., Mycerinus. See note on p. 69, l. 18.

6. ἡ θυγάτηρ ἀποθανοῦσα, ' the death of his daughter,' lit., ' his daughter having died.' Greek shares with Latin the dislike for verbal nouns of an abstract nature. Where we use such nouns followed by a genitive, the classical languages are likely to employ a noun with a participle in agreement. Cf. p. 7, b, l. 3, πληθούσης ἀγορᾶς; p. 26, d, l. 1, Σόλωνα οἰχόμενον; and such Latin expressions as *ab urbe condita*, ' from the founding of the city '; *urbs capta*, ' the capture of the city,' etc.

10. δεινόν. Δεινός, lit., ' fearful,' ' terrible,' ' awful ' (from δέος, ' fear,' ' terror,' ' awe '), is frequently used in Greek literature in a sense similar to that of the colloquial English words ' terrible;' ' dreadful,' ' awful.' It must be kept in mind, however, that the Greek δεινός was a literary word and is therefore not adequately represented by these English colloquialisms.

12. πάτρως, Chephren, the brother and successor of Cheops. He is responsible for the second of the three pyramids, and, like his brother, he kept the temples closed and forced the people to undergo all sorts of hardships in order that his pyramid might be completed. He reigned for fifty-six years.

17. τούτων ἕνεκα καί, ' for this very reason.' The καί here emphasizes what precedes rather than what follows.

21, 22. ὡς κατακεκριμένων ... τούτων. Ὡς is frequently attached to a causal participle to indicate that the reason given is that of the subject of the main verb or of some other person prominent in the sentence, and not necessarily that of the writer. (Cf. the Latin use of *quod* with the subjunctive.) So here the meaning is: it was because Mycerinus believed that his fate had been irrevocably decided that he determined to turn night into day and thus extract all the pleasure he could from his few remaining years.

22. ποιησάμενος. Notice the force of the middle, ' having made for himself.'

22, 23. ὅπως γίγνοιτο νύξ, ' whenever night came on.' The

optative expresses indefinite frequency in past time. Cf. πυνθάνοιτο in l. 25 below.

25. ἵνα γῆς κ.τ.λ., ' wherever in the land he heard that there were very suitable places of amusement.' The partitive genitive with the adverb (ἵνα γῆs) is found also in Latin, e.g., *ubinam gentium, ubicumque terrarum.* The expression is more or less equivalent to our ' where in the world.'

27. οἱ, dative of advantage; lit., ' that there might be for him,' i.e., ' that he might have.'

V. STORIES OF AMASIS

(a)

1. 'Απρίου δὲ καθῃρημένου. See Index of Names under *Ἄμασις*.

1, 2. τὰ ... πρῶτα, adverbial, ' at first.' This meaning is more commonly expressed by the neuter singular, πρῶτον, without the article.

3, 4. ἅτε ... ὄντα, ' since he was.' *Ἄτε* with the causal participle, unlike ὡς (see note on p. 70, ll. 21, 22), indicates that the reason given is accepted by the writer.

5, 6. ἦν αὐτῷ ἄλλα τε ἀγαθὰ μυρία καί. *Καί* after ἄλλος τε or ἄλλως τε places particular emphasis on what follows. Thus the meaning is, ' He had many other good things and *especially* a golden washbasin,' or, in more natural English, ' He had, in addition to many other good things, a golden washbasin.'

7. ἑκάστοτε, i.e., each time he had guests.

8. κατακόψας, ' cutting to pieces.' *Κατά* compounded with a verb often has an intensifying force, the literal meaning being ' right down to the end.' In English on the contrary we speak of ' cutting *up*.'

14, 15. ἐνεμοῖεν ... ἐναπονίζοιντο ... σέβοιντο, optative because the relative clause in which the verbs occur is in indirect discourse. With ἐναπονίζοιντο we must supply ἐν ᾧ, with σέβοιντο, ὄν.

15. ἔφη λέγων, ' he went on to say,' lit., ' he said as he spoke,' ' he said in his speech.' This pleonastic expression is quite common.

16. αὐτός. When the subject of an infinitive is omitted

because it is the same as the subject of the main verb, adjectives
and other words which would be in agreement with it are in
the nominative case, not the accusative. This also explains
βασιλεύς in l. 17.

πεπραγέναι. When a verb has two perfects, the second
perfect is usually intransitive. Thus πέπραγα means ' I have
fared,' πέπραχα, ' I have done '; ὅλωλα, ' I have perished,'
ὀλώλεκα, ' I have destroyed '; πέφηνα, ' I have appeared,'
πέφαγκα, ' I have shown.'

(b)

2, 3. ἐχρῆτο δὲ . . . τοιᾷδε, lit., ' he used the following arrangement of things,' i.e., ' he arranged his affairs as follows,'
or ' he followed this schedule.'

3. μέχρι πληθούσης ἀγορᾶς, ' until the filling of the market-
place,' lit., ' until the market-place being filled.' (For the construction see note on p. 70, l. 6.) Four divisions of the day are
given by Herodotus: ὄρθρος, early morning; ἀγορὰ πλήθουσα (or
πληθύουσα), forenoon; μεσημβρία, noon; ἀποκλινομένη ἡμέρα, afternoon.

4, 5. τὸ δὲ ἀπὸ τοῦδε, adverbial, ' after that ' or ' then.'

9. προύστηκας, contraction for προέστηκας.

τὸ ἄγαν φλαῦρον, ' too much frivolity,' ' an excess of frivolity.' Adverbs preceded by the article may be used to qualify
substantives, like attributive adjectives. Other examples are:
οἱ νῦν ἄνδρες, ' men of the present day '; ὁ πρὶν χρόνος, ' the former
time,' ' the past.'

10, 11. χρῆν . . . πράττειν, ' you should conduct.' The imperfect tense of impersonal verbs which denote obligation,
propriety, etc. is used without ἄν to form the apodosis of an
unfulfilled condition, the protasis being unexpressed. A
present infinitive in this construction represents present time
or repeated past action, an aorist infinitive simple past time.

17. εἰς τὸ δέον, ' for what was necessary ' (neuter participle
of δέω), i.e., ' when needed.'

19. τὸ μέρος, adverbial, ' in turn.'

(c)

4, 5. ἔκλεπτεν ἄν, ἦγον ἄν, ' he used to steal,' ' they used to
take him.' The imperfect and aorist indicative are sometimes

used with ἄν in what is known as an iterative sense to indicate a repeated action in past time. This ἄν is not to be confused with the ἄν of the apodosis of conditional sentences.

5, 6. μαντεῖον ὅπου ἑκάστοις εἴη, i.e., to the oracle which was nearest in each case.

8. ἐπεί . . . ἐβασίλευσεν, ' when he became king.' Greek here resembles English in using a simple past tense to express a time which is actually pluperfect. This use of the aorist in Greek is particularly common after conjunctions of time, such as ἐπεί, ἐπειδή, and ὡς. ῞Οσοι . . . ἀπέλυσαν (ll. 8, 9) and ὅσοι . . . κατέδησαν (l. 12), on the other hand, require a pluperfect in English although not in Greek: ' those who had acquitted him,' ' those who had convicted him.'

11. ὡς οὐδενὸς οὖσιν ἀξίοις, ' on the ground that or in the belief that they were worthless.' The meaning of ὡς in l. 13 is similar. See note on p. 70, ll. 21, 22.

VI. Arion saved by a Dolphin

1. Κιθαρῳδός, derived from κιθάρα, ' a lyre,' and ᾄδω, ' sing,' signifies ' one who sings to the lyre,' hence ' a lyric poet,' for in early times such poets not only composed poems capable of being set to music, but composed the music also, and sang their own songs to the lyre.

τὸν πολὺν τοῦ χρόνου, ' the greater part of his time.' Notice the partly adjectival, partly substantival value of πολύν here. It is substantival in that a noun in the genitive is dependent on it, adjectival in that it agrees in gender and number with the noun. ῞Ημισυς is used similarly, e.g., αἱ ἡμίσειαι τῶν νεῶν, ' half of the ships,' τὸ ἥμισυ τοῦ τείχους, ' half of the wall.'

2. Περιάνδρῳ. A favourable feature in the government of the Greek tyrants was the patronage they afforded to literature and the arts, especially to poetry. Periander at Corinth, Polycrates at Samos, Peisistratus and his sons at Athens, and Hiero at Syracuse entertained the most distinguished poets of their day at their courts.

3. Ἰταλίαν τε καὶ Σικελίαν. In visiting these countries Arion was not going among a foreign people. The coasts of Sicily

and of southern Italy were lined with cities founded by colonists from Greek states, and it was in these Greek-speaking cities that Arion displayed his poetical and musical talents. So numerous and important were these colonies in southern Italy that the whole region acquired the name of Magna Graecia.

5. οὐδαμοῖς. This word is frequent in Herodotus, but is not employed by later Greek authors, who use οὐδένες in its stead.

20. νόμον τὸν ὄρθιον, a high-pitched song or hymn in honour of Apollo. Its rhythm was solemn and stately.

ἔρριψεν, aorist of ῥίπτω. Verbs which begin with ρ double the ρ after the augment. Similarly, initial ρ is doubled when a vowel precedes it in forming a compound, e.g., ἀπόρρητος (p. 11, l. 1), ἀπορρίπτω (p. 26, c, l. 3), πρόρριζος (p. 26, l. 11), καταρρήγνυμι (p. 28, e, l. 13), etc.

22. ἀπέπλεον, imperfect of ἀποπλέω. See Vocabulary.

23. ὡς λέγουσι, ' as they say,' ' as the story goes.'

26. οὐδαμῇ μεθιείς, 'being in no way remiss,' i.e., ' carefully.'

27. ὡς δὲ ἄρα παρῆσαν, ' when they really came.' Arion had no doubt declared, in confirmation of his story, that the sailors would soon arrive at Corinth. But Periander did not believe him. Thus the particle ἄρα is appropriate, implying, as it frequently does, that a thing happens contrary to expectation.

28. εἴ τι λέγοιεν, ' if they had anything to say.'

29. περὶ Ἰταλίαν, 'somewhere in Italy,' implying that he was travelling around from city to city.

VII. STORY OF EUENIUS

(a)

1. ἱερὰ ἡλίου πρόβατα. Flocks sacred to the sun are mentioned in several passages by early Greek writers, in one of which they are said to number 350, corresponding, perhaps, to an old reckoning of the days of the year.

1, 2. τὰς μὲν ἡμέρας, τὰς δὲ νύκτας. The accusative is occasionally used, as in the present passage, to express ' time within which.'

4. Ἕκαστος, because of its collective sense, may be the subject of a plural verb. Occasionally, as in the present passage, it is in apposition to a plural noun.

4, 5. περὶ πολλοῦ ... ποιοῦνται, ' value highly.' Similar expressions are common in Greek, e.g., περὶ πλείονος ποιεῖσθαι, ' value more '; περὶ ὀλίγου ποιεῖσθαι, ' value lightly,' ' place little value on '; περὶ οὐδενὸς ποιεῖσθαι, ' place no value on.'

11. εἶχε σιγῇ, ' kept silent,' the intransitive use of ἔχω with an adverb.

14. ὑπαγαγόντες ... ὑπὸ δικαστήριον. We say ' before ' the court, or judge, and in Greek the more common preposition is εἰς, but ὑπό is employed in this passage somewhat as sub in the Latin sub iudice, ' under the consideration or decision of the judge.'

(b)

1. ἐπεὶ ... ἐξετύφλωσαν, pluperfect sense. See note on p. 73, l. 8.

2. αὐτοῖς, dative of advantage, ' didn't bear for them.'

5. οἱ θεοί, i.e., the priests or priestesses at the oracles who were supposed to speak the words with which the gods inspired them. As noted on p. 88, the authorities presiding over the oracles were usually staunch upholders of morality; so in this instance they condemn the blinding of Euenius as cruel and excessive.

7. οὐ πρότερόν τε. Τέ appears third in its clause instead of second because οὐ πρότερον is regarded as a unit. Notice the redundancy of πρότερον before πρίν, a common Greek construction.

8. πρὶν ἂν ... δῶτε. Πρίν meaning ' until ' is followed by the subjunctive only after negatives.

10. ἢν ἔχοντα κ.τ.λ., ' on the possession of which many men will congratulate him.'

πολλοὶ ἀνθρώπων. See note on τὸν πολὺν τοῦ χρόνου, p. 73, l. 1.

(c)

1. ἀπόρρητα. For the double ρ see note on ἔρριψεν, p. 74, l. 20.

2. προύθεσαν ... διαπρᾶξαι, ' assigned them (i.e., τὰ χρηστήρια)

to certain citizens to carry out.' Προὔθεσαν is contracted from προέθεσαν.

3. αὐτοῖς, ' for them,' i.e., the Apolloniates.

5. κατέβαινον συλλυπούμενοι, ' they ended by expressing sympathy for.' The verb κατέβαινον implies that they at length approached the subject which they really wanted to discuss, the preposition κατά expressing metaphorically gradual descent to a point aimed at.

5, 6. ταύτῃ δὲ ὑπάγοντες, 'leading him on in this way.' Ὑπό in composition may denote that an action is carried out by degrees, or secretly, with the intention of deception and possible treachery. Either meaning would be appropriate here.

17. ὡς ἐξαπατηθείς, ' feeling that he had been cheated.' See note on p. 70, ll. 21, 22.

18. ἔμφυτον μαντικήν, 'a naturally-inspired power of prophecy ' (in contrast to the same power acquired by education in the technicalities of signs and omens).

VIII. Story of Cyrus

A. INFANCY OF CYRUS

§ 1

7. πρᾶγμα δ ἂν προσθῶ, 'whatever task I impose upon you,' a conditional relative clause of the vivid future type, hence ἄν and the subjunctive. We might have had simply ὃ προστίθημι, ' the particular task that I am now imposing upon you,' but the king wishes to prepare Harpagus beforehand, as it were, for some unpleasant mission.

8. εἰς σεαυτοῦ, ' to your own house ' (understand οἰκίαν or some similar word). This is a common construction in English as well as in Greek, e.g., ' I went to Mr. Thompson's,' ' I was at Mr. Thompson's.'

9. ᾧτινι ἂν τρόπῳ αὐτὸς βούλῃ, a conditional relative of the same type as πρᾶγμα δ ἂν προσθῶ in l. 7 above.

10. φίλον, sc. ἐστί σοι, ' if it is pleasing to you,' ' if you want.'

10, 11. χρὴ δὴ τό γ' ἐμὸν ὑπηρετεῖσθαι, 'my service must certainly be performed,' ' my part must certainly be carried out.'

13. τὰ οἰκία. Both Greeks and Romans were fond of using a plural word to signify the collection of buildings which together made up a rich man's ' house.' Cf. *aedes* in Latin, and the custom of employing *domus, sedes,* etc. in the plural. The word for ' house ' in Attic Greek is ἡ οἰκία.

16. ᾗ, lit., ' how,' i.e., ' Not *what* Astyages ordered '; or (if the previous τί is regarded as adverbial and the question as meaning, ' In what way do you propose to act? '), ' Not in the way Astyages ordered.'

17, 18. οὐδ'εἰ . . . οὐκ. The second negative here repeats and strengthens the first. The two do not make an affirmative, as would be the case in English.

18. προσθήσομαι τῇ γνώμῃ αὐτοῦ, ' serve his purpose.'

20. αὐτῷ μοι. Observe the distinction between this form and ἐμαυτῷ. The latter is the reflexive pronoun, referring to the subject of the verb, whereas αὐτῷ μοι is simply the emphatic ' me myself.'

21. ἄπαις ἄρσενος γόνου. Adjectives compounded with the privative prefix ἀ are frequently followed by a genitive of separation.

24. τὸ ἐντεῦθεν, adverbial, ' in the future.'

25. ἐμοί, with ἀσφαλείας, ' security to myself,' ' my own security.'

26. τινὰ τῶν 'Αστυάγους, ' one of Astyages' servants.' See note on p. 67, l. 3.

§ 2

1, 2. βουκόλον τινὰ τῶν 'Αστυάγους, ' a certain herdsman from among the servants of Astyages.' Cf. above, l. 26.

2, 3. ὃν ἠπίστατο . . . ὄρη θηριωδέστατα, ' who, he knew, used as pasture-land very suitable grazing-places and mountains thickly infested with wild beasts.'

7. ὅπως ἂν τάχιστα διαφθαρείη. Purpose after a primary tense is usually expressed by ὅπως, ὡς, or ἵνα with the subjunctive. The use of the optative with ἂν after primary tenses

indicates a futurity of a somewhat vague or uncertain nature. It represents, in a sense, the apodosis of a conditional sentence, a protasis always being implied, if not actually expressed. Instances of this construction are also found where no uncertainty exists. This is particularly true when the reference is to something unpleasant, as in the present passage. Here the protasis or condition implied would be, 'if nothing unexpected happens.'

10. ἐκκείμενον, sc. τὸ παιδίον.

§ 3

2. τὴν αὐτὴν ὁδόν, cognate accusative after ᾔει, ' he went the same way.'

3. ἄρα, ' as it happened.'

5. ὅ τι, adverbial, ' why.'

7. ὃ μὴ ἰδεῖν ὤφελον, ' what I wish I had not seen,' lit., ' what I ought not to have seen.' Ὤφελον with the infinitive expresses an unfulfilled wish. The present infinitive in this construction indicates a wish for the present time, the aorist infinitive a wish for the past time.

8. κλαυθμῷ κατείχετο, ' was filled with weeping.'

13. εἴη. Although the infinitive after κελεύω does not represent indirect discourse, clauses dependent on such an infinitive nevertheless conform to the principles that apply to subordinate clauses in indirect discourse. This accounts for the optative in εἴη.

14, 15. καθ' ὁδόν, ' on the way,' or ' along the way.'

16. ὡς ἄρα . . ., ' that it was really . . .,' in apposition to λόγον.

18. ὅδε, not οὗτος, because he has not yet shown the child.

§ 4

3. λαβομένη τῶν γονάτων τοῦ ἀνδρός, not ' clasping the knees of her husband ' (which would require a second τῶν before τοῦ ἀνδρός), but ' clasping her husband by the knees.' The genitive is used after λαμβάνομαι when the meaning is ' take hold of.' Occasionally, as in this instance, there may be two genitives.

4, 5. οὐκ ἔφη οἷός τε εἶναι, ' said he couldn't.' When the indirect discourse dependent on φημί is negative, the negative word is attached to φημί rather than to the infinitive. Thus οὔ φημι is the equivalent of the Latin *nego*, and φημί... οὐ is avoided in Greek, as *dico* ... *non* is in Latin.

6. αὐτός. For the case see note on αὐτός, p. 71, l. 16.

9, 10. πᾶσα ἀνάγκη, sc. ἐστί, ' it is absolutely necessary.'

14. ἡμῖν ... βεβουλευμένον ἔσται, the impersonal passive; lit., ' it will have been planned by us,' i.e., ' we will have planned.' The agent is expressed by the dative (ἡμῖν) after the perfect tenses.

18. παῖδα. The antecedent is attracted into the relative clause.

24. εἰς τοῦ ' Αρπάγου. See note on p. 76, l. 8.

ἕτοιμος. For the case see note on αὐτός, p. 71, l. 16.

26, 27. εἶδέ τε διὰ τούτων, ' had him seen by means of them.' Cf. p. 13, l. 23, κτείνει... δι' ἐμοῦ, ' is having put to death by my agency.' Similarly in English we may say, ' He did it by proxy.'

B. BOYHOOD OF CYRUS

§ 1

1. δεκαετής. In Attic Greek this word signifies, not ' ten years old,' but ' ten years long.'

4. τὸν τοῦ ... παῖδα, ' the son of the herdsman, as he was called.' For the meaning of the adverbial use of ἐπίκλησιν, see Vocabulary.

6. ὀφθαλμὸν βασιλέως, evidently a familiar oriental expression, implying a confidential servant used by the king for secret inspection of his subjects and kingdom.

7. ὡς ἑκάστῳ. The use of ὡς with ἕκαστος indicates a distributive meaning: ' each separately.'

12, 13. ὡς ... παθών. See note on p. 70, ll. 21, 22.

§ 2

7, 8. ταῦτα τοῦτον ἐποίησα. When ποιέω has the meaning of ' do something to someone,' it may be followed by two accusatives. Frequently an adverb is used in place of the accusative of the thing, e.g., κακῶς or εὖ ποιῶ τινά.

9. ἐστήσαντο ἐμὲ βασιλέα, ' made me king.'

12. εἰς ὅ, ' until,' lit., ' until which (time).'

14. ὧδέ τοι πάρειμι, ' here I am,' ' here you have me.'

15, 16. τὸν Ἀστυάγη . . . αὐτοῦ, lit., ' recognition of him came to Astyages,' i.e., ' Astyages recognized him.' The usual Attic meaning of ἀνάγνωσις is ' reading '; for ' recognition ' ἀναγνώρισις is used.

17. ἐδόκει προσφέρεσθαι εἰς ἑαυτόν, ' seemed to resemble his own,' lit., ' seemed to resemble him.' This abbreviated form of expression is not uncommon after verbs of resembling and differing. (Cf. p. 49, l. 24, κεχωρισμένοις τῶν ἄλλων ἀνθρώπων.)

19, 20. ἐπὶ χρόνον, ' for a while.'

22. ταῦτα ποιήσω, ' I will settle this matter.'

24. πέμπει, ' sends away.' Ἀποπέμπει is more usual in this sense.

25, 26. ἐπεὶ δὲ ὑπελέλειπτο. The pluperfect with ἐπεί, ἐπειδή, and ὡς is not as common as the aorist. See note on p. 73, l. 8.

29. οὐκ ἔφη. See note on p. 79, ll. 4, 5.

31. ἅμα τε λέγων . . . ἐσήμαινε, ' while saying these words, he at the same time gave a sign. . . .' Greek usually connects ἅμα with the participial clause, while in English the corresponding adverb is taken with the principal verb.

33. τὸν ὄντα λόγον, ' the real story,' i.e., ' the truth.' κατέβαινεν εἰς λιτάς, ' he ended with prayers.' Cf. p. 11, c, l. 5 and note on that passage.

§ 3

1, 2. τοῦ μὲν βουκόλου . . . ἐκφήναντος, probably not genitive absolute, but simply dependent on λόγον, ' took less account of the herdsman, after he had revealed the truth.'

8. ἵνα μὴ ἐλεγχόμενος ἁλίσκηται, ' that he might not be confuted and detected (in deception).'

10. καθάπερ ἤκουσεν αὐτός, ' as he himself had heard.' Cf. note on p. 73, l. 8.

12. κατέβαινε λέγων, ' he ended by saying.' Cf. l. 33 above. λέγων ὡς, " Περίεστι κ.τ.λ.' Indirect discourse is frequently

introduced by the conjunctions ὡς and ὅτι, which correspond to the English ' that.' But these conjunctions may also be used, as in the present passage, to introduce the direct words of a speaker. In this function they have no English equivalent.

16, 17. τοῦτο μέν, . . . τοῦτο δέ, adverbial, ' in the first place, . . . in the second place.'

18, 19. πάρισθί μοι ἐπὶ δεῖπνον. Πάρειμι, whose literal meaning is ' I am present,' is often, as in this instance, used in the sense of ' I come to,' and in such cases it may be followed by εἰς, ἐπί, or πρός with the accusative, as if it were a verb of motion.

21, 22. εἰς δέον ἐγεγόνειν, ' had served his purpose.'

24. εἰς ' Ἀστυάγους. See note on p. 76, l. 8.

§ 4

7. τί, adverbial, ' at all.'

11. αὐτῶν, partitive genitive with ὅ, 'what he wanted of them.'

13. οὔτε . . . τε. Notice that the copulatives are not parallel. Instead of οὔτε . . . οὔτε (' neither . . . nor ') or τε καί (' both . . . and '), we have οὔτε . . . τε (lit., ' neither . . . and '). This is made possible by the fact that οὔτε is simply the negative of τέ. The copulatives then are τε . . . τε, with the first clause being negatived. It is impossible to bring out the full force of this combination in English. The best that can be done is to omit the first copulative: ' He was not startled, and he retained his self-control.'

§ 5

1. δίκην ταύτην. Attic prose would require ταύτην τὴν δίκην, unless we can regard δίκην as in apposition to ταύτην (' he imposed this as a punishment '), in which case the article would not be used.

1, 2. Κύρου δὲ πέρι. Dissyllabic prepositions, which usually accent the ultima, throw the accent back to the penult when they follow the noun they govern.

3. ἔκριναν, pluperfect meaning. Cf. note on p. 73, l. 8.

4. ταὐτά, for τὰ αὐτά, ' the same things,' i.e., the same as they had said before.

5. χρῆν ἄν, ' it would have been necessary,' an unfulfilled

condition in past time, where the imperfect represents a continuous action or state.

7. ἔστι τε . . . καὶ περίεστι, ' the boy lives and has survived,' i.e., ' he is still alive in spite of my efforts to get rid of him.'

8. ἐστήσαντο βασιλέα, ' made him king.' Cf. p. 16, l. 9.

14. μὴ ἐκ προνοίας τινός, i.e., unintentionally. 'Εκ with a substantive or its equivalent is frequently used in the place of a simple adverb, e.g., ἐκ τοῦ ἐμφανοῦς for ἐμφανῶς, ' openly.' The English use of ' of ' in such adverbial phrases as ' of course,' ' of one's own accord,' etc. is similar to this.

20. ἴθι χαίρων. The participle χαίρων, which usually means ' with impunity,' is also used in wishing someone well at parting. Thus ἴθι χαίρων is a close equivalent to the English ' farewell ' in its original meaning of ' may you fare well.'

21, 22. οὐ κατὰ Μιτραδάτην, ' not after the standard of Mithradates,' ' of a very different kind from Mithradates.'

C. MANHOOD OF CYRUS

§ 1

3, 4. πρὸ δ 'ἔτι τούτου, ' even before this.'

6. ἀνέπειθεν, ' kept urging them.' The prefix ἀνά (lit., ' up ') implies that the persuader had a difficult task. Our expression ' uphill work ' perhaps illustrates the force of the Greek preposition. The task of Harpagus was naturally a difficult one, since he had to persuade the Medes not only to revolt against their king, but to do so in favour of Cyrus, a member of the rival Persian race. The same word is used in l. 9, where the same connotation is implied.

6, 7. τὸν 'Αστυάγη . . . βασιλείας, ' to depose Astyages,' lit., ' to remove Astyages from the position of monarch.'

13. ἔφη λέγων. See note on p. 71, l. 15.

14. ἕκαστον, accusative in apposition to ὑμᾶς, the implied subject of the infinitive παρεῖναι. Similarly in l. 19 λελουμένους, for which we might have expected the dative in agreement with αὐτοῖς, is in the accusative to agree with the unexpressed subject of παρεῖναι.

18. εἰς τὴν ὑστεραίαν, sc. ἡμέραν, ' on the next day.' In expressions of time εἰς usually has the meaning of ' until.' It may also be used, however, to indicate that an action is per-

formed with a view to or looking ahead to a future occasion.
In this use it bears some resemblance to the Latin *in* with the
accusative and the English ' against ' in the meaning of ' in
preparation for ' or ' in provision for.'

20. ἐν δὲ τούτῳ, ' in the meantime.'

24, 25. ἐπεὶ δὲ ἀπὸ δείπνου ἦσαν, 'when they had finished
dinner,' a favourite idiom in Herodotus.

28. πάντα σφίσι κακὰ ἔχειν, ' brought them (*lit.*, had
for them) all sorts of evils.'

31, 32. οὕτως ὑμῖν ἔχει, ' this is the situation with you.'

33. ἔχουσι, dative plural of the participle with ὑμῖν.

§ 2

2. πάλαι δεινὸν ποιούμενοι, ' who had long been dissatisfied.'
Adverbs which refer to past time may be used with a present
tense to indicate an action begun in the past and continued in
the present. When used with the imperfect tense they denote
an action begun in the remote past (the time usually indicated
by the pluperfect) and continued in the less remote past (the
time usually indicated by the aorist). The former use is represented in English by the progressive perfect tenses (e.g., ' I
have been doing '), the latter by the progressive pluperfect
tenses (' I had been doing '). In the present passage the participle ποιούμενοι represents the imperfect tense, hence the
English ' had been ' (lit., ' had been making '). Cf. the use of
iam diu, iam pridem, and *iam dudum* in Latin with the present
and imperfect tenses. .

3, 4. ὡς ἐπύθετο . . . πράττοντα, ' when he learned that Cyrus
was doing these things.' Πυνθάνομαι, like various other verbs of
learning, perceiving, knowing, etc., takes the participle in indirect discourse.

10. τοῦ λόγου, ' the secret,' ' the conspiracy.'

15. χαιρήσει, ' go unpunished,' ' get away with it.' Cf. note
on p. 82, l. 20.

IX. SOLON AND CROESUS

(a)

4, 5. περιῆγον κατὰ τοὺς θησαυρούς, 'led him all around the
treasures.' Κατά (lit., ' down ') is frequently used with the

accusative to mean ' up and down,' ' all over,' e.g., κατὰ πόντον, κατὰ τὴν πόλιν.

8, 9. νῦν οὖν ἵμερος ἐπῆλθέ με, ἤδη . . . εἶδες, ' a desire has just now come upon me,' ' you have already seen.' With adverbs of time the Greek aorist may represent a present perfect, rather than a simple past action.

9. ἵμερος. In Attic this word is chiefly poetical. The prose equivalent is ἐπιθυμία.

9, 10. ἐπερωτᾶν εἴ τινα . . . ὀλβιώτατον, ' to ask who is the happiest person you have ever seen.' Εἴ τις (lit., ' if anyone ') is not infrequently used in the sense of the indirect interrogative ὅστις.

10. ἐλπίζων εἶναι, ' thinking that he was.' When ἐλπίζω means ' hope ' or ' expect,' it is followed by the future infinitive in indirect discourse. When it has its secondary meaning of ' think ' or ' believe ' (as in the present passage), the dependent infinitive is not in indirect discourse. The tense of the infinitive in such cases is determined by the type of action (aorist for instantaneous action, present for continued action).

ὀλβιώτατος. For the case see note on αὐτός, p. 71, l. 16.

12. τῷ ὄντι χρησάμενος, lit., ' using the real thing,' i.e., ' telling the truth.'

15, 17. τοῦτο μὲν . . . τοῦτο δέ, adverbial, ' in the first place . . . in the second place.'

15. καλοί τε κἀγαθοί. The phrase καλός τε κἀγαθός (also written καλὸς κἀγαθός) was used to imply the possession of all the qualities requisite in a gentleman. Hence οἱ καλοὶ κἀγαθοί often denoted simply members of the upper classes, whether they possessed the qualities implied by the term or not. The same is the case with the Latin optimates and the Greek οἱ ἄριστοι, ' the aristocracy ' (lit., ' the best men '). The reverse process has taken place with the English word ' gentlemen,' which from signifying simply men of good birth or family (gens, a ' tribe ' or ' clan ') has come to imply rather the possession of certain good qualities supposed to be characteristic of such persons.

19. ἀστυγείτονος, probably the Megarians, with whom the

Athenians carried on a long warfare during the lifetime of Solon.

(b)

1. τὰ κατὰ τὸν Τέλλον, ' Tellos's story.' For the lack of a substantive see note on p. 67, l. 3.

4. γένος, the accusative of specification or respect, which denotes the part, quality, or characteristic referred to: ' Argive with respect to their race ' (lit.), i.e., ' of Argive birth, nationality, etc.'

6. καὶ δὴ καί. This group of words is frequently used to introduce some additional fact on which greater emphasis is laid than on what has preceded: ' and moreover this story in particular.' Cf. also note on p. 71, ll. 5, 6.

7. Ἥρᾳ. For the relationship of Hera to Argos see Index of Names under Ἥρα.

7, 8. τὴν μητέρα αὐτῶν. She is said to have been one of the priestesses of Hera, by name Cydippe.

15, 16. ἄμεινον . . . μᾶλλον ἢ ζῆν. Strictly speaking, μᾶλλον is unnecessary after the comparative ἄμεινον; but the word ἄμεινον, like the Latin saepius, was often used almost in a positive sense (cf. p. 39, l. 9, οὐ γὰρ ἄμεινον, ' it is not well '), so that μᾶλλον became almost necessary to impart the full comparative signification. The sentiment expressed in this passage is a common one in Greek literature.

17, 18. τὴν μητέρα αὐτῶν (ἐμακάριζον) οἵων κ.τ.λ., ' congratulated their mother on being possessed of such children,' lit., ' on what sort of children she possessed.'

21, 22. ἔθυσαν, εὐωχήθησαν, pluperfect sense. See note on p. 73, l. 8.

24. ποιησάμενοι. Notice the middle, ' made for themselves,' or perhaps ' had made for themselves.' (Cf. διδάσκεσθαι, ' to have someone taught,' as distinct from διδάσκειν, ' to teach.')

24, 25. εἰς Δελφούς. The use of εἰς is permissible because motion is implied. The complete thought is, ' they brought them to (εἰς) Delphi and set them up there.'

25. ὡς. For the meaning of ὡς with a participle see note on p. 70, ll. 21, 22.

(c)

3. ἀπέρριπται εἰς τὸ μηδέν, lit., ' has been thrown away to nothing,' i.e., ' is considered worthless.'   For the double ρ of ἀπέρριπται see note on ἔρριψεν, p. 74, l. 20.

5–7. ἐπιστάμενον . . . πέρι.   It is convenient to turn this sentence slightly: ' Knowing well that the divine power is altogether envious (of human happiness) and disposed to bring trouble upon us, I am questioned by you. . . .'

10, 11. σκοπεῖν . . . τὴν τελευτὴν πῇ ἀποβήσεται, ' to consider how the end will turn out.'   When verbs of knowing, perceiving. etc. have an interrogative sentence dependent upon them, the subject of the dependent clause is usually introduced as the object of the principal verb.   Thus ' I know who you are ' becomes in Greek οἶδα σὲ ὅστις εἶ (lit., ' I know you who you are ').

11, 12. πολλοῖς . . . ἀνέτρεψε, ' to many men God gives but one short glimpse of happiness, and then destroys them utterly.'   The prefix ὑπό in verbal compounds such as ὑποδείξας may indicate that an action is of brief duration, gradual, or secret.   (Cf. ὑπάγοντες, p. 11, c, l. 6 and note on that passage.) For ἀνέτρεψε, the gnomic aorist where English uses a present, see note on p. 69, l. 19.

(d)

1. μετὰ δὲ Σόλωνα οἰχόμενον, lit., ' after Solon going away,' i.e., ' after Solon went away.' ' after Solon's departure.'   See note on p. 70, l. 6.

Νέμεσις is ' deserved retribution,' such as the Greeks held to be constantly brought upon a man by the gods, when excessive prosperity had led him to pride or presumption.   Solon (p. 26, c, l. 5) had described divine power as φθονερόν, ' envious,' implying that the gods took a malicious pleasure in overthrowing human prosperity, whether misused or not; he should rather, according to the more orthodox views of the ancients, have said νεμεσητικόν, ' retributive,' implying that the action of the gods was regulated by justice.

2. ὡς εἰκάσαι, ' as far as one may judge,' ' apparently,' ' presumably.'   This use of the infinitive in parenthetical expressions is not uncommon in Greek.   It occurs most frequently

in the phrase ὡς ἔπος εἰπεῖν or ὡς εἰπεῖν, 'so to speak,' 'if one may say so.'

8. ἐστῶτι. Beginners should be cautioned against regarding ἐστώς as a 'syncopated' form of ἐστηκώς, a term sometimes applied to it, erroneously. Ἐστώς is contracted from ἐσταώς, ἐστα- being the stem of the 2nd perfect, while ἐστηκώς is formed on ἐστηκ-, the stem of the 1st perfect.

9, 10. τὸ τοῦ Σόλωνος, subject of εἴη, while the clause, ὡς εἴη . . . εἰρημένον, is subject of εἰσῆλθε. For the genitive dependent on the article see note on p. 67, l. 3.

10, 11. τὸ " μηδένα . . . ὄλβιον." When a group of words performs the function of a substantive, it may take the neuter article. Here the substantival phrase, μηδένα . . . ὄλβιον, is in apposition to and explanatory of τὸ τοῦ Σόλωνος.

12. ἐκ πολλῆς ἡσυχίας, 'after a long silence.'

18. ἀποβεβήκοι, indirect discourse after ἔλεγεν ὡς and parallel to ἔλθοι and ἀποφλαυρίσειε.

18, 19. οὐδέν τι . . . λέγων ἤ, 'not speaking with reference to himself any more than,' i.e., 'not meaning himself any more than.'

20. παρ' ἑαυτοῖς, 'in their own eyes,' 'to themselves.'

(e)

5. εὐδαιμονίᾳ, dative of respect, a form of the dative of manner.

13. κατερράγη. For the double ρ see note on ἔρριψεν, p. 74, l. 20.

X. RESPECT FOR SUPPLIANTS

1. ᾤχετο φεύγων. The main idea here is contained in the participle, not the verb. English would simply say, 'he fled.'

3. ἐκδιδόναι κελεύων, sc. τοὺς Κυμαίους.

4. θεὸν τὸν ἐν Βραγχίδαις, Apollo. For the oracle referred to see Index of Names under Βραγχίδαι.

9. ἐπερωτῶσι, dative plural of the participle with αὐτοῖς.

13. ἔσχε μὴ ποιῆσαι . . . Κυμαίους, 'prevented the Cymeans from doing this.' Verbs which contain a negative idea (as of

hindering, preventing, refusing, denying, forbidding, distrusting, etc.) may be followed by an infinitive with μή, rather than the simple infinitive. Such a μή in no way alters the meaning of the sentence. It merely serves to emphasize the negative idea expressed by the leading verb.

15. τὸ δεύτερον, adverbial, ' the second time,' or, as we would be more likely to say, ' a second time.'

18. ἐκ πάντων, ' on behalf of them all,' lit. (chosen as spokesman) ' out of them all.'

22. εἰς τόδε, to be taken with πρίν, ' up to this point . . . until,' or simply ' until.'

23. τὸ ἀπὸ σοῦ, ' your wishes.'   See note on p. 67, l. 3.

29. ἄλλα ὅσα . . . γένη, ' all the other kinds . . . which.'   In Greek, as in Latin, the antecedent is frequently placed inside the relative clause, instead of outside it as in English.

This story illustrates for us the fact that the oracles of the Greeks, whatever their shortcomings, staunchly maintained, in early times at any rate, the highest principles in the code of Greek morality and religion. Cf. note on p. 75, b, l. 5.

XI. Captures of Babylon
A. FIRST CAPTURE, BY CYRUS

5. σιτία ἐτῶν κάρτα πολλῶν, ' provisions for very many years.'

7. τέλος, adverbial accusative, ' finally.'

13. τὴν λίμνην κ.τ.λ.   The lake, or marsh, referred to had been created by Nitocris as a temporary diversion for the Euphrates. As she wished to strengthen and fortify the banks of the river, whose course lay through the centre of Babylon, she had a large basin dug beside the river channel above the city, and the waters of the river diverted into this basin or ' lake.'   Then the empty bed within the city was strengthened with walls of brick, and the two portions of the city were united by a bridge over the river. These operations completed, the river waters were returned to their original channel, and the ' lake ' was dried up to the extent of becoming a ' marsh.'   Cyrus, by withdrawing a large part of the river water to the

lake once more, was able to lower the level of the river to the point where his soldiers could travel down it under the city walls and into the city. By this stratagem he captured Babylon.

17. ἐπ' αὐτῷ τούτῳ, ' for this very purpose.' With this usage of ἐπί (lit., ' on ') we may compare such English phrases as ' on this errand,' ' on this mission.'

18. ἀνδρὶ . . . μάλιστα, ' to about the middle of a man's thigh.' Both ὡς and μάλιστα, when used with numerals and other expressions of measure, make the number or amount approximate. With the adjectival use of μέσον cf. the Latin medius, summus, etc.

23. τὰς πυλίδας, the gates set where gaps were left in the masonry of the embankments, to admit of approach to the river from the streets.

27. τῶν, pronominal.

30. ἑορτή. It is generally supposed that this refers to the feast of Belshazzar, described in Daniel V.

τοῦτον τὸν χρόνον, ' during this time,' accusative of extent of time.

B. SECOND CAPTURE, BY DARIUS

§ 1

1. ἀπέστησαν οἱ Βαβυλώνιοι. This revolt was one of those occasioned by the changes of power after the death of Cambyses. See Index of Names under Δαρεῖος.

6. αὐτάς, i.e., the others.

10, 11. φροντίζοντας οὐδὲν κ.τ.λ. Their confidence on this as on the former occasion arose from the strength of their fortifications. In ancient times any well-fortified city, carefully guarded, seems to have been practically impregnable, and starvation or stratagem were usually the only means by which its capture could be effected.

15. Τότε anticipates and emphasizes ἐπήν: ' You will take us only when. . . .'

15, 16. ἐπὴν ἡμίονοι τέκωσι. Female mules rarely bear offspring.

17. ἐλπίζων ... τεκεῖν. For the tense of the infinitive see note on p. 84, l. 10.

22, 23. ἄλλοις τε ... καὶ δὴ καὶ τούτῳ. See notes on p. 71, ll. 5, 6 and p. 85, l. 6.

§ 2

1. τῷ Μεγαβύζου, 'son of Megabyzus.' See note on p. 67, l. 3.

4. ἀπειπὼν ... μηδενὶ φράζειν, 'forbidding them to tell anyone.' For the negative with the infinitive after verbs of forbidding see note on p. 87, l. 13.

6–8. σὺν γὰρ θεῷ ... τεκεῖν, 'for he thought that the man's remark, together with (τε ... καί) the fact of his mule having foaled, pointed to the intervention of providence'; lit., ' he thought that both the man spoke and his mule foaled under divine influence (σὺν θεῷ).'

10, 11. περὶ πολλοῦ ποιεῖται. See note on p. 75, ll. 4, 5.

12. πολλοῦ, genitive of price with τιμῶτο, ' valued highly.'

23. οὗτος ἀνήρ. Omission of the article with a demonstrative adjective indicates contempt.

32. πῶς οὐκ ... διαφθείρας. The meaning is, ' How can you expect to convince me that your mutilating yourself in this way was not simply a result of madness? ' (Lit., ' How did you not destroy yourself by having become mad? ")

34, 35. ἐπ' ἐμαυτοῦ βαλόμενος, ' on my own responsibility,' lit., ' casting it over in my own mind.' The phrase is not Attic.

35. ἐὰν μὴ τῶν σῶν δεήσῃ, ' if there is nothing lacking on your part (τῶν σῶν),' i.e., 'if you carry out properly your share in my stratagem.' The impersonal δεῖ is followed by a genitive of the thing needed.

§ 3

2. ὑπὸ σοῦ τάδε ἔπαθον, ' I suffered this treatment at your hands,' ' I was treated in this way by you.' As the verb ἔπαθον is used in a passive sense, the agent of the implied action is expressed by ὑπό and the genitive. For τάδε, ' such as follows,' we might have expected ταῦτα, ' such as you have seen,' but the meaning really is, ' such as I shall go on to describe to them.'

6. μοί, dative of advantage, meaning ' for my benefit.'

10. οἱ πρότεροι, οὗτοι, ' the former,' ' the latter.'

15, 16. τά τε ἄλλα . . . καὶ δὴ καί. See notes on p. 71, ll. 5, 6 and p. 85, l. 6.

16. τὸ δὲ ἐντεῦθεν, adverbial, ' as to what follows,' ' after that.'

§ 4

1. ἐπιστρεφόμενος, lit., ' turning around,' i.e., ' looking back.'

3. κατὰ τοῦτο, ' on this side,' ' in this position.'

3, 4. ὀλίγον τι, adverbial accusative, ' a little.'

4. τὴν ἑτέραν πύλην, ' one of the two gates.' Compare the use of *alter* in Latin, e.g. *alter consulum*, ' one of the two consuls.'

12. ἔφη λέγων. See note on p. 71, l. 15.

13, 14. ἀγαθόν, κακόν, substantives in apposition to ἐγώ.

14. οὐ γὰρ . . . καταπροΐξεται, lit., ' he will not go unpunished after having maimed me thus,' i.e., ' he will not have maimed me with impunity.' In colloquial language, ' he won't get away with it.'

23. τοῦτο, neuter, referring to the general idea expressed in ὧν ἐδεῖτο (l. 21), ' what he wanted.'

23, 24. παρέλαβεν, συνέθετο. For the use of the aorist with a pluperfect meaning see note on p. 73, l. 8.

27, 28. μαθόντες . . . παρεχόμενον, ' learning that he displayed deeds that matched his words.' Μανθάνω takes the participial construction in indirect discourse.

28. πᾶν, adverbial, ' in everything,' ' in every way.'

33. Ζώπυρον . . . στόμασιν, ' had the name of Zopyrus on their lips.'

36, 37. πάντα δὴ ἦν . . . Ζώπυρος, ' Zopyrus was everything to the Babylonians.'

45. τῶν δὲ Βαβυλωνίων, οἱ μὲν . . . οὗτοι, ' those of the Babylonians who. . . .'

46. Διός, genitive of Ζεύς.

46, 47. ἔμενον . . . ἕκαστος. For ἕκαστος with a plural verb see note on p. 75, l. 4.

47, 48. ἔμαθον προδεδομένοι. See note on ll. 27, 28 above.

§ 5

2. ἐκράτησε, pluperfect sense, as frequently after ἐπεί. See note on p. 73, l. 8.

5. μάλιστα εἰς τρισχιλίους, ' to the number of about 3,000.'

9. παρὰ Δαρείῳ κριτῇ, lit., ' before Darius as judge,' i.e., ' in the judgment of Darius.'

9, 10. οὔτε τῶν ὕστερον . . . οὔτε τῶν πρότερον, 'either of later or of earlier times.'   Οὔτε . . . οὔτε must not in this passage be translated ' neither . . . nor,' since we have already had one negative in οὐδείς.   Cf. the double negatives on p. 3, ll. 6, 7 and p. 12, ll. 17, 18.

13. ἀπαθῆ τῆς αἰκίας.   For the genitive see note on p. 77, l. 21.

15, 16. δῶρα . . . τιμιώτατα, ' (such) gifts as are held in most esteem among the Persians.'   Notice the imperfect ἐδίδου, of gifts renewed each year, in contrast to ἔδωκεν in the next line, of a gift given only once.

15. ἀνὰ πᾶν ἔτος; ' every year.'   See note on p. 67, l. 4.

XII. The Tomb of Nitocris, Queen of Babylon

3. κατεσκευάσατο.   The preposition κατά in this compound implies that the object which is built or prepared is intended as a fixed and permanent structure.   Similarly the related noun, κατασκευή, is used of immoveable articles or ' fixtures,' while παρασκευή designates moveable furniture or goods.

6. ὕστερον, a comparative without positive form (cf. προτέρους, p. 3, II, l. 5).   Ἐμοῦ is the genitive of comparison.

8. Μὴ σπανίσας γε is the equivalent of a conditional clause, ἐάν γε μὴ σπανίσῃ.   Hence μή and not οὐ is the appropriate negative.

9. ἄλλως, ' for any other reason.'

οὐ γὰρ ἄμεινον, sc. ἐστί, ' for it is not well,' lit., ' better,' but ἄμεινον in this phrase has almost lost its comparative force. Compare p. 25, b, l. 15, where ἄμεινον is strengthened by μᾶλλον to give it its full comparative signification.   The expression οὐ γὰρ ἄμεινον was evidently a stock phrase which had been in use long before the time of Herodotus. It is found in several passages of epic poetry, where it forms the last two feet of the hexameter.

11, 12. καὶ δεινὸν ... καί, χρημάτων κ.τ.λ. The first καί ('both') is somewhat misplaced, as it belongs, not to δεινὸν ἐδόκει, but to μηδὲν χρῆσθαι: 'it seemed a great pity both to make no use of these gates and. ...' For δεινόν see note on p. 70, l. 10. Μηδέν (like οὐδέν in l. 14) is the adverbial accusative, 'not at all.'

13. μὴ οὐ. The double negative is used with an infinitive after a verb which is itself negative or implies negation. Here δεινὸν ἐδόκει is the equivalent of οὐκ ἀγαθὸν ἐδόκει and hence a negative is implied.

15. ὅτι ὑπὲρ κ.τ.λ., 'because the corpse would be above his head as he passed through.' Διεξελαύνοντι is the equivalent of εἰ διεξήλαυνεν, so that the sentence is one which implies an unfulfilled condition.

18. ἄπληστος ... χρημάτων. See note on p. 77, l. 21.

19. ἀνέῳγες, imperfect of ἀνοίγω. It is doubly augmented, like ἑώρων (imperfect of ὁράω and ἑάλων (aorist of ἁλίσκομαι).

XIII. The Babylonian Wife-Market

1. κατὰ κώμας ἑκάστας, 'in each village.' Κατά with the accusative may mean 'up and down,' 'throughout' (cf. note on p. 83, ll. 4, 5), hence distributively of something that takes place in a number of individual instances. Κατὰ μίαν ἑκάστην, ll. 4, 5 ('one by one'), provides another illustration of this use.

2. ὡς αἱ παρθένοι γίγνοιντο. The optative implies indefinite frequency in past time: 'whenever the maidens became. ...' γάμων ὡραῖαι, 'ripe for marriage.'

5, 6. ἐπώλει, πραθείη. Of the three common verbs whose meaning is 'sell,' πωλέω or ἀποδίδομαι are used in the present, future, aorist active and middle, πιπράσκω in the perfects and in the aorist passive.

8. ἐπὶ συνοικήσει, 'for marriage.' (Cf. p. 32, l. 17, ἐπ' αὐτῷ τούτῳ).

12. ὡς ... διεξέλθοι. The aorist retains its pluperfect

meaning with ὡς (see note on p. 73, l. 8) even though it is in the optative mood to express indefinite frequency (see note on l. 2 above): ' after the herald had (on each occasion) sold off (lit., gone through in his sale) the most beautiful . . .'

14. ἄν. For the use of ἄν with the aorist to express a repeated action in past time see note on p. 72, c, ll. 4, 5.

17. ἐξεδίδοσαν, ' gave in marriage,' since the money by which the beautiful brides were bought made it possible for husbands in turn to be bought for the ugly.

XIV. Stories of the Alcmaeonid Family

(a)

10, 11. οὓς ηὕρισκεν . . . ὄντας, ' which he found to be.' For the construction see note on p. 68, ll. 24, 25.

15. πλησάμενος τοῦ χρυσοῦ. See note on p. 68, l. 12.

16. τοῦ ψήγματος, ' some of the gold dust,' partitive genitive.

(b)

3. γυναῖκα, in apposition to ταύτην, ' to bestow her as wife.'

4. 'Ολυμπίων. For this celebration see 'Ολύμπια in the Index of Names. As it was the most important festival of the Greeks, it was attended by men of the highest rank from all over the Greek world, and so provided an excellent opportunity for Cleisthenes to choose a husband for his daughter.

νικῶν. We might have expected the aorist νικήσας, ' having won,' but the present νικῶν perhaps expresses ' while celebrating his victory,' for such an event was usually followed by a feast and a thanksgiving service to a god, accompanied by songs which were composed especially for the occasion, often by the best living poets.

10. μνηστῆρες, in apposition to the ὅσοι clause, ' came as suitors.'

11, 12. ὁ 'Αλκμαίωνος, Τισάνδρου, sc. υἱός and see note on p. 67, l. 3.

13. τῶν ἄλλων . . . προφέρων. Verbs which imply comparison are followed by the genitive.

15. ἀνεπύθετο, ' made thorough inquiries about.' The prefix

ἀνά gives a verb an intensifying force, the literal meaning of
' up ' being readily transformed to ' right up to the end,'
' completely,' ' thoroughly.'

κατέχων ἐνιαυτόν, ' keeping them with him for a year.'

24. ἐδείπνησαν, pluperfect sense. See note on p. 73, l. 8.

μουσικῇ. The term includes singing, playing musical instruments, and even dancing. Contests in these accomplishments
were common among the Greeks from the earliest times, and
were particularly popular as an after-dinner amusement among
Greek gentlemen.

25. κατέχων, lit., ' restraining,' probably in the sense of
holding them spellbound.

28. καί πως . . . ὠρχεῖτο, ' and he danced in a way that was
pleasing to himself.'

34. ἀποστυγῶν κ.τ.λ., ' detesting the idea of Hippocleides'
becoming his son-in-law,' lit., ' hating that Hippocleides should
become. . . .'

40. φροντίς, sc. ἐστί.

41. σιγὴν ποιησάμενος, ' having procured silence.' The force
of the middle is that he procured silence for himself, i.e., to
make himself heard.

46. πᾶσι κατὰ νοῦν ποιεῖν, ' act according to the wishes of
everyone,' ' act so as to please everyone.'

47. τοῦδε τοῦ γάμου, dependent on ἀπελαυνομένοις.

48. ἑκάστῳ, in apposition to τοῖς . . . ἀπελαυνομένοις.

XV. EXPLORATION OF AFRICA

A. THE PYGMIES AND THE SOURCE OF THE NILE

1, 2. μέχρι μὲν . . . ὁ Νεῖλος, ' The Nile is known (i.e., has
been explored) for a distance of four-months' travel by land
and water (lit., up to four months of sailing and road).'

3. τὸ δ' ἀπὸ τοῦδε, ' what is beyond that.' For the use of the
article without a substantive see note on p. 67, l. 3.

9. ὡς, ' saying that,' λέγοντες being understood from λέσχην.

11. πλέον, i.e., more than was already known.

13, 14. ἄλλα τε . . . καὶ δὴ καί. See notes on p. 71, ll. 5, 6 and
p. 85, l. 6.

15. ὀψομένους, future participle to express purpose.

15, 16. τὰ μὲν κατὰ τὴν βορείαν θάλατταν, object of οἰκοῦσι, meaning either ' the parts (of Libya) that stretch *down to* . . . ,' or, more probably, ' the parts (of Libya) that stretch *along* the northern sea,' κατά signifying extension up and down. ' The northern sea ' is of course the Mediterranean.

18, 19. Ἕλληνες καὶ Φοίνικες, referring to the Greek and Phoenician colonies on the north coast of Africa, the chief of which were, respectively, Cyrene and Carthage.

19. τὰ δὲ καθύπερθε τούτων, adverbial accusative, ' in the regions beyond these.'

20. τῆς θηριώδους, sc. χώρας or γῆς.

20, 21. τε . . . καί. Notice that τε . . . καί in this passage connect, not similar parts of speech, as is usually the case, but a noun, ψάμμος, and an adjective, ἄνυδρος. This is possible because here ψάμμος is practically equivalent to the adjective ψαμμώδης.

21. ἄνυδρος δεινῶς, ' awfully dry,' i.e., ' very dry.' See note on p. 70, l. 10.

24. τῆς οἰκουμένης, sc. χώρας or γῆς; similarly χώραν or γῆν must be supplied with τὴν θηριώδη in l. 25.

30. ἄνδρες μικροί. Pygmies are mentioned by various ancient authors, beginning with Homer. They were thought to live in the distant south (i.e., Africa), although references to similar peoples in Asia are also found. Cranes supposedly migrated to the land of the pygmies for the winter, and fierce battles between pygmies and cranes were believed to be common and are depicted in ancient works of art. No doubt the pygmies referred to by Herodotus were the ancestors of the modern pygmies of central Africa.

33, 34. τὸ μέγεθος, χρῶμα, accusatives of respect, ' in size,' etc.

34, 35. ἔρρει, imperfect of ῥέω. For the double ρ see note on ἔρριψεν, p. 74, l. 20.

37, 38. ὁ μὲν δὴ . . . δεδηλώσθω, lit., ' Let the story of Etearchus have been told by me up to this point,' i.e., ' This is enough for me to tell about the story of Etearchus.' The perfect imperative occurs mainly in the third person singular of the passive, where its meaning is that an act shall be decisive and permanent.

41. Νεῖλον, partly from the fact of there being crocodiles in it and partly from the direction of its course from west to east. Herodotus goes on to use the following curious argument about the unknown course of the upper Nile: the Nile, the greatest river in Africa, must correspond, he says, to the Danube, the greatest river in Europe; and as the Danube flows for a long distance in its upper course from west to east, it is reasonable to conclude that the Nile does the same. The river here spoken of is more probably the Niger.

B. THE ETHIOPIANS

§ I

1, 2. τοὺς μακροβίους Αἰθίοπας, a mythical tribe.

4, 5. ὀψομένους ... τὴν ... τράπεζαν εἰ ἔστιν ἀληθῶς, ' to see if the so-called table of the sun . . . really existed,' lit., ' to see the so-called table . . . if it really existed.' This anticipatory accusative is common with verbs of perception (see note on p. 86, ll. 10, 11).

Τράπεζα in this passage has the sense of ' meal,' rather than the literal meaning of ' table.' The story of the ' table of the sun ' has been explained as being either an indication of offerings of food made to the dead, or simply a description of a region of great fertility.

6. τῷ λόγῳ, ' ostensibly.'

10, 11. τὰς μὲν νύκτας, τὰς δὲ ἡμέρας. See note on p. 74, ll. 1, 2.

18. ἀφίκοντο, pluperfect sense. See note on p. 73, l. 8.

20. εἷμα. Gifts of clothing have always been common among Oriental people. In the Old Testament, for instance, Naaman bestows two changes of raiment on Gehazi, Elisha's servant. Εἷμα and the nouns which follow are in apposition to δῶρα.

χρυσοῦν στρεπτὸν περιαυχένιον. When two adjectives modify a single noun they are usually connected by a conjunction, but in this instance στρεπτόν is taken so closely with περιαυχένιον that the two words form a single idea, ' a twisted-necklace.'

21. μύρου ἀλάβαστρον, another favourite gift among Orientals, the same present being offered to Our Lord in St. Matthew XXVI, 7: προσῆλθεν αὐτῷ γυνὴ ἔχουσα ἀλάβαστρον μύρου βαρυτίμου.

23, 24. νόμοις δὲ καὶ ἄλλοις . . . καὶ δὴ καὶ. See notes on p. 71, ll. 5, 6 and p. 85, l. 6.

24. κεχωρισμένοις τῶν ἄλλων ἀνθρώπων, 'different from those of other men ' (lit., ' different from other men '). See note on p. 80, l. 17.

26. κατὰ τὸ μέγεθος, ' in proportion to his size.'

31. εἰς λόγους ἐλθεῖν, ' get into a conversation.' Cf. ἀφικέσθαι εἰς λόγους and ἀφίκοντο εἰς λέσχην on p. 47, ll. 7 and 8.

32, 33. οἷς καὶ αὐτὸς . . . χρώμενος, ' in the use of which he also takes great pleasure,' lit., ' using which he himself also is greatly pleased.'

34. κατόπται, appositional, ' as spies.'

35. οὔτε κ.τ.λ. The negative properly belongs to βουλόμενος, ' neither did the king send you . . . because he wanted.'

39, 40. ἐπεθύμησε . . . ἦγεν. Notice the change of tense from the aorist to the imperfect. The imperfect is conative in meaning here: ' he would not have coveted land other than his own, nor would he be trying to lead into slavery . . .'

41. τόξον. The bows of the Ethiopians are described elsewhere by Herodotus (VII, 69) as being of four cubits in length and made of strips of palmwood.

43, 44. οὕτως εὐπετῶς, i.e., ' as easily as I do."

44. μεγέθει, dative of respect, a form of the dative of manner.

45, 46. ἐπὶ νοῦν . . . Αἰθίοψι, ' put it into the minds of the Ethiopians.'

§ 2

13, 14. ὁπόσον χρόνον μακρότατον, ' how much time at the longest,' or ' what was the longest time that. . . .

16. πλήρωμα, in apposition to ἔτη.

17. οὐδέν, adverbial, ' not at all.'

18. κόπρον, referring of course to the manure used in fertilizing the soil.

18, 19. οὐδὲ . . . ἔφη δύνασθαι, ' said they wouldn't be able.' See note on p. 79, ll. 4, 5.

20. φράζων τὸν οἶνον, ' referring to the wine.'

§ 3

2. ἔτη μὲν εἰς εἴκοσι καὶ ἑκατόν. It is unusual for a Greek preposition to be placed between its substantive and the adjectival modifier of the substantive. In this instance ἔτη μέν precedes so that it may be effectively contrasted with σίτησιν δέ in l. 4. Note how the constructions differ. While ἔτη is the object of εἰς, σίτησιν is the subject of εἶναι.

5. θαῦμα . . . ποιουμένων, for θαυμαζόντων. Similarly on p. 51, § 4, l. 2 ὀργὴν ποιησάμενος is the equivalent of ὀργισθείς. The force of the middle in such uses is that the subject produces the wonder, anger, etc. in himself. This is in contrast to its meaning on p. 45, l. 41, where σιγὴν ποιησάμενος signifies 'having procured silence for himself.'

6. αὐτοῖς ἡγήσατο. When the dative follows ἡγέομαι the meaning is 'lead' in the original sense of 'going before.' With the genitive the meaning is the derived one of 'leading' in the sense of 'commanding.' Ἡγέομαι is also used, like the Latin duco, to signify 'think' or 'consider.' This use is followed by the accusative case.

7. ὦζε, impersonal, 'there was a smell from it, as of violets.' The genitive (ἴων) is the usual case after verbs relating to the senses of smell, taste, touch, and hearing.

12, 13. διὰ τὸ ὕδωρ τοῦτο . . . μακρόβιοι ἂν εἶεν, 'they are likely to be long-lived on account of this water,' i.e., 'this water is likely to be, or probably is, the cause of their long life.' The optative indicates that the writer is uncertain, not about the fact of their long life, but about whether it is caused by the water. It is not the optative of a less vivid future condition, but the so-called 'potential' optative, which indicates the belief that a circumstance will probably turn out to be true in the present or to have been true in the past.

12. εἰ ἔστιν . . . λέγεται, 'if it (i.e., the water) is really as they say it is.'

14. ἀπὸ τῆς κρήνης δέ. Δέ is normally the second word in its clause. The fact of its following the phrase ἀπὸ τῆς κρήνης here indicates that these words are considered as a unit.

16. ἐδέδεντο, 'had been bound,' when put into prison; but

it is practically equivalent to simple past time, ' were bound,' or ' were lying bound.'

17. σπανιώτατον καὶ τιμιώτατον, 'the most scarce and valuable *thing*.' The neuters are used as predicate substantives; they are not modifiers of χαλκός.

§ 4

2. ὀργὴν ποιησάμενος. See note on p. 99, l. 5.

5. οἷα . . . ὤν, ' since he was.' The use of οἷα with a causal participle indicates that the writer vouches for the reason. Compare this with the use of ἅτε on p. 7, a, l. 3 and contrast with ὡς on p. 6, l. 21.

6. ἤκουσε, pluperfect sense. See note on p. 73, l. 8.

8. αὐτίκα . . . ἐπελελοίπειν. The pluperfect where we might have expected the aorist represents the situation more graphically: ' suddenly (they found that) the food had failed them.'

10, 11. εἰ . . . ἐγνωσιμάχει καὶ ἀπῆγεν κ.τ.λ., 'if he had. . . .' Unfulfilled conditions in past time are expressed by the aorist when the action would have been instantaneous, by the imperfect when it would have involved continuity. Thus the use of the imperfects in the present passage indicates that the action is conceived of as being continuous.

11, 12. ἐπὶ τῇ . . . ἁμαρτάδι. 'Επί is here temporal; from its basic meaning of ' upon,' it comes to mean ' following close upon,' ' behind,' hence ' after.'

12. νῦν δέ, ' but as it was.'

XVI. The Battle of Salamis

(a)

1. ἐξηγγέλθη, pluperfect sense. See note on p. 73, l. 8.

1, 2. ὡς ἔσχε τὰ περὶ κ.τ.λ., ' how things stood with regard to . . . ,' lit., ' how the situation with the Athenian Acropolis was.' For the use of the article without a substantive see note on p. 67, l. 3.

2, 3. εἰς τοσοῦτον . . . ὥστε, lit., ' arrived at such confusion (disturbance, etc.) that,' i.e., ' were so panic-stricken that.'

4. ὡς ἀποθευσόμενοι, ' with the intention of sailing away.'

5. τοῦ Ἰσθμοῦ, the Isthmus of Corinth.

12, 13. εἶπεν κ.τ λ. The suggestion that it was Mnesiphilus, rather than Themistocles, who saw the necessity of fighting at Salamis probably reflects the prejudice of Herodotus's Attic informants. For the hostility which developed against Themistocles after the Persian Wars see Θεμιστοκλῆς in the Index of Names.

οὗτοι . . . οὐδεμιᾶς. For the double negative see note on p. 68, ll. 6, 7.

Ἄρα gives the sense of ' contrary to expectation,' a frequent meaning of the word. (Cf. note on p. 74, l. 27.) Thus the significance of the passage is, ' You think you are going to fight for Greece at the Isthmus, but you will find that you have no country at all to fight for.'

14. κατὰ γὰρ . . . τρέψονται, ' each will betake himself to his own city.' For κατά in the distributive use see note on p. 93, l. 1. The plural ἕκαστοι signifies a *group* of people; in this instance, the group from each city is meant. Cf. the use of ἑκάτεροι on p. 3, III, l. 4.

(b)

3, 4. αὐτῷ κοινόν τι πρᾶγμα συμμῖξαι, ' to discuss with him a matter of common interest.'

5. εἴ τι ἐθέλει, sc. λέγειν, ' if he had something to say,' lit., ' if he wanted to say something.'

10. ὡς δὲ ἄρα, ' and when actually.' See note on ἄρα, ll. 12, 13 above.

11 τὸν λόγον (sc. τούτων) ὧν ἕνεκα συνήγαγε, ' his account of those things for the sake of which he had assembled,' i.e., ' his reasons for assembling.' Note that συνήγαγε has the pluperfect sense here (cf. note on p. 73, l. 8).

12. οἷα κάρτα δεόμενος. See note on p. 100, l. 5.

13. Ἀδείμαντος. It is probable that Adeimantus is being maligned here because of a prejudice on the part of the Athenians. His son Aristeas played a leading role in stirring up the Peloponnesian War. (Cf. the case of Themistocles noted above, ll. 12, 13.)

(c)

1. **Τότε μέν** is usually followed by ἔπειτα δέ, which indicates a later occasion. In this instance the later occasion is introduced by τότε δή (p. 55, l. 6).

3. **ἐν σοί . . . ἐστι,** ' it is in your hands,' ' it rests with you.'

6, 7. **ἦν τὰ εἰκότα . . . ἐκβαίνῃ,** lit., ' if what is likely comes out of the war,' i.e., ' if the war has the result that can be expected.'

7. **πολύ,** adverbial, ' we will win a great victory.'

7, 8. **τὸ . . . ναυμαχεῖν.** When the infinitive is used as a substantive it may be qualified by the neuter article.

8. **πρὸς ἡμῶν,** ' to our advantage.'

9. **περιγίγνεται,** ' escapes ' by not falling at once into the hands of the enemy, as would be the case if the Greeks withdrew to the Isthmus.

10–12. **ὁμοίως . . . Πελοποννήσου,** ' you will defend the Peloponnesus as well by staying here as by fighting off the Isthmus,' lit., ' equally by staying here and before the Isthmus.'

14. **ὑμῖν,** dative of disadvantage, ' to trouble you.'

14, 15. **εἰς τὸν Ἰσθμὸν παρέσονται.** See note on p. 81, ll. 18, 19.

15, 16. **ἑκαστέρω τῆς Αττικῆς,** ' beyond Attica.' Τῆς Ἀττικῆς is the genitive of comparison after the comparative adverb ἑκαστέρω.

(d)

2. **'Αδείμαντος.** See note on p. 101, l. 13.

6. **τότε δή,** ' then at last,' after previously restraining his anger. See note on l. 1 above.

11. **τῷ λόγῳ διέβαινεν εἰς,** ' passed over in his remarks to. '

12. **σὺ εἰ μενεῖς.** The apodosis is not expressed but it is clearly implied: ' if you stay here . . . (all will be well).' The vivid future condition is rendered even more vivid by the use of the future indicative with εἰ instead of the subjunctive with ἐάν.

15. **ὡς ἔχομεν,** ' just as we are,' i.e., without hesitation.

16. **ἡμετέρα.** It is not certain upon what foundation this claim rested.

20. ἀνεδιδάσκετο. For the force of ἀνά cf. note on p. 82, l. 6.

23. αὐτοῦ μένοντας διαναυμαχεῖν, explanatory of ταύτην τὴν γνώμην. Note the plural μένοντας, to indicate that the decision he makes is not for himself alone, but for all his troops.

(e)

3. εἰς τὴν ὑστεραίαν. See note on p. 82, l. 18.

14. πλοίῳ, 'in a boat,' but the dative is probably instrumental with πέμπει, 'sends by means of a boat.'

15. οἰκέτης, sc. Θεμιστοκλέους.

18, 19. τυγχάνει . . . βουλόμενος, 'happens to want,' i.e., 'wants.' When τυγχάνω is used with a participle it is the participle which contains the main thought.

19. καθύπερθε γίγνεσθαι, 'to prevail.'

22. κάλλ.στον, to be taken with ἐξεργάσασθαι, not with παρέχει: 'now you have an opportunity to do the best of all deeds.'

24. ἑαυτούς, for ἀλλήλους, 'each other.'

29. μέσαι νύκτες, 'midnight.' an expression which commonly occurs in the plural.

τὸ ἀφ' ἐσπέρας κέρας, 'the western wing,' more properly, the north-western wing. The Persian fleet had first taken up its position, according to Herodotus, off Phalerum, while the Greek fleet, as indicated in the Plan, lay in the harbour or bay off the town of Salamis. On receiving the message of Themistocles the whole Persian fleet was apparently moved upwards in a north-westerly direction so as to front the Greek fleet, cutting off also the chance of its retreat round the north of Salamis by the bay of Eleusis. It will be seen from the Plan that the south-eastern end could not be so closely occupied as the north-western, and thus Aristeides was able to elude the Persian vessels.

31. τῶνδε δὲ ἕνεκα, explained by ἵνα κ.τ.λ.

(f)

5. ἐξωστρακισμένος. Ostracism was a form of banishment practised at Athens. It was introduced by the legislator Cleisthenes for the purpose of preventing party strife from

breaking out into civil war. When the animosity between two political factions and their leaders became excessive, the citizens were ordered to meet and each to inscribe on a tile or potsherd (ὄστρακον) the name of any citizen whom he thought a possible source of danger to the peace of the state. The man against whom the majority of votes was recorded, provided the total against him reached a certain number, was forced to go into exile for ten years. His property, however, was not confiscated as in ordinary cases of banishment, and the decision against him probably brought him little discredit. Aristeides, who was the leader of what might be called the conservative party at Athens, had for three or four years been bitterly opposed to Themistocles, until the contention was ended by the ostracism of the former. It was Themistocles himself who, shortly before Salamis, had proposed the recall of all exiles, including Aristeides.

8. στὰς ἐπὶ τὸ συνέδριον, ' coming and standing before the council.' The ' coming ' is implied in the accusative after ἐπί.

10, 11. λήθην . . . ποιούμενος, ' assuming forgetfulness.' See note on p. 99, l. 5.

15, 16. ἔν τε τῷ ἄλλῳ . . . καὶ δὴ καὶ ἐν τῷδε. See notes on p. 71, ll. 5, 6 and p. 85, l. 6.

16, 17. περὶ τοῦ ὁπότερος . . . ἐργάσεται. The clause ὁπότερος . . . ἐργάσεται is treated as a substantive; hence the article τοῦ.

17. ἴσον, i.e., unimportant or indifferent.

(g)

1. χρηστὰ διακελεύει, i.e., with regard to their working together for the common good (ll. 15–17 above).

2. ἅ. Understand τούτων, dependent on αὐτόπτης, as the antecedent.

ἐδεόμην. Δέω, like most two-syllable verbs in εω, contracts only εε and εει.

13, 14. μόγις ἐκπλεῦσαι . . . ἐφορμοῦντας, ' had had difficulty sailing through the blockade without being seen.'

18. τὰ ἐξαγγελθέντα. Notice that when the meaning is ' obey,' the middle and passive forms of πείθω govern the dative, but when the meaning is ' believe,' they may govern

the accusative of the thing believed. Actually, the latter use involves the passive only, and the accusative represents the retention of one of the two accusatives of the active. For example, πείθω αὐτοὺς τὴν ἀλήθειαν, ' I persuade them of the truth,' becomes in the passive πείθονται τὴν ἀλήθειαν, ' they are persuaded of the truth,' ' they believe the truth.' The double accusative is common with verbs of teaching, asking, and related meanings.

(h)

2. ὡς ναυμαχήσοντες. 'Ως with the future participle simply emphasizes the idea of purpose contained in the participle.

4, 5. ἐπὶ πρύμναν ἀνεκρούοντο, ' began to back water,' lit., ' began to push (their ships) back sternwards.' In l. 11 the expression is varied slightly: πρύμναν ἀνακρούεσθε, lit., ' push back the stern.' The use of the imperfects in ἀνεκρούοντο and ὤκελλον denotes attempted or incipient action.

(i)

1. κατὰ ... 'Αθηναίους, ' opposite the Athenians.'

2. τὸ πρὸς ... κέρας, actually the wing on the north-west, which had been sent to cut off the retreat of the Greeks towards the Bay of Eleusis. Cf. note on p. 103, l. 29.

πρός, ' in the direction of,' ' towards.'

3, 4. τὸ πρὸς τὴν ἔω, sc. κέρας, actually the wing on the south-east, as the Plan indicates.

5. ἐν τῇ Σαλαμῖνι, in contrast to other vessels which were destroyed outside the straits while trying to escape from the scene of action to Phalerum. See p. 61, ll. 13, 14.

7. σὺν κόσμῳ. These words imply that the Greeks quickly recovered from their panic, and fought not only with bravery, but with discipline and coolness. The Persians, on the other hand, judging from the words οὔτε τεταγμένων ἔτι κ.τ.λ., seem to have lost heart quickly, and although they fought strenuously (ll. 10–13), they were apparently too excited to think of the proper tactics of naval warfare.

8. κατὰ τάξιν, ' in order ' in the sense of ' in battle-array,' while σὺν κόσμῳ, in the preceding line, means ' in an orderly manner.'

9, 10. ἤμελλε . . . ἀπέβη, ' it was natural that such a thing should happen to them as actually (πέρ) did happen.'

11. ταύτην τὴν ἡμέραν, accusative of extent of time.

μακρῷ, ' by far '; πολύ is more usual in Attic prose.

πρὸς Εὐβοίᾳ, referring to the engagements off Artemisium on the north coast of Euboea, where the Greek fleet had first been stationed.

(j)

2. ὁ Δαρείου. See note on p. 67, l. 3.

5. ἄτε. See note on p. 71, ll. 3, 4.

6. τισίν, dative of disadvantage. ' if any had their ships destroyed.'

10. ὡς, ' with the intention of.' See note on p. 70, ll. 21, 22.

14. ὑποστάντες, ' lying in wait.' 'Υπό in composition frequently denotes secrecy or deception. Cf. the meanings of ὑπάγοντες on p. 11, c, l. 6 and ὑποδείξας on p. 26, l. 11.

21. ὑπὸ τὸν πεζὸν στρατόν, ' under the protection of their land-force.' Ships-of-war were light enough to be beached and drawn up on the shore, and thus could be protected by a land-army.

XVII. Gold procured in India from Anthills

3. μέγεθος . . . κυνῶν . . . ἔλαττον, ' a size less than that of dogs.' Cf. p. 16, ll. 16, 17 and p. 49, l. 24.

8. εἶδος, ' in appearance,' accusative of respect or specification.

11. σειραφόρον. This term is usually applied to an outside horse in a chariot-team which pulls by the trace only and not by the yoke. In this instance it signifies ' a led-camel.' These two male led-camels do not assist, it will be noticed, in carrying either the man or the burden. They are taken partly as a means of arresting the pursuit (first one and then the other being sacrificed to the ' ants,' ll. 25-27) and partly, it would seem, because the female alone would endeavour to return home to her young ones before reaching the land of the ants at all.

12. **εἰς μέσον,** ' in the middle.'

14. **εἰς ταχυτῆτα,** ' with regard to swiftness,' ' in swiftness.'

15. **πολύ,** adverbial, ' by far.'

19. **ἀφανεῖς γίγνονται,** i.e., disappear.

21. **τῆς ψάμμου.** See note on p. 68, l. 12.

23, 24. **ταχυτῆτα,** accusative of respect, ' with respect to swiftness,' ' in swiftness.'

24. **οὐδενὶ ἑτέρῳ ὅμοιοι,** lit., ' like nothing else,' i.e., they are faster than anything else.

προυλάμβανον, contraction of *προελάμβανον.*

27. **παραλύονται κ.τ.λ.,** ' are let loose . . . (but) not both at the same time,' so that the pursuers may be twice delayed by a capture.

28. **ὧν ἔλιπον τέχνων,** for *τέκνων ἃ ἔλιπον.* Assimilation of the relative to the case of the antecedent is not uncommon in Greek. In this instance it is united with attraction of the antecedent into the relative clause.

XVIII. CURIOSITIES OF ARABIA

(a)

7. **τὸ μέγεθος, τὸ εἶδος,** accusatives of respect, ' in size,' ' in appearance.'

8. **πλήθει πολλοί,** ' many in number,' *πλήθει* being a dative of respect.

12. **βύρσαις καὶ δέρμασιν ἄλλοις.** Both *βύρσαις* and *δέρμασιν* mean ' hides,' but it is supposed that *βύρσαις* in this passage stands for ox-hides, the commonest kind, and *δέρμασιν ἄλλοις* for skins of other descriptions.

16. **τέτριγε δεινόν,** ' utter loud cries.' For *δεινόν* see note on p. 70, l. 10. The perfect *τέτριγε* has a present meaning, as is frequently the case with the perfects of verbs which express a sustained cry or sound. Cf. *κέκραγα, κέκληγα,* both of which mean ' I cry ' or ' I shout ' in the present.

26. **πρός,** ' against ' in the sense of ' to deal with ' this situation.

27, 28. **τὰ μέλη . . . ὡς μέγιστα,** ' cutting up the limbs in as large pieces as possible.'

32. καταρρήγνυνται. For the double ρ see note on ἔρριψεν, p. 74, l. 20.

(b)

3-5. ἃς εἴ τις κ.τ.λ., ' and if one were to allow them to drag *them*, they would have sores because of their tails' rubbing on the ground.' The relative is commonly used in both Greek and Latin where English uses ' and ' with a personal or a demonstrative pronoun. Notice the apparent pun of ἐφέλκειν and ἕλκη.

6. ἐπίσταται ... εἰς τοσοῦτο, ' understands carpentry up to this point,' i.e., sufficiently to prevent the tails from dragging; for τοσοῦτο, strictly speaking, refers not to what follows (in this case the manufacture of the little carts), but, like οὗτος, to what precedes.

8. φοροῦσι. From its original meaning of ' carry,' φορέω comes to mean ' wear,' and then simply ' have.' Cf. the meanings of the French *porter* and the Spanish *llevar*.

καὶ ἐπὶ πῆχυν πλάτος, ' even up to a cubit in width,' ' even as wide as a cubit.' Πλάτος is the accusative of respect.

XIX. Scythian Prophets

(a)

4. ἐπὶ μίαν ... τιθέντες, ' placing the wands one on top of another.' Ἐπί is used with cardinal numerals and other expressions of size or number to indicate ' so many deep,' e.g. ἐπὶ πολλοὺς τάττειν, ' to draw up a column many men deep '; ἐπὶ ὀκτὼ ναῦς, of a fleet eight ships deep. Both genitive and accusative cases are found in this usage.

4, 5. ἅμα τε λέγοντες ταῦτα, ' and while saying these things, they at the same time. . . .' See note on p. 80, l. 31.

6. κατὰ μίαν, ' one by one,' the distributive use of κατά. (Cf. note on p. 93, l. 1.)

11. ὡς τὸ ἐπίπαν, μάλιστα. These two expressions convey practically the same meaning: ' for the most part,' ' usually.'

12. λέγοντες ... λέγωσι, lit., ' mentioning of the townsmen whomever they do mention,' i.e., ' mentioning whoever of the townsmen it is.'

16, 17. ἐπιορκήσας φαίνεται, ' is shown (*not* seems) to have sworn falsely.' See Vocabulary for the distinction between φαίνομαι with the participle and with the infinitive.

18, 19. οὐ φάμενος ἐπιορκῆσαι, 'saying that he has not sworn falsely.' See note on p. 79, ll. 4, 5.

26. μάλα ἄλλοι, ' still others.'

27, 28. δέδοκται κ.τ.λ., ' it is decreed that the first prophets themselves be put to death.' The perfect δέδοκται is used here in a present sense, implying that the decree has been made and is still in force. The dative with the verb does not in this instance have its usual meaning of ' seem good to,' ' be decided by.' It means rather ' it is decreed *against*.'

(b)

2. ἐμποδίσαντες. The usual meaning of this word in Attic prose is ' hinder.'

XX. The Power of Custom

1. ἕκαστοι. For the meaning of the plural see note on p. 101, l. 14.

πολύ, adverbial, ' by far.'

2, 3. πολλοῖς τε ἄλλοις . . . καὶ δὴ καὶ τῷδε. See notes on p. 71, ll. 5, 6 and p. 85, l. 6.

4. ἐπὶ . . . ἀρχῆς, lit., ' in the time of his rule,' i.e., ' when he was king.'

5. ἐφ ' ὁπόσῳ ἂν χρήματι, ' for how much money,' ' for what price.'

11. κατακάειν πυρί. This was the Greek custom.

VOCABULARY

Principal parts of regular verbs are not given. Principal parts of irregular verbs will be found under the simple verb only, if it appears. If the simple verb is not listed, principal parts of irregular compound verbs will be found under the compound. Irregular parts which are not included in the vocabulary do not occur in the text.

Starred words and meanings are found rarely or not at all in Attic prose.

A

ἀβουλίᾱ, ᾱς, ἡ, lack of good counsel, imprudence.

ἀγαθός, ή, όν, good, brave; *comp.* ἀμείνων; *superl.* ἄριστος.

*ἀγαθουργίᾱ, ᾱς, ἡ, good deed, service.

ἄγαλμα, ατος, τό, statue, image.

ἄγᾱν, too much, too.

*ἀγγελιαφόρος, ου, ὁ, messenger.

ἀγγέλλω, ἀγγελῶ, ἤγγειλα, ἤγγελκα, ἤγγελμαι, ἠγγέλθην, give a message, report.

ἄγγελος, ου, ὁ, messenger.

*ἄγγος, ους, τό, receptacle of any kind: jar, pail, chest, box, etc.

*ἄγκιστρον, ου, τό, fish-hook.

ἀγνωμοσύνη, ης, ἡ, lack of judgment, senselessness, indiscretion.

ἀγορά, ᾶς, ἡ, assembly; place of assembly, *esp.* market-place.

ἀγορεύω (*lit., speak in the* ἀγορά), speak, say.

ἄγρᾱ, ᾱς, ἡ, *method of catching.

ἀγρός, οῦ, ὁ, field, country (*as opposed to city*).

*ἀγχοῦ, adv. and prep. with gen., near.

ἄγω, ἄξω, ἦχα, ἦγμαι, ἤχθην, 2nd aor. ἤγαγον, lead, take; hold, consider.

ἀγών, ῶνος, ὁ, assembly, *esp. for games;* contest, game.

ἀγώνισμα, ατος, τό, contest, combat.

ἀδελφός, οῦ, ὁ, brother.

ἀδικέω, do wrong, injure.

ἄδικος, ον, unjust, wicked; adv. ἀδίκως.

ἄδυτον, ου, τό, innermost shrine or sanctuary.

ᾄδω, ᾄσομαι, ᾖσα, ᾔσθην, sing.

ἀεί, always.

*ἆθλος, ου, ὁ, contest, *esp. for a prize;* task.

*ἀθλοφόρος, ον, winning prizes, victorious.

ἀθρόος, ᾱ, ον, all at once, altogether.

αἰθρίᾱ, ᾱς, ἡ, clear sky.

αἰκίᾱ, ᾱς, ἡ, insult, outrage.

αἷμα, ατος, τό, blood.

αἱμασίᾱ, ᾱς, ἡ, wall of loose stones.

*αἰνέω, αἰνέσω, praise.

αἴξ, αἰγός, ὁ, ἡ, goat.

*αἰπόλιον, ου, τό, herd of goats.

αἱρετός, ή, όν, verbal adj. of αἱρέομαι, to be chosen, preferable, desirable.

αἱρέω, αἱρήσω, ᾕρηκα, ᾕρημαι, ᾑρέθην, 2nd aor. εἷλον, take, capture; mid., take for oneself, choose.

αἴρω, ἀρῶ, ἦρα, lift, raise.

αἰσθάνομαι, αἰσθήσομαι, ᾔσθημαι, 2nd aor. ᾐσθόμην, perceive by the senses, learn, find out, discover.

αἰσχροκερδής, ές, shamefully greedy.

αἰσχρός, ά, όν, shameful, disgraceful; comp. αἰσχίων; superl. αἴσχιστος; adv. αἰσχρῶς.

αἰτίᾱ, ᾱς, ἡ, cause.

αἴτιον, ου, τό, cause.

αἰών, ῶνος, ὁ, space or period of time, esp. lifetime, life.

*ἀκανθώδης, ες, thorny.

ἀκίνητος, ον, unmoved, undisturbed, untouched.

ἄκος, ους, τό, cure, remedy.

ἀκούω, ἀκούσομαι, ἤκουσα, ἀκήκοα, ἠκούσθην, hear, with gen. of person and acc. of thing; κακῶς, εὖ, ἄμεινον etc. ἀκούειν, hear oneself called, have a bad (good, better) reputation.

ἄκρᾱ, ᾱς, ἡ, height, peak, promontory.

ἀκρῑβῶς, exactly.

ἀκρόπολις, εως, ἡ, upper part of the city, citadel; esp. the Acropolis of Athens.

ἄκων, ουσα, ον, unwilling.

ἀλάβαστρος, ου, ὁ, container for holding perfume.

ἀλγέω, be in pain, be ill.

*ἄλειψις, εως, ἡ, anointing, process of anointing.

ἀλήθεια, ᾱς, ἡ, truth.

ἀληθής, ές, true, real; adv. ἀληθῶς.

ἀληθινός, ή, όν, true, real.

*ἁλίᾱ, ᾱς, ἡ, assembly.

*ἁλίζω, gather together, collect.

ἅλις, adv. and prep. with gen., enough.

ἁλίσκομαι, ἁλώσομαι, ἑάλωκα and ἥλωκα, 2nd aor. ἑάλων and ἥλων, be caught or captured; be convicted.

*ἀλκή, ῆς, ἡ, physical strength, fighting-power.

*ἄλκιμος, ον, strong, brave.

ἀλλά, but.

*ἀλληλοφαγίᾱ, ᾱς, ἡ, cannibalism.

ἀλλήλων (no nom.), of each other, of one another.

ἄλλος, η, ο, other, another; ἄλλος ... ἄλλος, one ... another, one ... one; with article, the other, the rest of; adv. ἄλλως, otherwise.

ἀλλότριος, ᾱ, ον, belonging to someone else, strange, foreign; οἱ ἀλλότριοι, other people, strangers, foreigners.

ἄλσος, ους, τό, grove.

ἀλώπηξ, εκος, ἡ, fox.

ἁλώσιμος, ον, able to be captured, easy to take.

ἅλωσις, εως, ἡ, capture.

ἅμα, at the same time.

ἀμαθής, ές, ignorant.

ἄμαξα, ης, ἡ, wagon.

ἁμαξίς, ίδος, ἡ, little wagon, cart.

ἁμαρτάς, άδος, ἡ, mistake, wrong.

ἀμείβω, change, exchange; *mid.,* *answer, reply.

*ἀμήνῑτος,** ον, without resentment.

ἄμορφος, ον, misshapen, ugly.

ἀμύνω, ward off; *mid.,* ward off from oneself, defend oneself, resist.

ἀμφί, *prep. with gen., dat., acc.,* about; *with gen. and dat.,* about, concerning; *with acc.,* around, about, near. (*The use of the dat. after this prep. is not Attic.*)

ἀμφιδέαι, ῶν, αἱ (*lit., something bound around*), bracelets, anklets.

*ἀμφισβασίᾱ,** ᾱς, ἡ (*from ἀμφίς, apart, and root of βαίνω, go*), dispute.

ἀμφότερος, ᾱ, ον, both.

ἄν, *postpositive particle without English equivalent. Its chief uses are:* (1) *in the apodosis of contrary-to-fact and less-vivid-future conditional sentences;* (2) *with* εἰ, ἐπειδή, ὅτε, *and similar conjunctions when the reference is to future time, or to general conditions or circumstances. In this latter usage crasis occurs regularly (e.g.,* ἐάν, ἐπειδάν).

ἀνά, *prep. with acc.,* up; throughout; *for* ἀνά *in distributive uses see note on p.* 1, *l.* 4.

ἀναβαίνω, go up, mount; come in turn to.

ἀναβιβάζω, make ascend.

ἀναβοάω, -βοήσομαι, -εβόησα, cry out, shout out.

ἀναγιγνώσκω, aor. ἀνέγνωσα, *persuade.

ἀνάγκη, ης, ἡ, force, necessity; *plu.,* violence, physical pain, torture.

ἀνάγνωσις, εως, ἡ, *recognition.

ἀνάγω, bring up, lead forward.

ἀναδιδάσκω, teach again, teach better, win over by argument.

ἀναδίδωμι, give up; *of the earth,* give forth, yield, produce crops.

ἀναζεύγνῡμι, yoke again; ἀναζεύγνυμι ναῦς, set sail again.

ἀναίδεια, ᾱς, ἡ, shamelessness.

*ἀναισιμόω,** use up, consume.

ἀνακηρύττω, publish, proclaim, *put up for auction.

ἀνακρούω, push back; *mid.,* back water (*see note on p.* 105).

ἀνακῶς, carefully; ἀνακῶς ἔχειν, watch carefully for, *with gen.*

ἀναλαμβάνω, take up.

ἀναμιμνήσκω, remember, *with gen.*

ἄναξ, ἄνακτος, ὁ, lord, king.

ἀνάξιος, ον, *also* ᾱ, ον, unworthy, undeserving.

ἀναπείθω, persuade against one's will, persuade.

ἀναπετάννῡμι, -πετῶ, -επέτασα, -πέπταμαι, open up.

ἀναπηδάω, jump up.

*ἀναπτύσσω,** unfold, open.

ἀνάπτω, light.

ἀναπυνθάνομαι, inquire into; learn by inquiry.

ἀναρίθμητος, ον, countless, innumerable.

*ἀνάρσιος, ον, hostile, strange, monstrous.

*ἀνασκολοπίζω, fix on a pole or stake, impale.

*ἀναστενάζω, groan aloud.

ἀνατέλλω, rise, of the sun etc.

ἀνατίθημι, set up, esp. of a votive gift; offer.

ἀνατρέπω, overthrow.

*ἀνατρίβω, rub to pieces, wear away.

ἀναφέρω, carry up, bring up; refer to, consult; refresh, restore; intrans., refresh oneself, restore oneself, recover.

ἀναφορέω, carry up (used in Herod. as frequentative of ἀναφέρω).

*ἀναφύρω, mix up; stain.

ἀναχωρέω, go back, withdraw.

ἀνδραγαθίᾱ, ᾱς, ἡ, manhood, bravery, courage.

ἀνδρεῖος, ᾱ, ον, manly, brave.

*ἀνδρόω, bring up to manhood; pass., become a man, reach manhood.

ἄνεμος, ου, ὁ, wind.

ἀνευρίσκω, find out, discover.

ἀνήκεστος, ον, incurable; grievous, intolerable; adv. ἀνηκέστως.

ἀνηκουστέω, be unwilling to hear, disobey.

ἀνήρ, ἀνδρός, ὁ, man, as distinct from woman; husband.

ἀνθίστημι, set against; mid., pass., and intrans. tenses of act. (2nd aor. and perf.), stand against, withstand, resist, oppose.

ἀνθρώπειος, ᾱ, ον, belonging to man, human.

ἀνθρώπινος, η, ον, human, mortal.

ἄνθρωπος, ου, ὁ, man, human being.

ἀνίημι, send up or forth; let go, relax; of a bow, unstring.

ἀνίστημι, set up; put up for auction; pass. and intrans. tenses of act. (2nd aor., perf., pluperf.), get up. arise.

ἀνοίγω, -οίξω, -έῳξα, -έῳχα, -έῳγμαι, -εῴχθην, imperf. ἀνέῳγον, open up, open.

ἀνόσιος, ον, unholy, wicked.

ἀντέρομαι, ask in turn.

ἀντί, prep. with gen., instead of (originally against or over against).

ἀντικαθίστημι, put something in the place of something else, substitute.

*ἀντιμέμφομαι, blame in turn, retort.

ἀντίον, neut. of adj. ἀντίος, used as prep. with gen., before, in the presence of.

ἄντρον, ου, τό, cave.

*ἄνυδρος, ον, without water.

ἀξιόμαχος, ον, a match in battle.

ἄξιος, ᾱ, ον, of equal value, worth as much as, with gen.; worthy, deserving.

ἀξιόω, think fit or worthy; with infin., think someone worthy of doing or being something.

ἀοιδός, ου, ὁ, singer, minstrel.

ἀπαγγέλλω, take back a message, bring news, report.

ἀπάγω, lead back.

ἀπαθής, ές, without suffering, not having suffered, unharmed.

ἀπαίρω, take away, remove.

ἄπαις, gen. ἄπαιδος, childless.

ἀπαλλάττω, set free, get rid of; intrans., mid., and pass., go away, depart.

ἀπαμύνω, ward off from, keep from, repel.

ἀπανίστημι, take or send away, remove, withdraw.

ἅπαξ, once.

ἅπᾱς, ᾱσα, αν, all, all together (stronger than πᾶς).

ἀπάτη, ης, ἡ, deceit, trick.

*ἀπειλέω, force back, press hard.

ἀπειλέω, threaten.

ἄπειμι (Lat. ibo), go away, pres. with fut. meaning.

ἀπεῖπον (2nd aor., no pres.), forbid.

ἀπελαύνω, drive away; intrans., ride or march away, depart; pass., be driven away, be excluded from.

ἀπιστέω, disbelieve, distrust.

ἀπιστίᾱ, ᾱς, ἡ, disbelief.

ἄπληστος, ον, not to be filled, insatiable.

ἀπό, prep. with gen., from, away from, from the time of.

ἀποβαίνω, get off, disembark; come out, turn out.

ἀποβάλλω, throw away, lose.

ἀποδείκνῡμι, point out, make known, show, prove, declare, appoint; mid., show something belonging to oneself, display good qualities.

ἀποδίδωμι, give back, restore.

ἀποδοκιμάζω, reject after testing, reject.

ἀποθαυμάζω, be surprised at.

ἀποθέω, -θεύσομαι, run away.

ἀποθνῄσκω, die; also as pass. of ἀποκτείνω, be killed.

*ἀποικτίζομαι, complain.

ἀποκαλύπτω, uncover.

ἀποκλείω, shut off, close.

ἀποκληρόω, choose by lot.

ἀπόκρημνος, ον, precipitous, steep.

ἀποκρίνω, separate, select.

ἀποκρούω, beat off from; mid., beat off from oneself, repel.

ἀποκτείνω, kill.

ἀπολαμβάνω, take from; cut off, intercept.

ἀπολείπω, leave behind, leave, abandon.

ἄπολις, neut. ι, without a city or country.

ἀπόλλῡμι, -ολῶ, -ώλεσα, -ολώλεκα, 2nd aor. -ωλόμην, destroy, kill; lose completely; mid., perish, die.

ἀπολύω, set free, acquit; mid., defend oneself.

*ἀπονοστέω, return home.

ἀποπέμπω, send away, send; mid., dismiss.

ἀποπλέω, sail away (contracts only εε and εει).

ἀπόπληκτος, ον, struck out of one's senses, mad.

*ἀπόπλους, ου, ὁ, a sailing away.

ἀποπνίγω, choke.

*ἀποπυνθάνομαι, inquire of.

ἀπορέω, be at a loss, not know what to do.

ἀπορίᾱ, ᾱς, ἡ, resourcelessness, difficulty.

ἀπόρρητος, ον, not to be spoken of, secret.

ἀπορρίπτω, throw away, reject, renounce.

*ἀπορχέομαι, dance away, lose by dancing.

ἀποσπάω, -σπάσω, tear away, pull down, take away from.

ἀποστέλλω, send off, dispatch.

*ἀποστυγέω, hate; with infin., hate the thought that.

ἀποσῴζω, save, restore; pass., get away safely, escape.

*ἀποτακτός, όν, set aside for a special use, specially prepared.

ἀποτέμνω, -τεμῶ, -τέτμηκα, -τέτμημαι, -ετμήθην, 2nd aor. -έτεμον, cut off.

ἀποφεύγω, escape; be acquitted.

*ἀποφλαυρίζω, make light of.

ἀποχράω, be sufficient.

ἀπροσδόκητος, ον, unexpected; ἐξ ἀπροσδοκήτου, unexpectedly (see note on p. 19, l. 14).

ἅπτω, ἅψω, ἧψα, ἧμμαι, ἥφθην, light up, kindle; mid., touch, with gen.

ἄρα, postpositive particle, so then, therefore; really, actually.

ἀργύριον, ου, τό, piece of silver, money.

ἀρέσκω, ἀρέσω, ἤρεσα, ἠρέσθην, be pleasing, please.

ἀρεστός, ή, όν, verbal adj. of ἀρέσκω, pleasing, acceptable; adv. ἀρεστῶς.

ἀρκέω, be sufficient; partic. as adj., ἀρκῶν, sufficient, enough.

ἀρνέομαι, deny.

ἁρπαγή, ῆς, ἡ, seizure, robbery, plunder.

ἄρσην, εν, gen. ἄρσενος, male.

*ἄρτημα, ατος, τό, hanging ornament, earring.

ἄρτος, ου, ὁ, bread.

ἀρχαῖος, ᾱ, ον, old, ancient, former.

ἀρχή, ῆς, ἡ, beginning; first place, sovereignty, rule, dominion.

*ἀρχῆθεν, from the beginning.

ἄρχω, begin, be first, rule, command; mid., begin; with gen.

ἀσεβέω, act impiously, sin against the gods.

*ἄσημος, ον, meaningless, inarticulate.

ἀσθενής, ές, weak.

ἄσμενος, η, ον, pleased, glad.

ἀσπάζομαι, greet, welcome.

*ἀσπαίρω, gasp, struggle.

ἀστός, οῦ, ὁ, townsman, citizen.

ἀστράγαλοι, ων, οἱ, dice, the game of dice.

ἄστυ, εως, τό, town, city.

ἀστυγείτων, ονος, ὁ, neighbour.

ἀσφάλεια, ας, ἡ, safety.

*ἀσχάλλω, be annoyed, be grieved.

ἅτε, just as, as, as if; with partic., as, since.

ἀτελής, ές, exempt from taxation.

αὖθις, again.

αὐλέω, play on the flute.

αὐλητής, οῦ, ὁ, flute-player.

αὐλίζομαι (from αὐλή, courtyard), lie in the courtyard, lie out at night; take up one's abode, live, encamp.

αὐτίκα, at once, immediately.

αὐτόθι, on the very spot, here, there.

αὐτομολέω, desert.

αὐτόμολος, ου, ὁ, deserter.

αὐτόπτης, ου, ὁ (from αὐτός and root ὀπ, as in ὄψομαι, fut. of ὁράω), eyewitness.

αὐτός, ἡ, ό, self; when preceded by the article, the same; in the oblique cases also used as 3rd pers. pron., him, her, it.

αὐτοῦ, at the very place, here, there.

*ἀφανδάνω, displease.

ἀφανής, ές, unseen, invisible.

ἀφηγέομαι, relate, tell.

ἀφήγησις, εως, ἡ, a telling, narration.

*ἄφθογγος, ον, speechless.

ἀφίημι, send away, drive away, let loose; let go, abandon.

ἀφικνέομαι, -ίξομαι, -ῖγμαι, 2nd aor. -ἱκόμην, come to, arrive at, reach; ἀφικνεῖσθαι εἰς λόγους or εἰς λέσχην, get into a conversation.

ἀφίστημι, put away, remove, separate; mid. and intrans. tenses of act. (2nd aor., perf., pluperf.), revolt.

ἄχθομαι, ἀχθέσομαι, ἠχθέσθην, be grieved, be annoyed, be disgusted.

ἄχθος, ους, τό, weight, burden; sorrow, grief, trouble.

ἀχρεῖος, ον (from ἀ privative and χράομαι, use), useless, unserviceable.

ἀψευδής, ές, not lying, truthful.

B

βαθύς, εῖα, ύ, deep.

βαίνω, βήσομαι, βέβηκα, 2nd aor. ἔβην, go.

βαλανάγρᾱ, ᾱς, ἡ, key (actually a hook used to unlock a gate).

βάλλω, βαλῶ, βέβληκα, βέβλημαι, ἐβλήθην, 2nd aor. ἔβαλον, throw; mid., reflect, deliberate.

βάρβαρος, ου, ὁ, non-Greek, foreigner.

βαρύς, εῖα, ύ, heavy; adv. βαρέως; βαρέως φέρειν, take something badly, feel bad about.

βασανίζω, test, cross-examine.

βασίλεια, ᾱς, ἡ, queen.

βασιλείᾱ, ᾱς, ἡ, kingdom, monarchy.

βασίλειος, ᾱ, ον, royal; as subst., τὰ βασίλεια, palace.

βασιλεύς, έως, ὁ, king.

βασιλεύω, be king, become king.

βασιλικός, ή, όν, befitting a king, king-like, royal.

βαφή, ῆς, ἡ, process of dyeing, dye.

βέκος, ους, τό, bread.

βίαιος, ᾱ, ον, violent.

βιβλίον, ου, τό, paper, letter.

βιβρώσκω, perf. βέβρωκα, eat.

βίος, ου, ὁ, life; means of living, livelihood.

βιόω, βιώσομαι, 2nd aor. ἐβίων, live.

βλέπω, see, look.

βοηθέω, come to the aid of, assist, with dat.

βορᾱ, ᾶς, ἡ, food.

βόρειος, ᾱ, ον (*from* Βορέας, *the north wind*), northern.
βόσκω, βοσκήσω, feed, nourish; *mid.*, feed on, graze.
*βουκόλιον, ου, τό, herd of cattle.
βουκόλος, ου, ὁ, herdsman.
βούλευμα, ατος, το, decision, plan.
βουλεύω, take counsel, consider, plan, resolve, determine, decide; *similarly in mid.*
βούλομαι, βουλήσομαι, βεβούλημαι, ἐβουλήθην, wish, want.
βοῦς, βοός, ὁ, ἡ, ox, cow.
*βρέφος, ους, τό, new-born child, infant, baby; *also of animals.*
βυθός, οῦ, ὁ, bottom (*of a body of water*).
βύρσα, ης, ἡ, hide.
βύω, stuff full.

Γ

γάλα, γάλακτος, τό, milk.
γαμβρός, οῦ, ὁ, son-in-law.
γάμος, ου, ὁ, marriage, wedding.
γάρ, *conj.*, for.
γέ, *enclitic and postpositive intensive particle*, at least, at any rate, certainly.
γελάω, γελάσομαι, ἐγέλασα, ἐγελάσθην, laugh.
γέλως, ωτος, ὁ, laughter.
γένος, ους, τό, race, descent, family; kind, sort.
γέρων, οντος, ὁ, old man.
γῆ, γῆς, ἡ, earth, land.
γίγνομαι, γενήσομαι, γέγονα, γεγένημαι, 2nd aor. ἐγενόμην, come into being, be born, become, occur, happen, be; *of time*, come, go by.
γιγνώσκω, γνώσομαι, ἔγνωκα, ἔγνωσμαι, ἐγνώσθην, 2nd aor. ἔγνων, learn, get to know, know; recognize; decide.
γλῶττα, ης, ἡ, tongue; language.
γνώμη, ης, ἡ, opinion, sentiment; decision, intention, plan; vote.
*γνωσιμαχέω (*from* γνῶσις, opinion, *and* μάχομαι, fight), change one's mind.
γόης, ητος, ὁ, wizard.
γονεύς, έως, ὁ, father, ancestor; *plu.*, parents.
γόνος, ου, ὁ, ἡ, offspring, child.
γόνυ, γόνατος, τό, knee.
γοῦν (γέ, οὖν), at least, at any rate.
γράμμα, ατος, τό, letter of the alphabet; *plu.*, writing, inscription, records.
γράφω, write.
γυνή, γυναικός, ἡ, woman, wife.

Δ

δαιμόνιος, ᾱ, ον, *in vocative*, my good sir (*often ironic*), unhappy man, wretched creature.
δαίμων, ονος, ὁ, ἡ, god, goddess.
*δαίνυμι, give a feast; *mid.*, feast, eat.
δαιτυμών, όνος, ὁ, dinner guest, guest.
δακρύω, weep.

δέ, postpositive conjunctive particle, but; sometimes and; μὲν 'η8 ··· on the one hand ... on the other hand.

δείδω, δείσομαι, ἔδεισα, δέδοικα, fear (perf. has pres. meaning).

δείκνῡμι, δείξω, ἔδειξα, δέδειχα, δέδειγμαι, ἐδείχθην, point out, show.

δειμαίνω, fear.

*δεινολογέομαι, complain terribly.

δεινός, ή, όν, fearful, terrible; clever, skilful; δεινὸν ποιεῖσθαι, take badly, complain of, be indignant at; adv. δεινῶς.

δειπνέω, dine.

δεῖπνον, ου, τό, dinner.

δέκα, ten.

δεκαετής, ές, *ten years old.

*δεκάς, άδος, ἡ, group of ten.

δέκατος, η, ον, tenth.

δελεάζω, entice by bait, allure, catch; use as bait.

δέλφαξ, ακος, ὁ, young pig.

δελφίς, ῖνος, ὁ, dolphin.

δένδρον, ου, τό, tree.

δέος, δέους, τό, fear.

δέρμα, ατος, τό, skin, hide.

δεσμωτήριον, ου, τό, prison.

δεσπότης, ου, ὁ, master.

δευτερεῖα, ων, τά, second prize, second place.

δεύτερος, ᾱ, ον, second.

δέχομαι, δέξομαι, ἐδεξάμην, δέδεγμαι, ἐδέχθην, receive.

δέω, δήσω, ἔδησα, δέδεκα, δέδεμαι, ἐδέθην, bind.

δέω, δεήσω, want, lack, need, with gen.; similarly in mid.; δεῖ, impers., there is need, it is necessary, one should.

δή, postpositive intensive particle, now, indeed, in truth, so, then.

δηλόω, make clear, show.

δῆμος, ου, ὁ, the people, the nation; the common people.

δημοσίᾳ (adv. from δημόσιος), publicly, at public expense.

δημότης, ου, ὁ, one of the common people.

δῆτα, certainly, of course, then, so.

διά, prep. with gen. and acc., through; with gen., through; during; by the agency of, by; with acc., because of, on account of.

διαβαίνω, go over, cross.

διαβάλλω, accuse, slander.

διαβατός, ή, όν. verbal adj. of διαβαίνω, crossable, fordable.

διάγω, carry through, go through; with βίον understood, live.

*διαδείκνῡμι, make clear, show clearly.

διαδιδράσκω, -δράσομαι, -δέδρᾱκα, 2nd aor. -έδρᾶν, run away, escape.

διαζάω, live through, live; with partic., live by doing such-and-such a thing.

διαιρέω, take apart.

δίαιτα, ης, ἡ, way of living; food, diet.

διαιτάομαι, pass one's life, live.

διακελεύομαι, exhort, encourage, advise.

διακομίζω, carry across or over, carry.

διᾱκόσιοι, αι, α, two hundred.

*διαλαγχάνω, divide or distribute by lot.

διαλαμβάνω, seize.

διαλείπω, let go by (of time).

διαλύω, break up, scatter.

διαναυμαχέω, fight a naval battle through to the end.

διανέω, *swim across.

*διαπάττω, -πάσω, -έπασα, -επάσθην, sprinkle.

διαπειράομαι, make trial of, have experience of, with gen.

διαπράττω, go through, accomplish, carry out, complete; similarly in mid.

διατάττω, put in order, arrange; appoint to separate positions, order.

διατέμνω, -τεμῶ, -τέτμηκα, -τέτμημαι, -ετμήθην, 2nd aor. -έτεμον, cut through, cut into pieces.

διατίθημι, place separately, arrange; treat.

διατρίβω, rub away, consume, spend.

διαφεύγω, flee, escape.

διαφθείρω, destroy, kill; pass., perish, die.

διαχέω, aor. -έχεα (lit., pour apart), of plans, confound, confuse.

διαχράομαι, destroy, kill (lit., use up).

διδάσκω, διδάξω, ἐδίδαξα, δεδίδαχα, δεδίδαγμαι, ἐδιδάχθην, teach.

δίδωμι, δώσω, ἔδωκα, δέδωκα, δέδομαι, ἐδόθην, 2nd aor. ἔδομεν etc. in plu., give, offer.

διέξειμι (Lat. ibo), go out through, go right through.

*διεξελαύνω, go out through.

*διεξελίττω, unroll, untie.

διεξέρχομαι, go through.

διέξοδος, ου, ἡ, way out, passage; διέξοδοι βουλευμάτων, ins and outs of one's plans.

διέρχομαι, go through; of time, go by, pass.

διετής, ές, of two years.

διηγέομαι, relate, describe.

δίκαιος, ᾱ, ον, just.

δικαιόω, consider right, think fit, consent.

δικαστήριον, ου, τό, court of justice.

δίκη, ης, ἡ, right, justice; lawsuit, trial; just recompense, i.e., either penalty or compensation.

διότι, because.

διπλάσιος, ᾱ, ον, double, twice as many.

δίς, twice.

δισχίλιοι, αι, α, two thousand.

διώκω, pursue.

διῶρυξ, υχος, ἡ, trench, canal.

δοκέω, seem, appear, seem good, think; esp. in 3rd sing. impers. δοκεῖ, it seems good to, it is resolved by, e.g., ἔμοιγε δοκεῖ, I think; ἔδοξε αὐτῷ, he decided.

δόκιμος, ον, esteemed, honoured, notable.

*δολερός, ά, όν, deceitful, lying, false.

δόλος, ου, ὁ, trick, deceit.

δοριάλωτος, ον, captured by the spear, captured.

δορυφόρος, ον, spear-bearing; οἱ δορυφόροι, bodyguard.

δόσις, εως, ἡ, gift.

δουλεύω, be a slave, serve, obey.

δουλοπρεπής, ές, suitable for a slave, servile.

δοῦλος, ου, ὁ, slave.
*δουλοσύνη, ης, ἡ, slavery.
δρασμός, οῦ, ὁ, a running away, flight.
δρέπανον, ου, τό, sickle.
δρέπω, pluck, gather.
δύναμαι, δυνήσομαι, δεδύνημαι, ἐδυνήθην, be able, can.
δύναμις, εως, ἡ, power, strength; military strength, forces.
δυνάστης, ου, ὁ, master, ruler; ἄνδρες δυνάσται, men of the ruling class, aristocrats.
δυνατός, ή, όν, of persons, strong, able; of things, possible.
δύο, δυοῖν, two.
δυσμή, ῆς, ἡ, sinking, setting, esp. of the sun, usually in plu.
*δυσπετῶς, with difficulty.
δώδεκα, twelve.
δωρεά, ᾶς, ἡ, gift, present.
δωρέομαι, present with.
δῶρον, ου, τό, gift.

E

ἐάν (εἰ, ἄν), ἤν, if.
ἑαυτοῦ, ῆς, οῦ (no nom.), reflexive pron., 3rd pers., of himself, herself, itself.
ἐάω, ἐάσω, εἴασα, allow.
ἕβδομος, η, ον, seventh.
ἐγγυάω, hand over, betroth, engage, promise.
ἐγκαταλείπω, leave behind.
*ἐγκολάπτω, carve on, inscribe on.
ἐγχειρίδιος, ου, ὁ, dagger (lit., something held in the hand).
ἐγχειρίζω, put into someone's hands, entrust, deliver.

ἐγώ, ἐμοῦ, 1st pers. pron., I; ἔγωγε, emphatic form, I at least, I for my part.
ἐδώλιον, ου, τό, seat, rowing-bench.
ἐθελοκακέω, be wilfully bad or cowardly, play the coward.
ἐθέλω, ἐθελήσω, ἠθέλησα, ἠθέληκα, want, wish, be willing.
ἔθνος, ους, τό, race, tribe.
εἰ, if; in indirect questions, whether.
εἶδος, ους, τό, appearance; kind, sort.
εἰκάζω, liken, compare, infer from comparison, conjecture, guess.
εἴκοσι, twenty.
εἰκοστός, ή, όν, twentieth.
εἰκών, όνος, ἡ, likeness, image, statue.
*εἷμα, ατος, τό, robe, garment, cloak.
εἰμί, ἔσομαι (Lat. sum), be, exist.
εἶμι (Lat. ibo), go, pres. with future meaning.
εἴπερ, if at any rate, at least if.
εἶπον (2nd aor., no pres.), ἐρῶ, εἴρηκα, εἴρημαι, ἐρρήθην, say, tell, speak.
εἰς, prep. with acc., into, to, on to, against; toward, in relation to, with regard to; of the end or object, for; with numerals, up to, to the number of; εἰς ὅ, until.
εἷς, μία, ἕν, one.
εἰσαγγέλλω, announce, report.
εἰσάγω, lead into.
εἰσάπαξ, at once, at one time.
εἰσβαίνω, go into; go on board ship, embark.

εἰσβάλλω, throw into; enter into; *of a river*, flow into.

εἴσειμι (*Lat. ibo*), go into, enter.

εἰσέρχομαι, come into, go into.

εἰσίημι, send into, let into.

εἰσοράω, look into.

εἰσπίπτω, fall into, rush into, fall on.

εἰσφέρω, carry in, bring in.

εἴσω, *adv. and prep. with gen.*, inside.

εἴωθα (*perf. with pres. meaning*), be accustomed.

ἐκ, ἐξ, *prep. with gen.*, out of, from; *of time*, after; *of agency*, by.

*ἑκάς, *adv. and prep. with gen.*, far, far away, far from. *comp.* ἑκαστέρω.

ἕκαστος, η, ον, each, every.

ἑκάστοτε, each time.

ἑκάτερος, ᾱ, ον, each of two.

ἑκατέρωθεν, from each side, on each side.

ἑκατόν, a hundred.

ἐκβαίνω, go out; come out, result; disembark.

ἐκβάλλω, throw out.

ἐκγίγνομαι, *be born of.

ἐκδημέω, go abroad, travel.

ἐκδίδωμι, give up, surrender; give in marriage.

ἔκδοσις, εως, ἡ, a giving up, surrender.

ἐκεῖ, there.

ἐκεῖνος, η, ο, *demon. pron.*, that; *also as 3rd pers. pron.*, he, she, it.

*ἔκθεσις, εως, ἡ, a placing out, exposure.

ἐκκαλέω, call out; *mid.*, call *someone* to come out to oneself.

*ἐκκαλύπτω, uncover.

*ἔκκειμαι, lie out, be exposed.

ἐκλύω, loosen, unstring *a bow*.

ἐκπέμπω, send out, send away.

ἐκπηδάω, jump out.

ἐκπλέω, sail out, sail away; ἐκπλεῖν τῶν φρενῶν, go out of one's mind.

ἐκπλήττω, -πλήξω, -έπληξα, -πέπληγα, -πέπληγμαι, -επλάγην, strike out, drive out of one's senses, amaze; *pass.*, be amazed.

ἐκποδών, out of the way, away.

ἐκρήγνῡμι, break out, break off; *pass.*, break, *burst out in a passion.

ἐκστρατεύω, march out to battle, take the field; *similarly in mid.*

ἐκτίθημι, place out, expose.

ἐκτίνω, pay off, pay, *with acc. of the thing paid and gen. of the thing paid for.*

ἐκτυφλόω, make blind, blind.

*ἐκτύφλωσις, εως, ἡ, blinding.

ἐκφαίνω, bring to light, reveal, declare.

ἐκφέρω, carry out, carry.

ἑκών, οῦσα, όν, willing.

ἔλαιον, ου, τό, olive-oil, oil.

ἐλάττων, ον, *comp. adj.*, less, fewer, smaller; *superl.* ἐλάχιστος.

ἐλαύνω, ἐλῶ, ἤλασα, ἐλήλακα, ἐλήλαμαι, ἠλάθην, drive, ride, march; *of a wall*, build.

ἐλαφρός, ά, όν, light, easy; ἐν ἐλαφρῷ ποιεῖσθαι, make light of, bear easily.

ἐλέγχω, convict, refute; accuse.

ἐλεύθερος, ā, ον, free.

ἐλευθερόω, set free.

ἕλκος, ους, τό, wound, sore.

ἕλκω, ἕλξω, εἵλκυσα, εἵλκυκα, εἵλκυσμαι, εἱλκύσθην, drag, draw, pull, draw to oneself.

ἕλος, ους, τό, marsh.

ἐλπίζω, hope, expect; think, believe.

ἐμαυτοῦ, ῆς (no nom.), reflexive pron., 1st pers., of myself.

ἐμβάλλω, throw on; charge, attack.

*ἐμμανής, ές, mad.

ἐμμέλεια, ᾱς, ἡ, dancing-tune.

ἐμός, ή, όν, my, mine.

*ἔμπηρος, ον, crippled, deformed.

ἐμπίμπλημι, fill.

ἐμποδίζω (from ἐν and πούς), *fetter.

ἔμφυτος, ον, inborn, innate, natural.

ἐν, prep. with dat., in, on, among; of time, during; in the power of.

*ἐναπονίζω, wash off in, wash.

ἐνδίδωμι, give up, surrender; display, show.

ἔνδον, inside.

ἐνδύω, -δύσω, 2nd aor. -ἔδῡν, put a garment on someone; mid., with 2nd aor. and perf. act., put on oneself, wear.

ἕνεκα, prep. with gen., on account of, for the sake of.

*ἐνεμέω, vomit into.

ἐνέχω, hold in; pass., be caught in, be entangled in.

*ἐνηβητήριον, ου, τό, place of amusement.

ἔνθα, there, where; then, thereupon.

ἐνιαυτός, οῦ, ὁ, year.

ἔνιοι, αι, α, some.

ἐννοέω, have in mind, consider.

ἐνταῦθα, here, there; thereupon, then.

ἐντείνω, -τενῶ, -έτεινα, -τέτακα, -τέταμαι, -ετάθην, stretch tight, bend a bow.

ἐντέλλομαι, -ετειλάμην, -τέταλμαι, command, order.

ἐντεῦθεν, from this place, hence, thence; henceforth, thereupon, afterwards, next.

ἐντίθημι, put in, place in.

ἐντός, adv. and prep. with gen., inside, within; ἐντὸς ἑαυτοῦ γίγνεσθαι, retain one's self-control.

ἐντυγχάνω, come upon, meet, with dat.

ἐνύπνιον, ου, τό, dream.

ἕξ, six.

ἐξαγγέλλω, report.

ἐξάγω, lead out.

ἐξαίρετος, ον, picked out, chosen.

ἐξαιρέω, take away, remove; set aside, except.

ἐξαιτέω, demand from, request from; similarly in mid.

ἐξανάγω, bring up from; pass., put out to sea, set sail.

ἐξαπατάω, deceive.

ἐξαπίνης, suddenly.

ἐξαρτύω, get ready, fit out, provide with.

ἔξειμι (Lat. ibo), go out.

ἐξέλκω, draw or drag out.

ἐξεργάζομαι, work out, carry out, complete.

ἐξέρχομαι, come or go out.

ἔξεστι, impers., it is permitted, it is possible.

ἐξεύρεσις, εως, ἡ, a finding out, invention.

ἐξεύρημα, ατος, τό, something found out, invention, discovery.

ἐξευρίσκω, find out, discover, invent.

ἐξηγέομαι, lead the way, go first; explain.

ἐξήκοντα, sixty.

*ἐξημερόω, tame; of waste land, reclaim, make cultivable.

ἐξίημι, send out; intrans., of rivers, *flow out.

*ἐξογκόω, make swell; pass., be swollen, be filled with pride, be elated.

ἐξοστρακίζω, banish by ostracism (see note on p.103).

ἔξω, adv. and prep. with gen., outside, outside of.

ἐξωνέομαι, buy.

ἔοικα (perf. with pres. meaning), look like, resemble, with dat.; impers., be likely.

ἑορτή, ῆς, ἡ, feast, festival.

ἐπάγω, lead or bring to.

ἐπαινέω, praise, command.

ἐπακούω, listen to, with gen.

ἔπαυλις, εως, ἡ, hut, dwelling, living-quarters.

ἐπεί, when, since, after; ἐπεὶ τάχιστα, as soon as.

ἐπειδάν (ἐπειδή, ἄν), whenever, when.

ἐπειδή, when, after, since.

ἔπειμι (Lat. sum), be on.

ἔπειμι (Lat. ibo), go to, go against, attack.

ἐπείπερ, strengthened form of ἐπεί.

ἔπειτα, then, next, later.

ἐπελαύνω, march against.

ἐπέρομαι, ask.

ἐπέρχομαι, come or go to; come in addition.

ἐπερωτάω, ask, inquire.

ἐπήν (ἐπεί, ὅν), whenever, as soon as, when.

ἐπί, prep. with gen., dat., acc.; with gen., on, upon, in; in the time of; ἐφ' ἑαυτῶν, by themselves, alone; with dat., on, in; after; for the purpose of, for; with acc., on to, to, against, on, up to; of an object sought, for; of extent of time, for, during.

ἐπιβοάω, call upon, call to one's aid; similarly in mid.

ἐπιβουλεύω, plan or plot against.

ἐπίγαμος, ον, marriageable.

ἐπιγίγνομαι, happen to, come in addition to.

ἐπιδείκνυμι, point out, show off.

ἐπιδίδωμι, give in addition.

ἐπιζάω, survive.

ἐπιθυμέω, desire, want, be eager, with gen.

ἐπικαλέω, call on; mid., call to one's aid; invite.

ἐπίκειμαι, fall on, attack.

ἐπίκλησις, εως, ἡ, additional name, surname; acc. as adv., by name, in name only, nominally.

ἐπικρατέω, control, with gen.

ἐπιλαμβάνω, take hold of, seize; mid., get possession of, obtain.

ἐπιλέγω, say in addition; choose; *mid.*, choose; *read.

ἐπιλείπω, fail, run out on.

ἐπιμέλομαι, look after, take care of, *with gen.*

ἐπιμέμφομαι, blame.

*ἐπιμηχανάομαι, devise against, contrive as a preventive.

ἐπιορκέω, swear falsely, swear falsely by.

ἐπίπαν, on the whole, generally; ὡς τὸ ἐπίπαν, usually.

ἐπιπλέω, sail on, float on.

*ἐπίπλεως, ων, full of.

ἐπιπολῆς, *adv. and prep. with gen.*, on top of, above.

*ἐπισκευή, ῆς, ἡ, repair, restoration.

ἐπίσταμαι, ἐπιστήσομαι, ἠπιστήθην, *imperf.* ἠπιστάμην, understand, know; *with infin.*, know how to.

ἐπιστρέφομαι, turn oneself to, turn around.

ἐπιστρεφῶς, eagerly, earnestly.

ἐπιτάττω, order.

ἐπιτελέω, -τελέσω, complete, perform.

*ἐπιτεχνάομαι, contrive for a purpose.

ἐπιτήδειος, ᾱ, ον, useful, suitable, fit; τὰ ἐπιτήδεια, the necessities of life; *adv.* ἐπιτηδείως.

ἐπιτηδεύω, practise, pursue, attend to; *with ὅπως*, take care that, see to it that.

ἐπιτίθημι, place on; inflict on.

ἐπιτρέπω, turn over to, entrust to; *similarly in mid.*

ἐπίτροπος, ου, ὁ, one to whom something is entrusted, one who is in charge, steward.

·ἐπιτυγχάνω, come upon, meet with; ὁ ἐπιτυχών, the person who meets one, *i.e.*, an ordinary person, anyone.

ἐπιφαίνομαι, come into view, appear.

ἐπιφανής, ές, coming into view, visible; famous, outstanding.

ἐπιφέρω, attack.

ἐπιφοιτάω, come often to, visit, frequent.

ἐπιχώριος, ᾱ, ον, and ος, ον, belonging to a country, native.

ἐπιψηφίζω, put to the vote; *with dat.*, allow *someone* to vote.

ἕπομαι, ἕψομαι, 2nd aor. ἑσπόμην, follow.

ἔπος, ους, τό, word, remark, speech.

ἑπτά, seven.

ἐργάζομαι, work, do; χρήματα ἐργάζεσθαι, make money by working.

ἔργον, ου, τό, work, deed; fact, reality.

*ἔρδω, work, do, accomplish.

ἐρείδω, lean, press.

ἐρημίᾱ, ᾱς, ἡ, desert.

ἔρημος, η, ον, and ος, ον, deserted, empty, uninhabited, lonely; *with gen.*, destitute of; *as subst.*, ἡ ἔρημος (*sc.* χώρα), desert.

ἔρις, ιδος, ἡ, strife, rivalry, contest.

ἑρμηνεύς, έως, ὁ, interpreter.

ἔρομαι, ἐρήσομαι, 2nd aor. ἠρόμην (*pres. not Attic*), ask, inquire.

ἔρχομαι, ἐλήλυθα, 2nd aor. ἦλθον, come, go; εἰς λόγους ἔρχεσθαι, get into a conversation.

ἐρωτάω, ask a question, inquire.

ἐσθής, ῆτος, ἡ, clothing, dress.

ἐσθίω, ἔδομαι, 2nd aor. ἔφαγον, eat.

ἑσπέρα, ᾱς, ἡ, evening; west.

ἑστίᾱ, ᾱς, ἡ, hearth; home.

ἔσχατος, η, ον, farthest, extreme; as subst., τὸ ἔσχατον, extremity, edge.

ἕτερος, ᾱ, ον, the other, one of two; another, other; different.

ἑτέρωθι, elsewhere.

ἔτι, still, yet, any longer, any more.

ἕτοιμος, η, ον, ready.

ἔτος, ους, τό, year.

εὖ, well.

εὐδαιμονίᾱ, ᾱς, ἡ, good fortune, prosperity, happiness.

εὐδαίμων, ον, happy, prosperous, wealthy.

εὐδοκιμέω, have a good reputation, be famous.

εὐειδής, ές, good-looking.

εὐθύς, εῖα, ύ, straight, straightforward, honest, true; adv. εὐθύς and εὐθέως, immediately, at once.

*εὔμορφος, ον, well-formed, good-looking.

εὐπάθεια, ᾱς, ἡ, comfort, pleasure, enjoyment; ἐν εὐπαθείαις εἶναι, enjoy oneself, make merry.

εὐπαθέω, be well off, make merry, have a good time.

εὐπετῶς, easily.

εὑρίσκω, εὑρήσω, ηὕρηκα, ηὕρημαι, ηὑρέθην, 2nd aor. ηὗρον, find, discover; bring a price.

εὐρύς, εῖα, ύ, wide.

εὐρυχωρίᾱ, ᾱς, ἡ, free space, room; ἐν εὐρυχωρίᾳ, on the open sea.

εὐσεβής, ές, pious, holy.

εὐφημέω, properly speak words of good omen, but usually abstain from words of ill omen, be silent.

εὐχή, ῆς, ἡ, prayer.

εὔχομαι, pray.

εὐωχέω, entertain well, feast; pass., feast, fare sumptuously.

ἐφέλκω, draw, pull or drag behind.

ἐφθός, ή, όν, boiled.

ἐφίημι, allow.

ἐφοράω, look over, observe, superintend.

*ἐφορμάω, stir up, incite, urge on.

ἐφορμέω, of ships, lie in wait for, blockade.

ἐχθρός, ά, όν, hostile, hateful; as subst., enemy.

ἔχω, ἕξω, ἔσχηκα, ἔσχημαι, imperf. εἶχον, 2nd aor. ἔσχον, have, hold; restrain, prevent; be able; intrans. with adv., be in a certain state or condition; ὡς εἶχε, just as he was; ἔχων, having, with.

ἕψω, ἑψήσομαι, ἥψησα, boil.

ἕως, gen. and acc. ἕω, ἡ, dawn; the east.

ἕως, conj., as long as, while; until.

Z

ζάω, live (contracted forms have η for ā).

*ζεύγλη, ης, ἡ, strap of the yoke through which the oxen's heads were put; the yoke.

ζεύγνῦμι, ζεύξω, ἔζευξα, join, yoke; *similarly in mid.; used particularly of yoking or harnessing horses or other animals.

ζεῦγος, ους, τό, yoke or team of animals; carriage or wagon drawn by a team.

*ζεῦξις, εως, ἡ, method of yoking.

ζέφυρος, ου, ὁ, west wind.

ζητέω, seek, look for.

ζωγρέω, take prisoner.

ζωή, ῆς, ἡ, life.

ζωός, ἡ, όν, alive, living.

H

ἤ, or; ἤ ... ἤ, either ... or; after a comp., than; similarly after a positive adj. with comp. meaning, e.g., ἄλλος ἤ, other than.

ᾗ, where; how.

ἡγέομαι, lead, with dat.; think, consider, suppose.

ἤδη, already, by this time, now.

ἥδομαι, ἡσθήσομαι, ἥσθην, be glad or pleased; with dat., be pleased with, enjoy.

ἡδονή, ῆς, ἡ, pleasure.

ἥκω, have come, come.

ἡλικίᾱ, ᾱς, ἡ, time of life, age.

ἧλιξ, ικος, ὁ, ἡ, one of the same age, contemporary.

ἥλιος, ου, ὁ, sun.

ἡμεῖς, plu. of ἐγώ.

ἤμελλον, see μέλλω.

ἡμέρᾱ, ᾱς, ἡ, day.

ἡμέτερος, ᾱ, ον, our, ours.

ἡμίονος, ου, ὁ, ἡ, mule.

ἤν, see ἐάν.

ἤπερ (strengthened form of ἤ), just where, right where; just as.

ἤπιος, ᾱ, ον, and ος, ον, soft, gentle, kind; adv. ἠπίως.

ἡσυχίᾱ, ᾱς, ἡ, silence, quiet, rest; καθ' ἡσυχίαν, at leisure, at one's ease.

ἥσυχος, ον, quiet; ἥσυχος εἶναι, keep quiet.

ἤτοι, strengthened form of ἤ; ἤτοι ... ἤ, either ... or.

ἡττάομαι, be inferior; be defeated.

ἥττων, ον, worse, weaker, inferior.

Θ

*θᾱκέω, sit.

θᾶκος, ου, ὁ, seat.

θάλαττα, ης, ἡ, sea.

θάνατος, ου, ὁ, death.

θανατόω, put to death.

θάπτω, θάψω, ἔθαψα, τέθαμμαι, ἐτάφην, bury.

θαρσέω, be cheerful, be confident.

θάττων, see ταχύς.

θαῦμα, ατος, τό, wonder, amazement, marvel; θαῦμα ποιεῖσθαι, express or show amazement.

θαυμάζω, be surprised.

θαυμαστός, ἡ, όν, to be wondered at, amazing, surprising.

θεάομαι, θεάσομαι, look at, see.

θεῖος, ᾱ, ον, divine; as subst.,

τὸ θεῖον, the divine power, God.

*θεοβλαβής, ές, stricken by the gods, distraught, mad.

*θεοπρόπιον, ου, τό, prophecy.

*θεοπρόπος, ου, ὁ, messenger sent to consult an oracle.

θεός, οῦ, ὁ, ἡ, god, goddess.

θεράπων, οντος, ὁ, servant, attendant.

θερμός, ή, όν, warm, hot.

*θεσπίζω, prophesy.

θήκη, ης, ἡ, box, chest; grave, tomb.

θῆλυς, εια, υ, female.

θηρευτής, οῦ, ὁ, hunter.

θηρεύω, hunt, catch.

θηρίον, ου, τό, wild animal.

θηριώδης, ες, infested with wild animals.

θησαυρός, οῦ, ὁ, treasure, treasury.

θνήσκω, θανοῦμαι, τέθνηκα, 2nd aor. ἔθανον, die; perf., be dead.

θοίνη, ης, ἡ, meal, feast.

θόρυβος, ου, ὁ, uproar, tumult, confusion, disturbance.

θρίξ, τριχός, ἡ, hair.

θρόνος, ου, ὁ, seat, throne.

θυγάτηρ, θυγατρός, ἡ, daughter.

θυλάκιον, ου, τό, small bag.

θυμιάω, burn as incense, burn.

θυμός, οῦ, ὁ, soul, heart; courage.

θύρα, ᾱς, ἡ, door.

θυρωρός, οῦ, ὁ, door-keeper.

θυσίᾱ, ᾱς, ἡ, sacrifice.

θύω, sacrifice.

I

ἰδιώτης, ου, ὁ, private citizen.

ἱδρύω, establish, set up.

ἱερεῖον, ου, τό, sacrifice.

ἱερός, ά, όν, holy, sacred; as subst., τὸ ἱερόν, temple.

ἵημι, ἥσω, ἧκα, εἷκα, εἷμαι, εἵθην, 2nd aor. εἷμεν etc. in plu., send; of sounds, send forth, utter; mid., rush, charge, move, go.

ἱκέτης, ου, ὁ, suppliant, fugitive.

*ἵμερος, ου, ὁ, desire.

ἵνα, conj., so that, in order that; adv., where, wherever.

ἴον, ου, τό, violet.

ἵππος, ου, ὁ, ἡ, horse.

ἰσθμός, οῦ, ὁ, isthmus, esp., as proper noun, the Isthmus of Corinth.

ἴσος, η, ον, equal, like.

ἵστημι, στήσω, ἔστησα, ἔστηκα, ἔσταμαι, ἐστάθην, 2nd aor. ἔστην, 2nd perf. ἔσταμεν etc. in plu., make stand, place; pass. and intrans. tenses of act. (2nd aor., perf., pluperf.), stand.

ἱστίον, ου, τό, sail.

ἰσχυρός, ά, όν, strong, severe.

ἰσχύς, ύος, ἡ, strength.

ἴσχω (a form of ἔχω found only in pres. and imperf.), have, hold.

*ἰτέϊνος, η, ον, made of willow.

K

κάδος, ου, ὁ, jar, cask.

καθαιρέω, take down, subdue, depose; similarly in mid.

καθάπερ, just as.

κάθημαι, sit down.

καθίζω, set down, station.

καθίστημι, set down, arrange, appoint; *pass. and intrans. tenses of act.* (*2nd aor., perf., pluperf.*), take one's place, be established, be customary.

καθοράω, look down on, view, examine.

*καθύπερθε(ν), *adv. and prep. with gen.*, above, beyond.

καί, and, also, even; καὶ . . . καί, τε . . . καί, both . . . and; καίτοι, and yet.

καίπερ, although.

καίριος, ᾱ, ον, opportune, suitable.

καιρός, οῦ, ὁ, right time, opportunity, occasion.

κακός, ή, όν, bad; *as subst.*, τὸ κακόν, evil, misfortune; *adv.* κακῶς.

κακόω, treat badly, harm, afflict.

καλέω, καλῶ, ἐκάλεσα, κέκληκα, κέκλημαι, ἐκλήθην, call.

*καλλιστεύω, be the most beautiful.

καλός, ή, όν, beautiful, honourable, noble, good; *comp.* καλλίων; *superl.* κάλλιστος; *adv.* καλῶς, rightly, well, nobly.

κάμηλος, ου, ὁ, ἡ, camel.

κάμνω, καμοῦμαι, κέκμηκα, *2nd aor.* ἔκαμον, be tired *or* ill; *be annoyed *or* distressed.

κανοῦν, οῦ, τό, basket.

καπνός, οῦ, ὁ, smoke.

καρπός, οῦ, ὁ, fruit, produce.

*κάρτα, very much, very.

κάρφος, ους, τό, dry stick, chip, twig.

κασίᾱ, ᾶς, ἡ, cassia, *a spice.*

κατά, *prep. with gen. and acc.*, down; *with gen.*, down from;

with acc., down, down towards, in the direction of, to, against; down along, along beside; opposite; with regard to, in relation to, concerning, towards; in accordance with; *for κατά in distributive uses see note on p. 93.*

καταβαίνω, go *or* come down, descend.

καταβιβάζω, make descend, bring down.

καταγελάω, laugh at, *with dat.*

καταδέω, bind down, bind; *convict.

κατακαλύπτω, cover up.

κατακάω, burn down, burn.

κατακλείω, shut up.

κατακλίνω, -κλινῶ, -ἔκλῑνα, make *someone* lie down *or* recline, *esp. for a meal.*

κατάκλισις, εως, ἡ, a reclining *or* sitting for a meal; κατάκλισις τοῦ γάμου, marriage feast, celebration of a wedding.

κατακοιμάω, put to sleep; *pass.*, go to sleep, sleep.

κατακόπτω, cut to pieces.

κατακρίνω, condemn; *pass.*, be assigned as penalty.

καταλέγω, go through, relate in detail.

καταλείπω, leave behind, leave over.

καταπέτομαι, fly down.

καταπίνω, drink down, gulp *or* swallow down.

καταπλάττω, -πλάσω, spread over, plaster.

καταπροΐξομαι(*fut. only*), go unpunished.

καταρρήγνῡμι, break down; *pass.*, break out, burst forth, fall down.
κατασβέννῡμι, quench, put out.
*κατασῑτέομαι, eat up.
κατασκευάζω, prepare, build, construct.
κατάσκοπος, ου, ὁ, spy.
*κατασκώπτω, make jokes on, make fun of.
*κατασπουδάζομαι, be serious about, be serious.
κατάστασις, εως, ἡ, arrangement, setup; nature.
κατατρέχω, run down.
*καταφονεύω, slaughter, kill.
καταχράομαι, use up; do away with, dispose of, kill.
*κατειλέω, force into a place, coop up.
κατείργνῡμι, shut in, confine.
κατεργάζομαι, effect, accomplish; *destroy.
κατέρχομαι, come *or* go down, return, go home.
κατεσθίω, eat up.
κατέχω, hold down, hold, restrain, detain; have the upper hand, outdo; *intrans.*, restrain oneself.
*κατοικτίζω, pity; *mid.*, bewail, lament.
*κατόνομαι, blame, slight, despise.
*κατόπτης, ου, ὁ, spy.
*κατορρωδέω, be afraid.
*κατορχέομαι, dance in defiance at.
κάτω, down.
καῦμα, ατος, τό, heat.
κάω (*not contracted*), καύσω;

ἔκαυσα, κέκαυκα, κέκαυμαι, ἐκαύθην, burn.
κεῖμαι, κείσομαι, be laid, lie.
κελεύω, order, bid.
*κεραΐζω, ravage, destroy.
κέρας, κέρως *and* κέρᾱτος, τό, wing (*of an army or fleet*).
κεφαλή, ῆς, ἡ, head.
κήρυγμα, ατος, τό, public announcement.
κῆρυξ, ῦκος, ὁ, herald.
κιθάρᾱ, ᾱς, ἡ, lyre, lute.
κιθαρῳδός, οῦ, ὁ, one who sings and plays on the lyre at the same time.
κινάμωμον, ου, τό, cinnamon.
κινδῡνεύω, incur danger, run a risk, take a chance.
κίνδῡνος, ου, ὁ, danger.
*κλαυθμός, οῦ, ὁ, weeping, lamentation.
κλάω (*not contracted*), weep.
κλέπτω, steal.
κνήμη, ης, ἡ, part of the leg between the knee and the ankle.
*κνύζημα, ατος, τό, inarticulate noise, babbling, whimpering.
κόθορνος, ου, ὁ, buskin, high boot.
κοινός, ή, όν, common, public; *as subst.*, τὰ κοινά, public authorities, assembly.
*κόλπος, ου, ὁ, fold of a garment.
κόμη, ης, ἡ, hair.
κομίζω, κομιῶ, ἐκόμισα, κεκόμικα, κεκόμισμαι, ἐκομίσθην, carry; *pass.*, be carried, travel, betake oneself *to*.
κόπρος, ου, ἡ, dung, manure.
*κορυφαῖος, ου, ὁ, leader.

κοσμέω, arrange, adorn.

κόσμος, ου, ό, order; adornment, dress.

κρατέω, rule, conquer, *with gen.*; prevail.

*κραυγανάομαι, cry, wail.

κρέας, κρέως, τό, flesh, meat; *often in plu.*

κρήνη, ης, ή, fountain, spring.

κρίνω, κρινῶ, ἔκρῑνα, κέκρικα, κέκριμαι, ἐκρίθην, distinguish, decide, judge; *of a dream,* interpret.

κριτής, οῦ, ό, judge.

κροκόδειλος, ου, ό, crocodile.

κρύπτω, conceal.

κτάομαι, κτήσομαι, ἐκτησάμην, κέκτημαι, procure, acquire; *perf. with pres. meaning,* possess.

κτείνω, κτενῶ, ἔκτεινα, ἔκτονα, kill.

κτίζω, found, occupy, inhabit.

κύβος, ου, ό, cube, die.

κύκλος, ου, ό, circle, ring; *dat. as adv.,* κύκλῳ, in a circle, all around.

κυκλόω, surround; *similarly in mid.*

*κυρέω, come upon, meet with, obtain, *with gen.*

κύριος, ᾱ, ον, ruling, having authority; *of time,* fixed, appointed.

κῡρόω, make good, ratify, decide.

κύρτη, ης, ή, wicker basket for catching fish.

κύων, κυνός, ό, ή, dog.

κώμη, ης, ή, village.

Λ

*λάβρος, ον, furious, violent.

λάθρᾳ, *adv. and prep. with gen.,* secretly, without the knowledge of.

λαμβάνω, λήψομαι, εἴληφα, εἴλημμαι, ἐλήφθην, 2nd aor. ἔλαβον, take, receive, get; *mid.,* take hold of, clasp, *with gen.*

λαμπρός, ά, όν, bright, illustrious, distinguished.

λανθάνω, λήσω, λέληθα, λέλησμαι, 2nd aor. ἔλαθον, escape the notice of; *with partic.,* do something unawares *or* unobserved.

λέγω, speak, say, tell; call; εὐδαίμονά σε λέγω, I call you happy.

*λεῖμμα, ατος, τό, what is left, remains.

λειμών, ῶνος, ό, meadow.

λείπω, λείψω, λέλοιπα, λέλειμμαι, ἐλείφθην, 2nd aor. ἔλιπον, leave behind, leave; *pass.,* remain.

*λελογισμένως (*adv. formed from perf. partic. of* λογίζομαι), deliberately.

*λέσχη, ης, ή, talk, conversation.

λεώς, λεώ, ό, people.

λεωφόρος, ον, bearing people, populous, frequented.

λήδανον, ου, τό, ladanum, *a kind of gum.*

λήθη, ης, ή, forgetfulness.

λιβανωτός, οῦ, ό, frankincense.

λιβανωτοφόρος, ον, incense-bearing.

λίμνη, ης, ή, lake, marsh.

λῑμός, οῦ, ό, hunger, famine.

λῑπαρέω, *hold out, endure.

λιπαρός, ά, όν, shiny, sleek, bright.

*λίσσομαι, beg, beseech.

*λιτή, ῆς, ἡ, prayer, entreaty, supplication.

λογίζομαι, calculate, consider.

λόγιον, ου, τό, saying; oracle.

λόγος, ου, ὁ, word, talk; story, report, account; *plu.*, conversation; λόγον ποιεῖσθαι (*with gen.*), λόγον ἔχειν (*with gen.*), λόγου τινὰ ποιεῖσθαι, pay attention to, attach importance to, be concerned about; λόγον ἑαυτῷ διδόναι, think something over.

λοιπός, ή, όν, remaining; *as subst.*, τὰ λοιπά, the remains, the rest; *as adv.*, τὸ λοιπόν, in the future.

λούω, wash.

λύκος, ου, ὁ, wolf.

λύχνος, ου, ὁ, *plu.* τὰ λύχνα, light, lamp.

λωβάομαι, mutilate.

λώβη, ης, ἡ, mutilation, maiming.

M

μαίνομαι, μανοῦμαι, *aor. pass.* ἐμάνην, be mad.

μακαρίζω, *fut.* μακαριῶ, call *or* consider happy, congratulate, *with gen. of that on which one is congratulated.*

*μακρόβιος, ον, long-lived.

μακρός, ά, όν, long; *dat. as adv.*, μακρῷ, by far.

μάλα, very, very much; *comp.* μᾶλλον, more, rather, somewhat, too much; μᾶλλον ἤ, rather than, than; *superl.* μάλιστα, most, very much; *with numerals and expressions of size or quantity*, at

most, about; τὰ μάλιστα, very much, especially.

μαλακός, ή, όν, soft, gentle, easy; relaxed, remiss; μαλακὸν οὐδέν, no sign of flagging.

μανθάνω, μαθήσομαι, μεμάθηκα, *2nd aor.* ἔμαθον, learn, discover.

μαντεῖον, ου, τό, oracle, seat of an oracle, shrine.

μαντεύομαι, prophesy.

μαντική, ῆς, ἡ, power of divination, ability to prophesy; method of divination; divination.

μάντις, εως, ὁ, prophet, seer.

μαστιγόω, whip.

μάστιξ, ῑγος, ἡ, whip.

μάταιος, ᾱ, ον, idle, trifling, foolish, useless.

μάχη, ης, ἡ, battle.

μάχομαι, fight in battle.

μεγαλοπρεπῶς, magnificently.

μέγας, μεγάλη, μέγα, large, great; *comp.* μείζων; *superl.* μέγιστος; *adv.* μεγάλως.

μέγεθος, ους, τό, size.

μεθίημι, send forth, let down, cast, let go; *intrans.*, slacken, be careless.

μεθίστημι, put in another place, remove, change; *mid.*, *pass.*, *and intrans. tenses of act. (2nd aor., perf., pluperf.)*, change; depart.

μέλᾱς, μέλαινα, μέλαν, black.

μέλει, μελήσει, *impers.*, it concerns, it is the business of, *with dat.*

μέλλω, μελλήσω, ἐμέλλησα, *imperf.* ἔμελλον *and* ἤμελλον, be about to, be going to, be likely to, be destined to.

μέλος, ους, τό, limb; κατὰ μέλη, limb by limb.

μέμνημαι, perf. of μιμνήσκω with pres. meaning, remember, with gen.

μέμφομαι, blame, with dat. of person.

μέν, postpositive conjunctive particle, used to distinguish the word or clause with which it stands from a word or clause that follows, and commonly answered by δέ after the corresponding word or in the corresponding clause, on the one hand; ὁ μὲν ... ὁ δέ, the one ... the other.

μέντοι, really, certainly; however, nevertheless.

μένω, μενῶ, ἔμεινα, μεμένηκα, remain; trans., wait for.

μέρος, ους, τό, part, share.

μέσος, η, ον, middle; as subst., τὸ μέσον, the space between, the difference.

μετά, prep. with gen. and acc.; with gen., with, in company with; with acc., after; *as adv., afterwards, later, then, next.

μεταβουλεύομαι, change one's plans.

μεταγιγνώσκω, change one's mind.

μετάγνωσις, εως, ἡ, change of mind.

μεταπέμπομαι, send for, summon.

μετέχω, share in, with gen.

μετέωρος, ον, in the air, off the ground, above the head.

μέτριος, ᾱ, ον, moderate, of medium size.

μέχρι, prep. with gen., until, as long as, during; as far as, up to or to a place; μέχρι οὗ (conj.), until; μέχρι πόσου, how long.

μή, not, in prohibitions, final clauses, conditional clauses, etc.

μηδαμῶς, by no means.

μηδέ, but not, and not, nor, not even.

μηδείς, μηδεμία, μηδέν, not one, not any, none, no, no one, nothing.

μήν, postpositive intensive particle, certainly, indeed; καὶ μήν, and besides, moreover.

μήν, μηνός, ὁ, month.

μηρός, οῦ, ὁ, thigh.

μήτε, and not, nor; μήτε ... μήτε, neither ... nor.

μήτηρ, μητρός, ἡ, mother.

μηχανάομαι, contrive, devise.

μηχανή, ῆς, ἡ, contrivance, device, way, means.

μῑκρός, ά, όν, small.

μισθόω, let for hire or rent; mid., hire, rent.

*μνηστήρ, ῆρος, ὁ, suitor.

μόγις, with difficulty.

μοῖρα, ᾱς, ἡ, fate, lot; ἐν μοίρᾳ ἄγειν, hold in respect, respect.

μονογενής, ές, only-begotten, only.

μόνος, η, ον, alone, only.

μονόω, make solitary; pass., be left alone, be deserted, be deprived of, with gen.

*μόρος, ου, ὁ, fate, destiny; death.

*μόρσιμος, ον, destined, fated.
μουσική, ῆς, ἡ, music, poetry,
the arts.
μῡρίος, ᾱ, ον, countless, in-
finite; *usually in plu.*
μύρμηξ, ηκος, ὁ, ant.
μύρον, ου, τό, sweet oil,
unguent, perfume.

N

ναί, certainly, yes.
ναυμαχέω, engage in a sea-
fight.
ναυμαχίᾱ, ᾱς, ἡ, sea-fight.
ναῦς, νεώς, ἡ, ship.
νεᾱνίᾱς, ου, ὁ, young man.
νέηλμς, υδος, ὁ, ἡ, newcomer;
also as adj.
νεκρός, οῦ, ὁ, dead body,
corpse.
νέκυς, υος, ὁ, dead body,
corpse.
νέμεσις, εως, ἡ, vengeance,
retribution.
νέμω, νεμῶ, ἔνειμα, νενέμηκα,
νενέμημαι, ἐνεμήθην, distribute,
assign, allot; pasture cattle
or sheep; *mid.*, have assigned
to one, possess; inhabit,
occupy; rule.
νεογνός, όν, newborn.
νέος, ᾱ, ον, young.
νεοττεύω, hatch.
νεοττιά, ᾶς, ἡ, nest of young
birds, nest.
νέφος, ους, τό, cloud.
νέω, swim (*contracts only* εε
and εει).
νεώς, νεώ, ὁ, temple.
νηνεμίᾱ, ᾱς, ἡ, calm.
νῑκάω, win, conquer.
νομή, ῆς, ἡ, pasture, pasture-
land.

νομίζω, νομῶ, ἐνόμισα, νενόμικα,
νενόμισμαι, ἐνομίσθην, think,
consider.
νόμος, ου, ὁ, custom, law;
strain of music.
νοστέω, return home.
νότιος, ᾱ, ον, southern.
νουθετέω, remind, admonish.
νοῦς, νοῦ, ὁ, mind, sense; ἐν νῷ
ἔχειν, have in mind, intend.
νυκτερίς, ίδος, ἡ, bat.
νῦν, *adv. of time,* now; *enclitic*
νύν, now then, therefore, so
then.
νύξ, νυκτός, ἡ, night.
νῶτον, ου, τό, back.

Ξ

ξενίζω, entertain, receive as
guest.
ξένος, ου, ὁ, guest, host; anyone entitled to rights of
hospitality, friend, stranger.
ξύλον, ου, τό, wood.
*ξυλουργέω, do carpentry
work.

O

ὁ, ἡ, τό, *definite article,* the; *as
demon. pron. with* μέν *and*
δέ, ὁ μέν... ὁ δέ, the one...
the other; ὁ δέ, *without preceding* ὁ μέν, but he, and he,
he.
ὀγδοήκοντα, eighty.
ὅδε, ἥδε, τόδε, *demon. pron.,*
this, the following.
ὁδός, οῦ, ἡ, way, road, journey.
ὄζω, smell, smell of, *with gen.;*
impers. ὄζει, there is a smell
of.
οἶδα (*perf. with pres. meaning*),
know; χάριν οἶδα, be grateful.

οἰκεῖος, ᾱ, ον, belonging to one's house *or* household, related.

οἰκειόω, make one's own; *mid.*, claim.

οἰκέτης, ου, ὁ, member of one's household (*either slave or one of the family*).

οἰκέω, live, dwell, inhabit.

οἴκησις, εως, ἡ, place to live, house, home.

οἰκίᾱ, ᾱς, ἡ, house, household, family; *similarly in plu.*

οἰκίον, ου, τό (*usually in plu.*), house, dwelling, palace with group of buildings.

οἰκοδομέω, build a house, build.

οἶκος, ου, ὁ, house, household, home.

οἶνος, ου, ὁ, wine.

οἷος, ᾱ, ον, of what kind, such as, as; οἷός τε, able, possible; *neut. plu. as adv.*, οἷα, as, since.

οἷς, οἰός, ὁ, ἡ, sheep.

οἴχομαι, be gone, depart.

ὀκέλλω, run aground.

*ὄλβιος, ᾱ, ον, happy, prosperous, rich.

*ὄλβος, ου, ὁ, happiness.

ὄλεθρος, ου, ὁ, destruction, death.

ὀλίγος, η, ον, little, small; *plu.*, few; *neut. as adv.*, ὀλίγον, a little.

ὅλος, η, ον, whole, entire.

ὅμιλος, ου, ὁ, crowd.

ὄμνῡμι, swear, swear by.

ὅμοιος, ᾱ, ον, like, resembling, similar, equal, *with dat.*; *adv.* ὁμοίως, in the same way, similarly, equally.

ὁμοῦ, together, at the same time.

*ὁμοφρονέω, agree, *with dat.*

ὅμως, nevertheless.

ὀνειδίζω, blame, reproach, impute as blame.

*ὀνείδισμα, ατος, τό, reproach.

*ὀνειροπόλος, ου, ὁ, interpreter of dreams.

ὄνειρος, ου, ὁ, dream.

ὄνομα, ατος, τό, name.

ὀνομάζω, name, call on.

ὀνομαστός, ή, όν, famous.

ὄνος, ου, ὁ, ass, donkey.

ὅπη, in what way, how; where

ὄπισθε(ν), *adv. and prep. with gen.*, behind.

ὀπίσω, behind; back; again.

ὁπλίζω, arm.

ὅπλον, ου, τό, implement; *plu.*, arms.

ὁπόθεν, from what place.

ὁποῖος, ᾱ, ον, of what kind.

ὁπόσος, η, ον, of what size, how much, how many, as much as, as many as.

ὁπότερος, ᾱ, ον, which of two.

ὅπου, where, wherever.

ὀπτάω, roast.

ὅπως, that, so that; how; when, whenever.

ὁράω, ὄψομαι, *aor. pass.* ὤφθην, 2nd *aor.* εἶδον, see.

ὀργή, ῆς, ἡ, temperament, disposition; anger; ὀργὴν ποιεῖσθαι, become angry.

ὀρέγω, stretch out.

ὄρθιος, ᾱ, ον, steep; *of sounds*, high-pitched, shrill, clear.

ὄρθριος, ᾱ, ον, at dawn, in the morning, early; *neut. as adv.*, ὄρθριον *or* τὸ ὄρθριον.

ὀρθῶς, rightly.

ὅρκος, ου, ὁ, oath.
ὁρμάω, set in motion, hurry, rush; mid., and pass., start; be eager, want or intend to do.
ὄρνις, ὄρνῑθος, ὁ, ἡ, bird.
ὄρος, ους, τό, mountain.
ὀρρωδίᾱ, ᾱς, ἡ, shuddering, trembling, fear.
ὀρχέομαι, dance.
ὄρχησις, εως, ἡ, dancing, dance.
ὅς, ἥ, ὅ, rel. pron., who, which.
ὀσμή, ῆς, ἡ, smell.
ὅσος, η, ον, how much, how many, as much as, as many as; plu. also those who, all who.
ὅσπερ, ἥπερ, ὅπερ (strengthened form of ὅς), the very one who, the very thing which, who, which.
ὅστις, ἥτις, ὅ τι, indirect interrog. pro., who, which, what; also indef. rel. pro., whoever, etc.
ὅταν (ὅτε, ἄν), whenever.
ὅτε, when; since, because.
ὅτι, that (after verbs of saying, knowing etc.); because; ὅτι μή, unless, except, except that; with superl., as . . . as possible, e.g., ὅτι τάχιστα, as quickly as possible.
οὐ, οὐκ, οὐχ, not.
οὗ οἷ, ἕ, enclitic 3rd pers. pron. sing., indirect reflex., of himself, etc.
οὐδαμῇ, nowhere, in no way.
*οὐδαμός, ή, όν, no, no one, none.
οὐδαμοῦ, nowhere.
οὐδαμῶς, in no way, not at all.
οὐδέ, but not, and not, nor; not even.

οὐδείς, οὐδεμία, οὐδέν, not one, not any, none, no, no one, nothing.
οὐδέτερος, ᾱ, ον, neither of two.
οὐκέτι, no longer, not any more.
οὔκουν, not therefore, so not.
οὖν, therefore, then, accordingly, so.
οὔπω, not yet.
οὐρά, ᾶς, ἡ, tail.
οὖς, ὠτός, τό, ear.
οὔτε, and not; οὔτε . . . οὔτε, neither . . . nor.
οὔτοι, (οὐ, τοί), not therefore, certainly not.
οὗτος, αὕτη, τοῦτο, demon. pron., this; also as 3rd pers. pron., he, she, it.
οὕτω, οὕτως, in this way, thus, so.
ὀφείλω, ὀφειλήσω, 2nd aor. ὤφελον, owe, be bound.
ὀφθαλμός, οῦ, ὁ, eye.
ὄφις, εως, ὁ, snake.
ὀχέω, bear; pass., with fut. mid., be borne or carried, ride.
ὄψις, ὄψεως, ἡ, vision, dream; power of seeing, eyesight.

Π

πάθος, ους, τό, experience, suffering, affliction, trouble.
*παιγνίᾱ, ᾱς, ἡ, game.
*παιγνιήμων, ον, fond of a joke, playful, gay.
παιδαγωγός, οῦ, ὁ, slave who escorted boy to and from school; tutor, teacher.
παίδευσις, εως, ἡ, training, education.

παιδίον, ου, τό (dimin. of παῖς), small child, baby.

παίζω, play.

παῖς, παιδός, ὁ, ἡ, child, boy, girl, son, daughter.

πάλαι, long ago, formerly.

παλαιός, ά, όν, old, ancient; ἐκ παλαιοῦ, from of old, from ancient times.

πάλιν, back, again.

πανήγυρις, εως, ἡ (πᾶς, ἀγορά), assembly of all the people, festival.

πανταχόθεν, from all sides, on all sides.

παντοῖος, ᾱ, ον, of all kinds, manifold.

πάντως, by all means.

πάνυ, very, altogether; certainly.

παρά, prep. with gen., dat., acc., beside; with gen., from beside, from; with dat., beside, at the side of, with; in the eyes of, in the judgment of; with acc., to a position beside, to the side of, to, beside, near, along.

παραγγέλλω, give orders, order.

παραγίγνομαι, be at hand; appear, arrive.

*παραγυμνόω, reveal, disclose.

παραδίδωμι, hand over, surrender.

παραινέω, recommend, advise.

παραιτέομαι, beg from, earnestly ask for.

παρακλίνω, -κλινῶ, -έκλῑνα, turn aside, open a little.

παρακρίνω, separate, draw up, array.

παραλαμβάνω, receive or take from someone; learn, hear.

παραλύω, loose from, detach.

παραμένω, stay with; survive, remain alive.

παραπλήσιος, ᾱ, ον, and ος, ον, similar, like.

*παρασάττω, stuff in beside.

παρασκευάζω, make preparations, prepare; similarly in mid.

παρασκευή, ῆς, ἡ, preparation.

παρατίθημι, place beside or before.

παραφέρω, bring to, bring in.

*παραφρονέω, be out of one's mind, be mad.

*παραχράομαι, misuse, neglect.

*πάρεδρος, ον, sitting beside.

πάρειμι (Lat. sum), be present; be with, with dat.; impers. πάρεστι, it is possible; παρών, as adj., present; ἐν τῷ παρόντι, at present; τὰ παρόντα, the present circumstances or situation.

πάρειμι (Lat. ibo). go along, go ahead, advance.

*παρέκ, παρέξ, prep. with gen., outside, beyond, besides.

*παρέλκω, draw beside, pull.

παρέρχομαι, go by or beside; come to, arrive at.

παρέχω, furnish, supply, provide; similarly in mid.; impers. παρέχει, it is allowed, it is possible, one has the opportunity.

παρθένος, ου, ἡ, maiden.

παρίζομαι, sit beside.

παρίστημι, place beside; pass. and intrans. tenses of act.

(2nd aor., perf., pluperf.), stand by, be near, be at hand; aid; surrender.

πᾶς, πᾶσα, πᾶν, all, every.

πάσχω, πείσομαι, πέπονθα, 2nd aor. ἔπαθον, experience, suffer.

πατήρ, πατρός, ὁ, father.

*πάτρᾱ, ᾱς, ἡ, fatherland.

πατρίς, ίδος, ἡ, fatherland.

πατρῷος, ᾱ, ον, coming from a father, hereditary.

πάτρως, ωος, ὁ, paternal uncle.

παύω, make stop from, with acc. of person and gen. of thing; mid., stop.

πέδη, ης, ἡ, fetter, chain.

πεδίον, ου, τό, plain.

πεζός, ή, όν, on foot; as subst., ὁ πεζός, the infantry.

πείθω, πείσω, ἔπεισα, πέπεικα, πέπεισμαι, ἐπείσθην, persuade; mid. and pass., obey, with dat.; believe.

πειράομαι, πειράσομαι, πεπείραμαι, ἐπειράθην, try, attempt.

πέλαγος, ους, τό, sea.

πέμπτος, η, ον, fifth.

πέμπω, send, send away.

πέντε, five.

πεντήκοντα, fifty.

πέρ, enclitic particle which adds emphasis to the preceding word to which it is frequently attached, e.g., ὅσπερ, the very one who.

περί, prep. with gen., dat., acc., around, about; with gen., about, concerning; with dat., around; on behalf of, for; with acc., around, near, by; about, with regard to.

περιάγω, lead around.

περιαιρέω, take away all around, pull down, remove.

περιαυχένιος, ον, for wearing around the neck; as subst., τὸ περιαυχένιον, necklace.

περιγίγνομαι, be superior, prevail over, with gen.; survive, escape.

περίειμι (Lat. sum), survive.

περίειμι (Lat. ibo), go around.

περιέπω, -έψω, imperf. -εῖπον, 2nd aor. -έσπον, treat, handle.

περιέρχομαι, come around to, come into the hands of.

*περιέσχατα, ων, τά, edges, extremities.

περιέχω, surround.

*περιημεκτέω, be annoyed.

περιίστημι, place around; pass. and intrans. tenses of act. (2nd aor., perf., pluperf.), stand around, come around.

*περικάω, burn around.

*περικείρω, clip all around, clip.

περικυκλέομαι, surround.

*πέριξ, adv. and prep. with gen., around, all around.

περιοράω, look on; allow.

περιπίπτω, fall around, fall against, collide with.

περιποιέω, make survive, save.

περιττός, ή, όν, beyond measure, excessive; strange, unusual.

περιυβρίζω, treat insolently, grossly outrage.

περιχαρής, ές, very glad.

πεττοί, ῶν, οἱ, men for playing a game similar to checkers or chess; the game itself.

πῇ, how.

πηγή, ῆs, ἡ, fountain, spring; source.

πηλός, οῦ, ὁ, mud, clay.

πῆχυς, εωs, ὁ, cubit.

πικρός, ά, όν, bitter, harsh.

πίμπλημι, πλήσω, ἔπλησα, πέπληκα, πέπλησμαι, ἐπλήσθην, fill, with gen. of that with which a thing is filled.

πίνω, drink.

πιπράσκω, aor. pass. ἐπράθην, sell.

πίπτω, πεσοῦμαι, πέπτωκα, 2nd aor. ἔπεσον, fall.

πιστεύω, trust in, put faith in, with dat.

πιστός, ή, όν, trustworthy, faithful; credible.

πλανάω, make wander; pass., wander, roam.

πλάνη, ηs, ἡ, wandering, travel.

πλάτος, ουs, τό, width.

πλάττω, πλάσω, ἔπλασα, πέπλασμαι, ἐπλάσθην, form, mould; make up, invent.

πλατύς, εῖα, ύ, wide, flat.

πλέω, πλεύσομαι, ἔπλευσα, sail (contracts only εε and εει).

πλῆθος, ουs, τό, crowd, large number, majority.

πλήθω, be full, become full.

πλήν, prep. with gen., except.

πληρόω, fill; of a ship, man.

πλήρωμα, ατοs, τό, that which fills up, a full measure; ζωῆς πλήρωμα μακρότατον, the longest span of life.

πλοῖον, ου, τό, boat, ship.

πλοῦς, πλοῦ, ὁ, sailing.

πλουτέω, be rich.

πλοῦτος, ου, ὁ, wealth.

ποδανιπτήρ, ῆροs, ὁ, basin for washing feet.

ποιέω, do, make; mid., make for oneself; regard, consider; μεγάλα ποιεῖσθαι, be greatly pleased; δεινὸν ποιεῖσθαι, take badly, complain of, be indignant at; λόγον ποιεῖσθαι (with gen.), λόγου τινὰ ποιεῖσθαι, pay attention to, attach importance to.

ποίησις, εωs, ἡ, making, manufacture.

*ποιηφαγέω, eat grass.

ποικίλος, η, ον, many-coloured, spotted.

ποιμήν, ένοs, ὁ, shepherd.

ποίμνη, ηs, ἡ, flock of sheep.

πολέμιος, ᾱ, ον, hostile; as subst., enemy.

πόλεμος, ου, ὁ, war.

πολιορκέω, besiege.

πολιορκίᾱ, ᾶs, ἡ, siege.

πόλις, εωs, ἡ, city.

πολίτης, ου, ὁ, citizen.

πολλάκις, often.

πολύς, πολλή, πολύ, much, many; comp. πλείων and πλέων; superl. πλεῖστος.

*πομπός, οῦ, ὁ, guide, escort.

πόνος, ου, ὁ, labour, toil, trouble, struggle.

πορεύομαι, proceed.

πορθμεύς, έωs, ὁ, boatman, sailor.

*πορθμός, οῦ, ὁ, strait.

πόρος, ου, ὁ, means of crossing, ford; way or means of doing, resource, solution of a difficulty.

πορφύρᾱ, ᾶs, ἡ, purple.

πορφυροῦς, ᾶ, οῦν, purple.

πόσις, εωs, ἡ, drinking, drink.

πόσος, η, ον, how much, how many, how large; μέχρι πόσου, how long.

ποταμός, οῦ, ὁ, river.

πότε, when; enclitic ποτέ, at some time, at any time, once, at last.

πότερος, ᾱ, ον, which of two; πότερον ... ἤ, whether ... or.

πού, enclitic adv., anywhere, somewhere; to some extent, somehow, perhaps, I suppose, of course.

πούς, ποδός, ὁ, foot.

πρᾶγμα, ατος, τό, deed, thing, matter, affair, business.

πράττω, πράξω, ἔπρᾱξα, πέπρᾱγα and πέπρᾱχα, πέπρᾱγμαι, ἐπράχθην, do; intrans., fare.

πρέσβυς, εως, ὁ, old man.

πρεσβύτης, ου, ὁ, old man; also as adj., πρεσβύτης ἀνήρ.

πρίν, before, until; πρὶν ἤ with infin., sooner than, before; τὸ πρίν, formerly.

πρό, prep. with gen., before (of both place and time); for, in behalf of, in defence of.

προαγορεύω, proclaim, order.

προάγω, lead forward, lead on.

προακούω, hear beforehand.

προάστειον, ου, τό, suburb.

προβαίνω, go ahead, proceed.

πρόβατον, ου, τό, usually in plu. πρόβατα, domestic animals, esp. sheep; flock of sheep.

προδίδωμι, betray.

πρόειμι (Lat. ibo), go forward, go ahead.

προεῖπον (2nd aor., no pres.), tell beforehand, foretell, proclaim, order.

προεξανίσταμαι, get up and go

ahead of time, start before the signal.

προθῡμέομαι, be eager or zealous.

προθύμως, eagerly, zealously.

προΐημι, send out; give up.

προΐστημι, set before; mid., choose as leader; pass. and intrans. tenses of act. (2nd aor., perf., pluperf.), stand before, be set over, be ahead of, guide, conduct, with gen.

πρόκειμαι, lie before, lie in view; be set before, be appointed.

προλαμβάνω, take beforehand; προλαμβάνειν τῆς ὁδοῦ, get a head start.

προμαχεών, ῶνος, ὁ, bulwark, rampart.

προμηθέομαι, show respect for, with gen.

*προναυμαχέω, fight a naval battle for, with gen.

πρόνοια, ᾱς, ἡ, foresight, foreknowledge; ἐκ προνοίας, on purpose, intentionally (see note on p. 19, l. 14).

προπέμπω, send forward, escort.

προπυνθάνομαι, learn beforehand.

πρόρριζος, ον, by the roots, root and branch, utterly.

πρός, prep. with gen., dat., acc.; with gen., over against, towards; from; at the hands of; with dat., near; on; in addition to; with acc., to, towards, against; in reply to; in relation to, according to; πρὸς ταῦτα, considering this, therefore; in answer to this.

προσάγω, lead to; *mid.*, lead to oneself, win over.

προσβάλλω, strike against, attack.

πρόσβασις, εως, ἡ, means of approach, access.

προσβολή, ῆς, ἡ, attack.

προσγίγνομαι, come to, be added, be in addition *or* besides.

*προσείκελος, η, ον, resembling.

πρόσειμι (*Lat.* sum), be at *or* near; be added to *or* be in addition to.

πρόσειμι (*Lat.* ibo), go to.

*προσεξαιρέομαι, choose for oneself.

προσέρχομαι, come *or* go to.

προσέτι, besides.

πρόσθεν, before, forwards; τὸ πρόσθεν, the front.

πρόσθιος, ᾱ, ον, front.

πρόσκειμαι, lie beside; belong to, fall to; attach oneself to, make overtures to.

προσκτάομαι, acquire in addition to, *with dat.*

προσκυνέω, prostrate oneself before, do obeisance to.

προσπίπτω, fall against, fall at a person's knees in supplication.

*προσπλάττω, form *or* mould on, build on.

προστάτης, ου, ὁ, one who stands before, leader.

προστάττω, assign (*as a task*), order.

προστίθημι, place before, add, attribute, consign to; *mid.*,

assent to; προστίθημι γυναῖκα, give as wife.

προσφέρω, bring to, bring before; *pass.*, *resemble, followed by* εἰς.

προσφιλής, ές, well-liked, popular.

πρόσω, forward; εἰς τὸ πρόσω, forward, ahead.

πρόσωπον, ου, τό, face.

προτεραῖος, ᾱ, ον, on the day before; *as subst.*, ἡ προτεραία (*sc.* ἡμέρα), the day before.

πρότερος, ᾱ, ον, before, earlier, previous, first, former; *neut. as adv.*, πρότερον, formerly, before, first; πρότερον ἤ, sooner than.

προτίθημι, place before, propose; lay out, expose; assign to.

προφέρω, excel, surpass, *with gen.*

πρύμνα, ης, ἡ, stern of a ship.

πρῶτος, η, ον, first; *neut. as adv.*, πρῶτον and τὰ πρῶτα, at first.

*πτερωτός, ή, όν, winged.

πύλη, ης, ἡ, gate.

πυλίς, ίδος, ἡ, little gate.

*πυλωρός, οῦ, ὁ, gate-keeper.

πυνθάνομαι, πεύσομαι, πέπυσμαι, 2nd *aor*. ἐπυθόμην, ask, inquire; learn by asking, find out.

πῦρ, πυρός, τό, fire.

πυρά, ᾶς, ἡ, pyre.

πύργος, ου, ὁ, tower.

πῦρός, οῦ, ὁ, wheat.

πώ, *enclitic adv.*, yet.

πωλέω, sell.

πῶμα, ατος, τό, drink.

πῶς, how; *enclitic* πώς, somehow, in any way, at all.

P

ῥάβδος, ου, ἡ, stick, wand.
ῥαπίζω, hit with a stick, beat.
*ῥεῖθρον, ου, τό, river, stream.
ῥεῦμα, ατος, τό, stream.
ῥέω, flow.
ῥήγνῡμι, ῥήξω, ἔρρηξα, aor. pass.
ἐρράγην, break, let break forth; ῥήγνυμι φωνήν, utter a sound or word.
ῥῆμα, ατος, τό, what is said, word, statement.
ῥίπτω, ῥίψω, ἔρριψα, throw, hurl.
ῥίς, ῥῑνός, ἡ, nose.
*ῥῡμός, οῦ, ὁ, pole of a wagon or other horse-drawn vehicle.
*ῥύομαι, draw to oneself, draw out of danger, rescue, deliver.
*ῥωμαλέος, ᾱ, ον, strong.
ῥώμη, ης, ἡ, physical strength.

Σ

σαφῶς, clearly, for certain.
σβέννῡμι, σβέσω, ἔσβεσα, ἔσβηκα, ἐσβέσθην, quench, put out.
σεαυτοῦ *and* σαυτοῦ, ῆς (*no nom.*), *reflexive pron.*, 2nd pers., of yourself.
σέβομαι, worship.
σειρᾱφόρος, ον, having a rope attached, led by a rope; *of horses*, drawing by the trace, not by the yoke.
σεμνός, ή, όν, holy, stately, majestic.
σημαίνω, σημανῶ, ἐσήμηνα, make a sign, signify, indicate, reveal.
σῑγάω, be silent.

σῑγή, ῆς, ἡ, silence; *dat. as adv.*, σιγῇ, in silence, silently.
σῑτέομαι, σῑτήσομαι, ἐσῑτήθην, take food, eat; *with acc.*, feed on, eat.
σίτησις, εως, ἡ, eating; food.
σῑτίον, ου, τό, *usually in plu.* σιτία, bread, food, provisions.
σῑτοδείᾱ, ᾱς, ἡ, scarcity of food, famine.
σῑτοποιός, όν, bread-making; *as subst.*, ἡ σιτοποιός, breadmaker.
σῖτος, ου, ὁ, grain, food, supplies.
*σῑτοφόρος, ον, grain-carrying.
σκέλος, ους, τό, leg.
σκευή, ῆς, ἡ, equipment, attire, dress.
σκοπέω, look at, see; consider.
σμύρνα, ης, ἡ, myrrh.
σός, σή, σόν, your, yours (*sing.*).
σοφίᾱ, ᾱς, ἡ, cleverness, skill, wisdom.
σοφίζω, devise.
σόφισμα, ατος, τό, clever device, trick.
σοφός, ή, όν, clever, skilful, wise.
σπανίζω, want, need, *with gen.*
σπάνιος, η, ον, rare, scarce.
*σπέρχω, σπέρξω, aor. pass. ἐσπέρχθην, drive, urge on; *pass.*, hurry; σπερχθείς, hastily, quickly.
σπεύδω, hasten.
σπουδή, ῆς, ἡ, haste, eagerness.
στάδιον, ου, τό, *plu.* τὰ στάδια *and* οἱ στάδιοι, stade(*a measure of distance of about 600 feet*).
σταθμάω, measure; *mid.*, measure, estimate, judge.
σταθμόω, put on the scales; *mid.*, infer, conjecture.

στασιάζω, quarrel, disagree, be at variance.

*στέγη, ης, ἡ, roof, covered place, shelter, room.

στέλλω, send.

στενός, ή, όν, narrow; ἐν στενῷ, in a narrow place, in a strait.

στερέω, deprive of, with gen.

στεφανόω, crown, esp. with a wreath of victory; pass., be crowned, win.

στόλος, ου, ὁ, expedition.

στόμα, ατος, τό, mouth.

*στομόω, gag.

*στρατάρχης, ου, ὁ, commander of an army.

στρατείᾱ, ᾶς, ἡ, expedition.

στράτευμα, ατος, τό, army.

στρατεύω, serve as a soldier, go on a military expedition; similarly in mid.

στρατηγός, οῦ, ὁ, general.

στρατιᾱ, ᾶς, ἡ, army.

στρατιώτης, ου, ὁ, soldier.

στρατόπεδον, ου, τό, camp; army.

στρατός, οῦ, ὁ, army.

στρεπτός, ή, όν, and ός, όν, easily bent or twisted; as subst., ὁ στρεπτός, collar, necklace.

στρουθός, οῦ, ὁ, small bird, sparrow.

στύραξ, ακος, ἡ, storax, a kind of gum; the tree which produces it.

σύ, σοῦ, 2nd pers. pron., you.

συγγενής, ές, of the same family, related.

συγγνώμη, ης, ἡ, forgiveness, pardon.

συγκαλέω, call together, summon.

συγκατακάω, burn up with.

σύγκειμαι, lie with; be agreed on.

*συγκυρέω, happen, occur.

συγχωρέω, agree.

συλλαμβάνω, help.

συλλέγω, collect, bring together.

σύλλογος, ου, ὁ, meeting.

συλλῡπέομαι, sympathize with, condole.

συμβαίνω, coincide with, agree with.

συμβάλλω, compare; join battle; mid., conjecture.

συμβουλεύω, advise, with dat.

συμβουλή, ῆς, ἡ, advice.

σύμμαχος, ου, ὁ, ally.

*συμμίσγω, -μίξω, mix with, communicate to; intrans., mingle with, associate with, converse with.

*συμπαίζω, play with.

συμπλέκω, aor. pass. -επλάκην, plait together; pass., be locked together or entangled, be engaged in close combat.

συμπότης, ου, ὁ, fellow-drinker, boon-companion.

συμπράκτωρ, opos, ὁ, helper.

συμφέρω, bring together; happen.

σύν, prep. with dat., with.

συνάγω, bring together.

συνᾱλίζω, gather together, collect.

συνέδριον, ου, τό, assembly, meeting, council.

*συνειλέω, gather together, pick up.

συνίημι, send or put together; understand, perceive.

συνίστημι, place together; pass. and intrans. tenses of act. (2nd aor., perf., pluperf.), stand together, meet, join battle; συνεστηκότων τῶν στρατηγῶν, while the generals were arguing.

*συννέω, pile up.

συννοέω, consider, reflect.

συνοικέω, live with, marry.

συνοίκησις, εως, ἡ, a living together, marriage.

*συνταχύνω, hasten on, hasten to an end.

συντίθημι, put together; mid., agree on.

συντρέχω, run together, gather.

σφάζω, σφάξω, cut the throat, slaughter.

σφαῖρα, ᾱς, ἡ, globe, sphere, ball.

σφεῖς, σφῶν, σφίσι, σφᾶς, 3rd pers. pron. plu., they; oblique cases as indirect reflex., of themselves.

σχέτλιος, ᾱ, ον, wretched, miserable.

*σχημάτιον, ου, τό, dance figure.

σῴζω, σώσω, save.

σῶμα, ατος, τό, body.

σωρός, οῦ, ὁ, heap.

σῶς, σᾶ, σῶν, safe.

σῶστρα, ων, τά, thank-offering for deliverance from a danger.

T

τάλαντον, ου, τό, talent (a sum of money equivalent to 60 minas).

τἆλλα, crasis for τὰ ἄλλα.

τάξις, εως, ἡ, arrangement, order; post, position.

ταραχώδης, ες, fond of causing trouble, trouble-making.

ταρῑχεύω, embalm (of mummies).

τάττω, τάξω, ἔταξα, τέταχα, τέταγμαι, ἐτάχθην, arrange, order, draw up, marshal.

ταὐτά, crasis for τὰ αὐτά; ταὐτό, for τὸ αὐτό.

ταύτῃ, fem. dat. of οὗτος used adverbially, in this way.

ταφή, ῆς, ἡ, burial.

τάφος, ου, ὁ, burial; tomb.

ταχύς, εῖα, ύ, quick; comp. θάττων; neut. sing. as adv., θᾶττον; superl. τάχιστος; τὴν ταχίστην (sc. ὁδόν), the quickest way, with the greatest speed; neut. plu. as adv., τάχιστα; ἐπεὶ τάχιστα, as soon as; adv. ταχέως.

ταχυτής, ῆτος, ἡ, swiftness, speed.

τέ, enclitic particle, and; τε . . . τε, τε . . . καί, both . . . and.

τέθριππον, ου, τό, four-horse chariot.

τεῖχος, ους, τό, wall.

*τειχοφύλαξ, ακος, ὁ, one who guards the walls, sentinel.

τεκμήριον, ου, τό, evidence, proof.

τέκνον, ου, τό, child.

τέλειος, ᾱ, ον, complete, fulfilled.

τελειόω, accomplish, effect.

τελευτάω, bring to an end, kill; come to an end, die; be the end of, with gen.

τελευτή, ῆς, ἡ, end.

τελέω, fulfil, accomplish.

τέλος, ους, τό, end; highest office, full power or authority; οἱ ἐν τέλει ὄντες, those in power or authority.

τέρας, ατος, τό, wonder, marvel.

τέταρτος, η, ον, fourth.

τετρακισχίλιοι, αι, α, four thousand.

τετράπουν, ποδος, τό, quadruped.

τετταράκοντα, forty.

τέτταρες, α, four.

τετταρεσκαίδεκα, fourteen.

τέως, for a while.

τίθημι, θήσω, ἔθηκα, τέθεικα, τέθειμαι, ἐτέθην, 2nd aor. ἔθεμεν etc. in plu., put, place.

τίκτω, τέξομαι, τέτοκα, 2nd aor. ἔτεκον, give birth, bear young.

τῑμάω, honour, value.

τῑμή, ῆς, ἡ, honour.

τίμιος, ᾱ, ον, honoured, valued.

τῑμωρέω, help, avenge, with dat.

τίνω, τίσω, ἔτισα, τέτικα, pay; mid., take vengeance on, punish.

τίς, τί, gen. τίνος, interrog. pron., who, which, what; neut. as adv., τί, why.

τὶς, τὶ, gen. τινός, enclitic indef. pron., any, some, a certain, anyone, anything, someone, something.

τίσις, εως, ἡ, recompense, usually in the sense of penalty or punishment, but also reward; τίσιν δίδωμι, undergo punishment, be punished.

τοί, enclitic particle, therefore, so, then, really.

τοίνυν, so then, therefore.

τοιόσδε, τοιάδε, τοιόνδε, of such a kind, such, as follows.

τοιοῦτος, τοιαύτη, τοιοῦτο, of such a kind, such, usually referring to what has preceded.

τολμάω, dare, venture, have the courage or effrontery.

τόξον, ου, τό, bow.

τοσοῦτος, τοσαύτη, τοσοῦτο(ν), so large, so much, so many.

τότε, then, at that time.

τράπεζα, ης, ἡ, table; meal.

τρᾱχέως, roughly.

τρεῖς, τρία, three.

τρέπω, turn; τρέπειν ἐπὶ νοῦν, put into someone's mind; mid., turn, betake oneself; εἰς φυγὴν τρέπεσθαι, be put to flight, flee.

τρέφω, θρέψω, ἔθρεψα, τέτροφα, τέθραμμαι, ἐτράφην, nourish, raise, rear, bring up, produce.

τρέχω, δραμοῦμαι, δεδράμηκα, δεδράμημαι, 2nd aor. ἔδραμον, run.

*τρίζω, τέτρῑγα (perf. with pres. meaning), squeak.

τριήρης, ους, ἡ, trireme, ship-of-war with three banks of oars.

τρίς, three times.

τρισχίλιοι, αι, α, three thousand.

τρίτος, η, ον, third.

τρίχας, see θρίξ.

τροπή, ῆς, ἡ, rout, flight, defeat.

τρόπος, ου, ὁ, way, manner, means; character, disposition.

τρύω, rub, wear out, afflict, distress.

τυγχάνω, τεύξομαι, τετύχηκα, 2nd aor. ἔτυχον, get, obtain, with gen.; happen (esp. with partic.).

τύπτω, strike, beat.

τυραννίς, ίδος, ἡ, sovereignty.

τύραννος, ου, ὁ, king, tyrant.

τύχη, ης, ἡ, fortune, luck, chance.

Υ

ὑβριστής, οῦ, ὁ, overbearing, intemperate person; as adj., unruly, ungovernable.

ὕδωρ, ὕδατος, τό, water.

υἱός, οῦ, ὁ, son.

ὑμεῖς, plu. of σύ.

ὑμέτερος, ᾱ, ον, your, yours (plu.).

ὑπάγω, lead under, bring before a judge; lead on by degrees.

ὕπειμι (Lat. sum), be under, be at hand, be at one's command.

ὑπέκκειμαι, be put away in safety.

ὑπέρ, prep. with gen. and acc., over, above; with gen., over, above; for the sake of, on behalf of; with acc., above, beyond, exceeding.

ὑπερβάλλω, throw beyond; exceed, surpass; outbid.

ὑπερήδομαι, be very pleased, be delighted.

*ὑπερτίθημι, entrust or refer to someone, disclose; consult, ask for advice.

ὑπηρετέω, row; serve; pass., be done as service.

ὑπό, prep. with gen., dat., acc., under; with gen. also by (of agency), because of.

ὑποδείκνῡμι, show secretly, give a glimpse of.

ὑποδέχομαι, promise.

ὑποδέω, bind or tie under; mid., bind under oneself, put on shoes.

ὑποδύω, 2nd aor. -έδῡν, slip under, go under, take on one's shoulders.

*ὑποζεύγνῡμι, put under the yoke.

ὑποζύγιον, ου, τό, beast of burden, baggage animal.

ὑποθήκη, ης, ἡ, suggestion, advice.

ὑποθωπεύω, flatter, slightly.

ὑπόκρισις, εως, ἡ, reply, answer.

ὑπολαμβάνω, take up, support; answer, retort.

ὑπολείπω, leave behind.

ὑπονοστέω, go down, sink.

*ὑποπίμπρημι, -πρήσω, -έπρησα, set fire to.

ὑπόπτερος, ον, winged.

ὑποπτεύω, suspect, regard with disfavour.

ὑποχείριος, ᾱ, ον, under one's hands, under one's power or control; ὑποχείριον ποιεῖν, capture or subdue.

ὗς, ὑός, ὁ, ἡ, pig.

ὑστεραῖος, ᾱ, ον, on the day after; as subst., ἡ ὑστεραία (sc. ἡμέρα), the next day.

ὕστερος, ᾱ, ον, later; neut. as adv., ὕστερον, later, afterwards.

ὑφίστημι, place under; pass. and intrans. tenses of act.

(2nd aor. and perf.), stand under; undertake, promise; lie in wait.

ὕω, rain; impers. ὕει, it rains.

Φ

φαίνω, φανῶ, ἔφηνα, aor. pass. ἐφάνην, reveal, disclose, make known; mid. and pass., be shown, be seen, appear, seem; with infin., e.g., φαίνομαι εἶναι, I seem to be; with partic., e.g., φαίνομαι ὤν, I am shown to be, I obviously am.

φάκελος, ου, ὁ, bundle.

φάσμα, ατος, τό, apparition, phantom.

φέρω, οἴσω, ἤνεγκα, ἐνήνοχα, ἐνήνεγμαι, ἠνέχθην, 2nd aor. ἤνεγκον, carry, bring, take; bear, produce; lead, tend; mid., win; pass., be carried along, be hurried, rush.

φεύγω, φεύξομαι and φευξοῦμαι, πέφευγα, 2nd aor. ἔφυγον, flee.

φήμη, ης, ἡ, report, reputation.

φημί, φήσω, ἔφησα, imperf. ἔφην (often used as aor.), say.

φθείρω, φθερῶ, ἔφθειρα, ἔφθαρκα, ἔφθαρμαι, ἐφθάρην, destroy, ruin.

φθονερός, ά, όν, envious, grudging.

φιλοπότης, ου, ὁ, lover of drinking.

φίλος, η, ον, dear, friendly; pleasing; as subst., friend.

*φιλοσκώμμων, ον, fond of joking; also as subst.

φλαῦρος, ᾱ, ον, worthless, paltry, trifling.

φοβέω, frighten; pass., be frightened, fear:

φοινίκειος, ᾱ, ον, of or from the palm-tree.

φοιτάω, go to and fro, go frequently to, visit.

φονεύς, έως, ὁ, murderer.

*φονεύω, kill, murder.

φόνος, ου, ὁ, murder.

φορέω (frequentative of φέρω), bear or carry constantly; wear; have, possess.

φράζω, tell, speak, say; mid., think.

*φρενήρης, ες, of sound mind, sane.

φρήν, φρενός, ἡ, mind.

φρονέω, think; εὖ φρονεῖν, be sensible; τὰ ὑμέτερα φρονεῖν, hold your views, be on your side.

φροντίζω, think, consider.

φροντίς, ίδος, ἡ, thought, care, concern.

φρύγανον, ου, τό, dry stick; usually in plu. meaning firewood.

φυγή, ῆς, ἡ, flight.

φυλακή, ῆς, ἡ, guard, custody, keeping guard; ἐν φυλακῇ ἔχειν, have under guard; ἐν φυλακαῖς εἶναι, be on guard.

φύλαξ, ακος, ὁ, guard.

φυλάττω, guard, watch; mid., guard against.

φύσις, εως, ἡ, nature.

φύω, bring forth, make grow; mid., pass., and intrans. tenses of act. (2nd aor., perf., *pluperf.*), grow, be produced, come into being, be.

φωνέω, speak, say.

φωνή, ῆς, ἡ, sound, voice, cry.

φώρ, φωρός, ὁ, thief.

X

χαίρω, χαιρήσω, κεχάρηκα, *aor. pass.* ἐχάρην, rejoice, be glad; go unpunished; *similarly in pass.*

χαλκός, οῦ, ὁ, copper, bronze.

χαμαί, on the ground.

χαρακτήρ, ῆρος, ὁ, stamp, mark, distinguishing characteristic.

χαρίζομαι, *fut.* χαριοῦμαι, please, gratify, *with dat.*

χάρις, ιτος, ἡ, grace, favour, gratitude; χάριν οἶδα, be grateful.

χεῖλος, ους, τό, lip; edge; bank (*of a river*).

χειμών, ῶνος, ὁ, winter; storm.

χείρ, χειρός, ἡ, hand.

χειροήθης, ες (*lit.*, *accustomed to the hand*), manageable, tame.

χειρονομέω, move the hands, gesticulate.

χειρόω, take in hand, master, subdue.

***χθιζός**, ή, όν, of yesterday, yesterday's.

χίλιοι, αι, α, a thousand.

χιτών, ῶνος, ὁ, undergarment, shirt, tunic.

***χόλος**, ου, ὁ, anger.

χορεύω, dance.

χράομαι, χρήσομαι, ἐχρησάμην, κέχρημαι, ἐχρήσθην, use, *with dat.* (*contracted forms have* η *for* ᾱ).

χρεών, τo, *indecl.*, fate, necessity; χρεών ἐστι, it is fated *or* necessary.

χρή, *impers.; imperf.* χρῆν *and* ἐχρῆν, *subj.* χρῇ, *opt.* χρείη, *infin.* χρῆναι, it is necessary, one must.

χρῄζω, want, need; ask, demand.

χρῆμα, ατος, τό, thing; *plu.*, things, property, money.

χρησμός, οῦ, ὁ, oracular response, oracle.

***χρηστηριάζομαι**, consult an oracle.

χρηστήριον, ου, τό, seat of an oracle, shrine, oracle.

χρηστός, ή, όν, useful, good.

χρόνος, ου, ὁ, time, period.

χρῡσίον, ου, τό, piece of gold, gold.

***χρῡσῖτης**, ου, *fem.* χρυσῖτις, ιδος, containing gold.

χρῡσός, οῦ, ὁ, gold.

χρῡσοῦς, ῆ, οῦν, of gold, golden.

χρῶμα, ατος, τό, skin; colour of skin, complexion; colour.

χώρᾱ, ᾱς, ἡ, place, land, country.

χωρέω, go; have room for, hold.

χωρίζω, divide, separate; *pass.*, differ, *with gen.*

χωρίον, ου, τό, place, spot.

χωρίς, aside, apart, to one side, besides.

χῶρος, ου, ὁ, place, space.

Ψ

ψάμμος, ου, ἡ, sand.

ψαμμώδης, ες, sandy.

ψέλιον, ου, τό, bracelet.

ψευδής, ές, lying, false.

ψεύδομαι, ψεύσομαι, ἐψευσάμην, ἔψευσμαι, ἐψεύσθην, lie, deceive.

*ψευδόμαντις, εως, ὁ, false prophet.

*ψῆγμα, ατος, τό, shavings; ψῆγμα χρυσοῦ, gold dust.

ψῡχή, ῆς, ἡ, life, soul.

Ω

ὦ, exclamation, oh.

ὧδε, thus, as follows.

ὠθισμός, οῦ, ὁ, struggling, wrestling; ὠθισμὸς λόγων, debate, argument.

ὦμος, ον, ὁ, shoulder.

ὦναξ, crasis for ὦ ἄναξ.

ὠνέομαι, ὠνήσομαι, aor. ἐπριάμην, buy.

ὥρᾱ, ᾱς, ἡ, time, period, season, hour, the right time.

ὡραῖος, ᾱ, ον, seasonable, ripe.

ὡς, conj. and adv., as, since, when, whenever; so that (with subj. or opt.); that (introd. indirect disc.); as, as if; with superl., as . . . as possible, e.g. ὡς μέγιστα, as large as possible, ὡς τάχιστα, as quickly as possible; also ὡς τάχιστα as conj., as soon as; with partic., as, since, in the belief that, on the grounds that; with numerals, about.

ὧς, so, in this way.

ὡσεί, as if, as though.

ὥσπερ, just as, as if, as it were.

ὥστε, so that, so as to, with infin. or indic.

ὦτα, see οὖς.

INDEX OF NAMES

Where genitives and gender are not indicated, they were not found.
The numbers refer to the pages.

A

family was banished, although it was later recalled from exile. The most famous members of the family were Cleisthenes (son of Megacles and Agariste), Pericles, and Alcibiades. 41.

Ἄμᾱσις, εως, ὁ, *Amasis*, king of Egypt from 570 to 526 B.C. When his predecessor Apries sent him to put down a revolt, the soldiers who were in rebellion chose Amasis as their king, and Apries was thus deposed. At first Amasis treated Apries kindly, but he was eventually persuaded to give him up to the people, who killed him. Amasis had a long and prosperous reign. He cultivated close relationships with the Greeks and other foreigners. These alliances were intended as a defence against the Persians, but they proved fruitless, since, six months after Amasis' death, Egypt was defeated by Cambyses and thus became subject to Persian rule. 6–8.

Ἀμεινίας, ου, ὁ, *Ameinias*, an Athenian who distinguished himself at the battle of Salamis. He is reported by some to have been a brother of Aeschylus. 59.

Ἄμμων, ωνος, ὁ, *Ammon*, originally the god of Thebes in upper Egypt. After the rise and growth of the Egyptian Empire he became the most famous of the Egyptian and Libyan deities and was worshipped throughout North Africa and the Near East. His most famous oracle was at the oasis of Siwa, near the Egyptian-Libyan border. It is said to have been visited by Alexander the Great. 47.

Ἀμμώνιος, ου, ὁ, an *Ammonian*, i.e., a worshipper of Ammon; also, an inhabitant of Ammonium, a city in Libya. 47, 48.

Ἀπόλλων, ωνος, ὁ, *Apollo*, one of the most important of the Greek divinities. He was the god of youth, beauty, poetry, music, healing, archery, prophecy, and the sun. 28.

Ἀπολλωνίᾱ, ᾱs, ἡ, *Apollonia*, a city in the southern part of Illyria a few miles from the Adriatic Sea. It was founded by the Corinthians in the days of Periander. 10, 11.

Ἀπολλωνιᾶται, ῶν, οἱ, the *Apolloniates*, i.e., the citizens of Apollonia. 10, 11.

Ἀπρίης, ου, ὁ, *Apries*, the fourth king of the 26th Egyptian dynasty. He reigned from 589 to 570 B.C. For his deposal and death see "*Ἄμασις*. 6.

Ἀραβίᾱ, ᾱs, ἡ, *Arabia*. 62.

Ἀράβιοι, ων, οἱ, the *Arabians*. 63.

Ἀργεῖος, ᾱ, ον, *Argive*, of Argos, the chief city of the district of Argolis in the north-eastern Peloponnesus. 25, 26.

Ἀριαβίγνης, ὁ, *Ariabignes*, a Persian general, son of Darius and brother of Xerxes. He was commander of the Ionian and Carian ships at the battle of Salamis. 61.

Ἀριστείδης, ου, ὁ, *Aristeides*, an Athenian statesman and general. He was in command of a contingent at the battle of Marathon, and was elected archon for the following year. He aimed at making Athens a strong land power, opposing the naval policy of Themistocles. As a result of this conflict Aristeides was ostracized, but he returned in time to help defend Greece at Salamis and Plataea. At Salamis he gave loyal support to Themistocles, whom he had previously opposed. He was given the title of ' the Just ' because of his honesty. 57, 58.

Ἀριστόδικος, ου, ὁ, *Aristodicus*, a Cymean, son of Heracleides. 28, 30.

Ἀρίων, ονος, ὁ, *Arion*, a semi-legendary poet and musician who lived at the end of the 7th century B.C. He was a friend of Periander, tyrant of Corinth. He is said to have invented the dithyramb, but no work of his has survived. 8–10.

Ἅρπαγος, ου, ὁ, *Harpagus*, a Median noble who betrayed his king, Astyages, to Cyrus. Later, as a general in Cyrus's army, he won the Ionian cities of Asia Minor for the Persians. 12–15, 17–19, 23.

Ἀρτεμβάρης, ους, ὁ, *Artembares*, a Median noble. 15, 16.

Ἀρτεμίσιον, ου, τό, *Artemisium*, a promontory at the north end of the island of Euboea, so called from a temple of Artemis which was located in the vicinity. Here the Greek fleet first met the Persians in their invasion of Greece in 480 B.C. Although the naval battle was indecisive, the annihilation of the Greek land forces at near-by Thermopylae made it necessary for the fleet to retreat to Salamis. 57.

Ἀσσύριοι, ων, οἱ, the *Assyrians*. 35.

Ἀστυάγης, ους, ὁ, *Astyages*, the last king of the Medes. After a reign of approximately 35 years he was defeated and taken prisoner by Cyrus in 550 B.C. Cyrus is said to have kept him in his home and treated him kindly until he died a natural death. 12–20, 22, 23.

Ἀττικός, ή, όν, *Attic*, i.e., belonging to Attica, the district of which Athens was the chief city; hence ἡ Ἀττική (SC. γῆ), Attica. 44, 55.

Ἄτυς, υος, ὁ, *Atys*, a king of the Maeonians, who were later called Lydians after Atys' son Lydus. 1.

B

Βαβυλών, ῶνος, ἡ, *Babylon,* the chief city of Babylonia. It extended along both sides of the Euphrates River. 30, 32, 33, 35, 38, 39.

Βαβυλώνιος, ου, ὁ, a *Babylonian.* 30, 32–38, 41.

Βηλεύς, fem. *Βηλίς,* gen. *ίδος,* of *Belus* or *Baal.* 36, 38.

Βῆλος, ου, ὁ, *Belus,* the Greek form of Baal, an oriental word for ' god.' It was sometimes combined with the name of another deity (e.g., *Ζεὺς Βῆλος*) as a general epithet for the divine. 38.

Βίτων, ωνος, ὁ, *Biton* of Argos, brother of Cleobis. 25, 26.

Βουτώ, οῦς, ἡ, *Buto,* a city in the Nile delta. It was famous for its oracle of the goddess Buto, whom the Greeks identified with Leto. A yearly festival was held there in her honour. Herodotus comments elsewhere (II, 155) on the remarkable construction of the temple, whose walls and ceiling were made each of a single slab of stone. 6.

Βραγχίδαι, ῶν, αἱ, *Branchidae,* the seat of an oracle of Apollo, near Miletus in Asia Minor. Its original name was Didyma, but it was also called Branchidae after its priests, who claimed descent from a youth named Branchus, who was loved by Apollo. The oracle was consulted by all the inhabitants of Ionia and Aeolia, and also by Croesus, who made rich gifts to the temple. After the revolt and subsequent capture of Miletus, the temple was burned by the Persians. Some time later it was rebuilt on a very ambitious scale. Magnificent ruins of it may still be seen. 28.

Δ

Δᾶρεῖος, ου, ὁ, *Darius,* king of Persia after Cambyses. At the death of Cambyses the government was in the hands of a usurper, who claimed to be Cambyses' murdered brother, Smerdis. Darius, a member of the royal family, was assisted by six other nobles to overthrow the usurper and become king himself. These changes in power occasioned general unrest throughout the empire, and a number of revolts had to be suppressed by the new king. This was successfully accomplished in 520 and 519 B.C.

The administration of Darius was well-organized and just. He introduced coinage into the eastern parts of his empire, where it had not previously been used. He dug a canal from the Nile to the Red Sea. He attempted to develop commerce, establishing relations with Carthage and exploring the shores of Sicily and Italy. He had the Egyptian calendar adopted in his native Persia. He built temples in Egypt and maintained good relations with the religious leaders of all his subject peoples.

When the Ionian states in Asia Minor were assisted in their revolt against Persia by the Greeks on the European mainland, Darius organized an expedition to punish the European Greeks. The first Persian attempt to invade Greece met with failure through shipwreck. A second expedition was organized in 490 and defeated at Marathon. Before a third expedition could be prepared, a revolt broke out in Egypt (486). In the following year Darius died. The war against Greece was continued by his son Xerxes. 33–35, 37–39, 61, 65, 66.

Δελφοί, ῶν, οἱ, *Delphi*, the seat of the most important temple and oracle of Apollo and the most famous of all Greek oracles. It was located in the district of Phocis, on the lower southern slopes of Mt. Parnassus about six miles from the Gulf of Corinth. Its site was believed to be the centre of the earth and it was therefore called the ὀμφαλός (navel). 11, 26.

Δωδώνη, ης, ἡ, *Dodona*, a town in the mountains of Epirus in northwest Greece. It was famous as the seat of an ancient and venerable oracle of Zeus. 10.

E

'Ελευσίς, ῖνος, ἡ, *Eleusis*, a town in Attica opposite the island of Salamis. It was famous for the mysteries which were celebrated there in honour of Demeter and Persephone. 25, 59.

'Ελεφαντίνη, ης, ἡ, *Elephantine*, a city in southern Egypt, situated on an island in the Nile just below the first cataract. 4, 49.

'Ελλάς, άδος, ἡ, *Greece*. Hellas was the name by which the Greeks themselves called their country, our word ' Greece ' being derived from the Latin name of ' Graecia.' 53–55.

Έλλην, ηνος, ὁ, a *Greek*. 1, 42, 47, 53, 55–59, 61, 62, 65, 66.

'Ελληνικός, ή, όν, *Greek*. 58.

'Ετέαρχος, ου, ὁ, *Etearchus*, a king of the Ammonians. 47, 48.

Εὔβοια, ᾶς, ἡ, *Euboea*, a large island in the Aegean, stretching along the coasts of Attica, Boeotia, and Locris. 59.

Εὐήνιος, ου, ὁ, *Euenius*, a distinguished citizen of Apollonia. 10, 11.

Εὐρυβιάδης, ου, ὁ, *Eurybiades*, a Spartan nobleman, commander of the combined Greek fleet during the invasion of Xerxes. Although the Athenians furnished a larger number of ships than the Spartans, and although Themistocles was the superior strategist, the post was given to Eurybiades because the Spartans would not consent to fight under an Athenian. 53–55, 58.

Εὐφράτης, ου, ὁ, the *Euphrates*, the longest river of western Asia. It is the more westerly of the two rivers (the other being the Tigris) which flow through Mesopotamia into the Persian Gulf. Babylon was built on its banks. 32.

Z

Ζεύς, Διός, ὁ, *Zeus*, the chief Greek god. He was often identified with the major god of the peoples with whom the Greeks came in contact, e.g., Ammon in North Africa, Baal in the East, and later Jupiter in Rome. 38.

Ζώπυρος, ου, ὁ, *Zopyrus*, a Persian in the army of Darius at the seige of Babylon. 34–38.

H

Ἥρᾱ, ᾱς, ἡ, *Hera*, the sister of Zeus and the chief Greek goddess. She is most frequently represented in Greek literature as the jealous wife, resentful of her husband's numerous affairs. In her own right she was worshipped as the goddess of marriage and of the various phases (e.g. childbirth) of a woman's life. In Argos and Samos she had a special function, performing there the role of patron-goddess which was performed by Athena at Athens. In Argos her agricultural character was particularly manifest. The first oxen used in ploughing were dedicated to her and she was worshipped as the goddess of flowers. 25.

Θ

Θεμιστοκλῆς, έους, ὁ, *Themistocles*, a famous Athenian statesman. It was he who persuaded the Athenians, during the interval between the invasion of Darius and that of Xerxes, to build a fleet, so that they might meet the Persian forces by sea as well as by land. Although the combined Greek fleet was nominally under the command of the Spartan Eurybiades, it was Themistocles who was responsible for the battles of Artemisium and Salamis. After the departure of the Persians, Themistocles succeeded in having the walls of Athens rebuilt against the opposition of Sparta. He was also responsible for the building and fortifying of the harbour of the Peiraeus, and for the plan of constructing the Long Walls between the Peiraeus and Athens, although the latter project was not carried out in his own time.

His fellow Athenians turned against Themistocles after the Persian Wars, with the result that he was ostracized. During his absence he was charged with treason, so that he was never able to return to his native city. He took refuge among the Persians in Asia Minor, where he lived until his death at the age of 65. 53–58.

Θῆβαι, ῶν, αἱ, *Thebes*, an important city in upper Egypt. The area is famous for its temples and tombs. (Not to be confused with the city of the same name in Boeotia, Greece.) 3, 52.

I

'Ινδοί, ῶν, οἱ, the *Indians*. 61, 62, 66.

'Ιπποκλείδης, ὁ (dat. η, acc. η), *Hippocleides*, an Athenian suitor for the daughter of Cleisthenes, tyrant of Sicyon. 42, 44, 45.

'Ιταλίᾱ, ᾱς, ἡ, *Italy*. 8, 10, 55.

'Ιχθυοφάγοι, ων, οἱ, the *Ichthyophagi* or *Fish-Eaters*, a descriptive term applied to people who lived in various coastal areas of Asia and Africa. 49–51.

Ἴωνες, ων, οἱ, the *Ionians*, one of the major divisions of the Greek people, to which the Athenians belonged. The territory which was named after them, Ionia, consisted of the southern part of the Aegean coast of Asia Minor. The Ionic cities in this area, which were twelve in number, did not form a political unit, although they frequently followed similar patterns of behaviour, e.g. in their revolt against the Persians. 28, 59.

K

Καλλατίαι, ῶν, οἱ, the *Callatiae*, a tribe of Indians who, according to Herodotus, ate their dead. 66.

Καμβύσης, ου, ὁ, I. *Cambyses*, father of Cyrus. 14, 19.

II. *Cambyses*, son of Cyrus and his successor as head of the Persian Empire. He undertook the conquest of Egypt, the only state of the eastern world which was independent at the death of his father. The expedition to Egypt took place in 525 B.C., shortly after Amasis had been succeeded by his son Psammetichus III. The Egyptians were deteated and Psammetichus executed. From Egypt Cambyses attempted the conquest of Ethiopia, but the desert forced him back. During his absence from Persia his throne was usurped by a Magian who claimed to be Cambyses' dead brother, Smerdis (the so-called ' false Smerdis '). Cambyses made an unsuccessful attempt to overthrow him and then committed suicide in 521 B.C. 48, 49, 51, 52.

Κίσσιος, ᾱ, ον, Cissian, of Cissia in southern Persia. 36, 38.

Κλεισθένης, ους, ὁ, Cleisthenes, a famous tyrant of Sicyon, who ruled from about 600 to 570 B.C. He was the grandfather of Cleisthenes of Athens. 42, 44, 45.

Κλέοβις, εως, ὁ, Cleobis, an Argive youth, brother of Biton. 25, 26.

Κορίνθιος, ᾱ, ον, Corinthian. 9, 54, 55, 58.

Κόρινθος, ου, ὁ and **ἡ,** Corinth, a city in the Peloponnesus just south of the Isthmus of the same name. It became important and prosperous under the tyrants, particularly Periander, and its strategic location helped to make it a great commercial centre at an early date. 8, 9.

Κροῖσος, ου, ὁ, Croesus, last king of Lydia (560–546 B.C.). He completed the conquest of the Ionian cities on the coast of Asia Minor and also extended his kingdom to the east. After the Median Empire was overthrown by Cyrus and the Persians became a threat to the rest of the civilized world, Croesus formed an alliance with Egypt, Babylonia, and Sparta against Cyrus, and made an attack on him. But he was driven back to his capital Sardis, which was captured, while he himself was taken prisoner. The manner of his death is uncertain.

Many legends about Croesus were current in ancient times. His wealth was proverbial. For the chronological impossibility of the visit from Solon described in Selection IX, see Σόλων. 23, 25–28, 41, 42.

Κὒμαῖοι, ων, οἱ, the Cymeans, the inhabitants of Cyme. 28, 30.

Κὺμη, ης, ἡ, Cyme, an important Greek city on the coast of Asia Minor opposite the island of Lesbia. 28.

Κυρηναῖοι, ων, οἱ, the Cyrenaeans, or inhabitants of Cyrene. Their city was an important Greek colony near the North-

African coast. It was the capital of Cyrenaica and was founded about the middle of the 7th century. 47, 48.

Κῦρος, ου, ὁ, *Cyrus*, the founder and first king of the Persian Empire. His people had been subject to the Medes before Cyrus led them in revolt. The success of the revolt and the capture of Astyages, the last Median king, in 550 were followed by a rapid expansion and consolidation of Persian rule. Croesus, king of Lydia, who had màde alliances with Babylonia, Egypt, and Sparta against the common foe, was defeated and captured at Sardis in 546. Babylon surrendered in 539. Other conquests followed, until the Persians were supreme throughout the East.

The facts about Cyrus's parentage and early childhood are obscure. The legend related by Herodotus — that he was the grandson of Astyages — is only one of several. About his death, however, there is general agreement: he was killed in battle while on an expedition against the East in 529 B.C. 12, 15, 16, 18–20, 22, 23, 27, 28, 30, 32, 34, 38.

Λ

Λακεδαιμόνιοι, ων, οἱ, the *Lacedaemonians* or *Spartans*. Lacedaemon was the name of the man who founded the city, Sparta that of his wife. 59.

Λακωνικός, ή, όν, *Laconian*, i.e., belonging to Laconia, the south-eastern district of the Peloponnesus, of which Sparta was the chief city. 44.

Λιβύη, ης, ἡ, *Libya*, the Greek name for the continent of Africa, which was originally thought to be a part of Asia. When its separateness was established (about 500 B.C.), the boundary between the two continents was at first considered the Nile, or the western border of Egypt. It was not until after the time of Herodotus that the boundary was fixed at Suez. 47, 48.

Λίβυς, υος, ὁ, a *Libyan*, i.e., an African. 47.

Λῡδίᾱ, ᾱς, ἡ, *Lydia*, an important kingdom in the west of Asia Minor. Its capital was Sardis and Croesus was its last king. After Croesus it became the chief Persian satrapy. 1.

Λῡδός, οῦ, ὁ, a *Lydian*. 1, 2, 27, 28, 41.

Λυσίμαχος, ου, ὁ, *Lysimachus*, an Athenian, father of Aristeides. 57.

M

Μάγοι, ων, οἱ, the *Magi* or *Magians*. These were the hereditary priestly class, first of the Medes, later also of the Persians. They were greatly respected and had considerable influence in both public and private affairs. Our word ' magic ' is derived from their name, since they were believed to have supernatural powers. 12, 18, 19, 23.

Μαζάρης, ους, ὁ, *Mazares*, a Mede, a general of Cyrus. 28.

Μανδάνη, ης, ἡ, *Mandane*. According to Herodotus, she was the daughter of Astyages and the mother of Cyrus. There is no evidence to substantiate this story, however. See *Κῦρος*. 12, 14.

Μάνης, ου, ὁ, *Manes*, the mythological founder and first king of the people who were later called Lydians. His son Atys was the second king. 1.

Μεγάβυζος, ου, ὁ, *Megabyzus*, a Persian, father of Zopyrus. 34.

Μεγακλῆς, έους, ὁ, *Megacles*, son of Alcmaeon and member of the Alcmaeonid family of Athens. He was the son-in-law of Cleisthenes of Sicyon and the father of the Athenian statesman Cleisthenes. Political difficulties during his archonship forced him and his family into exile. 41, 42, 45.

Μεγαρεῖς, έων, οἱ, the *Megarians*, the inhabitants of Megara, which is the chief town of Megaris, the district to the west of Attica. 56.

Μηδικός, ή, όν, *Median*. 23.

Μῆδοι, ων, οἱ, the *Medes*, the inhabitants of Media, a country which occupied what is now the north-west portion of Iran. 12, 15, 19, 22, 23, 56, 58, 61.

Μιτραδᾶτης, ου, ὁ, *Mitradates*, foster-father of Cyrus, according to Herodotus. 13, 19.

Μνησίφιλος, ου, ὁ, *Mnesiphilus*, a prominent Athenian who took part in the battle of Salamis. 53, 54.

Μοῖρις, εως, ἡ, Lake *Moeris*, the largest lake in Egypt. It is west of the Nile valley and is supplied with water by the Nile during the flood season. 3.

Μουνυχία, ᾶς, ἡ, *Munychia*, one of the two smaller harbours of the Peiraeus. 57.

Μυκερῖνος, ου, ὁ, *Mycerinus*, an Egyptian king, son of Cheops and nephew of Chephren. He built the third pyramid at Giza, but did not oppress his subjects as his father and uncle had done. He reopened the temples and allowed the people to resume their former occupations. (For Cheops and Chephren see notes on p. 69 and p. 70.) 4, 6.

N

Νασαμῶνες, ων, οἱ, the *Nasamones*, an African tribe who are believed to have lived on the shores of the Great Syrtis (the modern Gulf of Sidra off the coast of Libya). 47, 48.

Νεῖλος, ου, ὁ, the *Nile.* 45, 47, 48.

Νίνιοι, ων, οἱ, the *Ninevites* or inhabitants of Nineveh, the capital of Assyria. The city was also called Ninus after its founder. 36.

Νίτωκρις, ἡ, *Nitocris*, one of the two queens of Babylon, according to Herodotus, Semiramis being the other. She diverted the waters of the Euphrates into an artificial lake which she had dug, and while the river channel was thus empty she had its walls lined with bricks. She also had a bridge built across the Euphrates to connect the two parts of Babylon. For details, see note on p. 88, l. 13. 39.

Ξ

Ξέρξης, ου, ὁ, *Xerxes*, king of Persia, son of Darius. At the time of his accession (485) Egypt was in revolt against Persian rule. After suppressing this revolt Xerxes proceeded to organize a powerful force to carry out his father's project of punishing Greece for its assistance in the Ionian rebellion. In 480 the invasion began, and at first the Persians' advance was attended with success everywhere. A battle was won at Thermopylae and the Greek fleet had to abandon its position at Artemisium; Attica was ravaged and the Greeks were forced to withdraw to Salamis and the Isthmus of Corinth. At Salamis, however, the tables turned and the Greeks won a decisive victory over the Persian fleet. In the following year the Persian army was defeated at Plataea. Of Xerxes' later life little is known. He was murdered in 464. 58, 61.

O

Ὀλύμπια, ων, τά, the *Olympic* games. This event, the chief national festival of the Greeks, took place every four years. It was a religious celebration in honour of Zeus and was therefore held at his chief place of worship, which was Olympia, in the district of Elis in the north-west part of the Peloponnese. According to tradition, the games were established in 776 B.C. They lasted five days, and were concluded on the fifth day with sacrifices, a banquet at which the victors were entertained, and prizes consisting of crowns of wild olives. 42.

Π

Παχτύης, ου, ό, *Pactyes*, a Lydian. He was charged with collecting the revenue of Lydia after the defeat of that country by Cyrus. But he induced the Lydians to revolt and used the money to hire mercenaries. Cyrus sent an army against him, and when Pactyes learned of its approach, he fled to Cyme. The Cymeans, not wanting to surrender Pactyes and afraid to keep him, sent him on to Mytilene. From Mytilene he was sent to Chios and the Chians surrendered him to the Persians. 28, 30.

Παλληνεύς, έως, ό, a *Pallenian*, i.e., an inhabitant of Pallene, a deme or ' township ' of Attica. 59.

Παναίτιος, ου, ό, *Panaetius*, a native of Tenos and commander of a ship in the army of Xerxes. Just before the battle of Salamis he deserted to the Greeks and confirmed the news that they were surrounded by the Persians. 59.

Πειραιεύς, έως, ό, the *Peiraeus*, a town on the coast of Attica and the main port of Athens after the time of Themistocles. It consisted of one large harbour and two smaller harbours. 59.

Πελοποννήσιοι, ων, οί, the *Peloponnesians*. 56.

Πελοπόννησος, ου, ή (i.e., Πέλοπος νῆσος, island of Pelops), the *Peloponnesus* or *Peloponnese*, the part of Greece south of the Isthmus of Corinth. 53, 54, 56, 58.

Περίανδρος, ου, ό, *Periander*, tyrant of Corinth from 625 to 585 B.C. Although he had a reputation for cruelty, his contributions to the progress of Corinth are undisputed. He carried on various colonizing activities and laid the foundations for the commercial prosperity of his city. He maintained friendly relations with the tyrants of Miletus and Mytilene, and with the kings of Egypt and Lydia. He was a patron of literature and the arts, and was considered one of the seven sages of Greece. A collection of maxims in 2,000 verses is ascribed to his authorship. 8, 9.

Πέρσης, ου, ό, a *Persian*. 19, 20, 22, 23, 26, 28, 30, 32, 33, 35-38, 49, 50, 56, 61, 62.

Σ

Σαλαμίς, ῖνος, ἡ, *Salamis*, an island off the west coast of Attica, the scene of the famous battle of Salamis of 480 B.C. 53, 54, 56, 57, 59, 61.

Σάρδεις, εων, αἱ, *Sardis*, chief city and capital of the kingdom of Lydia. 23, 26, 41.

Σεμίραμις, εως, ἡ, *Semiramis*, a queen of Babylon, according to Herodotus, who says that she erected embankments along the Euphrates to keep it from overflowing. She lived five generations before Nitocris, the second queen of Babylon. 36.

Σικελίᾱ, ᾱς, ἡ, *Sicily*. 8.

Σίκιννος, ου, ὁ, *Sicinnus*, a slave of Themistocles. 57.

Σικυών, ῶνος, ἡ and ὁ, *Sicyon*, a city in the northern Peloponnese, west of Corinth and about two miles from the Gulf. Its greatest power was reached under the tyrant Cleisthenes. 42.

Σικυώνιος, ᾱ, ον, *Sicyonian*. 42, 44.

Σῖρις, εως, ἡ, *Siris*, a Greek colony in the south of Italy, situated on the Gulf of Tarentum at the mouth of the Siris River. 55.

Σκύθαι, ῶν, οἱ, the *Scythians*, a general term for the nomadic tribes to the north and north-east of the Black and Caspian Seas. 64.

Σολόεις, εντος, *Soloeis*, a promontory in the extreme west of North Africa. It is generally thought to have been the modern Cape Spartel (near Tangier), though some authorities identify it with Cape Cantin, which is farther south on the coast of Morocco. 47.

Σόλων, ωνος, ὁ, *Solon*, a great Athenian statesman, often regarded as the father of the Athenian constitution. His first service to his state was the recovery of Salamis, which had fallen into the hands of the Megarians. He was then elected archon in 594, with powers to bring about much-needed constitutional and economic reforms. During his archonship he freed those peasants who had been enslaved for debt and revoked the law which permitted such enslavement; he encouraged industry and trade; his new constitution gave every citizen the right to vote, and trial by jury was instituted. At the end of his archonship Solon left Athens for a period of ten years in order to give his reforms a chance to take effect. His supposed visit to Croesus is not possible chronologically, since Croesus did not become king of Lydia until about twenty-five years after Solon's return to Athens. In his youth Solon wrote amatory poetry; later he wrote patriotic and didactic poems. He was considered one of the seven sages of Greece. 23, 25–27.

Σωσιμένης, ους, ὁ, *Sosimenes*, a Tenian, father of Panaetius. 59.

T

Ταίναρος, ου, ἡ and ὁ, also Ταίναρον, τό, *Taenarus* or *Taenarum*, a promontory at the southern tip of Laconia in the Peloponnese. The name was also used occasionally to include the peninsula north of the promontory, which is the central one of the three southern peninsulas of the Peloponnesus. 9.

Τάρας, αντος, ὁ, *Tarentum*, an important Greek city in southern Italy on the gulf of the same name. It was founded by the Spartans. 9, 10.

Τέλλος, ου, ὁ, *Tellus*, an Athenian. 25.

Τήνιος, ᾱ, ον, *Tenian*, i.e., belonging to Tenos, an island in the Aegean Sea. 59.

Τίσανδρος, ου, ὁ, *Tisander*, an Athenian, father of Hippocleides. 42, 44, 45.

Φ

Φάληρον, ου, τό. *Phalerum*, a small town and port on the west coast of Attica. It served as the harbour of Athens until the early 5th century, when the Peiraeus took over this function. 61.

Φοῖνιξ, ικος, ὁ, a *Phoenician*. Phoenicia was the name given to the part of Syria which bordered on the Mediterranean. Its chief cities were Tyre and Sidon. The Phoenicians were a sea-faring people, who explored the Mediterranean from one end to the other, establishing colonies and carrying on trade in Cyprus, Sicily, Africa, and Spain. From the late 7th century to the year 538 Phoenicia was under Chaldean domination. In 538 it passed to the Persians, to whom it remained subject until the 2nd century B.C. The Phoenicians took an active part in the Persian Wars against the Greeks. 47, 59, 63.

Φρύξ, Φρυγός, ὁ, a *Phrygian*. The Phrygians are believed to have arrived in Asia Minor, where they made their home in the country named after them, some time between 2,000 and 1,500 B.C. 3.

X

Χαλδαῖοι, ων, οἱ, the *Chaldeans*. The word included different groups at different periods of time and in different authors. In one of its earlier applications it was synonymous with ' Babylonians.' Later it came to designate only the priestly class of the Babylonians, who had powers similar to those of the Persian Magi. In some authors its meaning is simply ' astrologers ' or ' astronomers.' 36.

Ψ

Ψαμμήτιχος, ου, ὁ, *Psammetichus* I, a king of Egypt, the first of the 26th dynasty. He had a long and prosperous reign (664–610 B.C.), during which he maintained close relationships with the Greeks. 2, 3.